Drawing for
Landscape Architecture

Drawing for Landscape Architecture

Edward Hutchison

Sketch to Screen to Site

Thames & Hudson

Previous pages: This quick drawing was part of a series
of six sketches that explored the different qualities of
an urban area (Brook Green, in London), where a new
nursery school was planned.

2B pencil, Daler sketchbook; 10 minutes.

First published in the United Kingdom in 2011
by Thames & Hudson Ltd, 181A High Holborn,
London WC1V 7QX

Designed by Susan Scott: www.design514.com

British Library Cataloguing-in-Publication Data
A catalogue record for this book is available
from the British Library

ISBN 978-0-500-34271-8

Printed and bound in China by 1010 Printing Ltd

To find out about all our publications,
please visit **www.thamesandhudson.com**.
There you can subscribe to our e-newsletter,
browse or download our current catalogue,
and buy any titles that are in print.

The Palm House

KEW GARDENS, LONDON

The avenue of Holm oak trees, planted by Capability Brown in the
18th century, emphasizes the delicacy of Decimus Burton's structure.

Winsor & Newton watercolours on A3 paper; 3 hours.

Contents

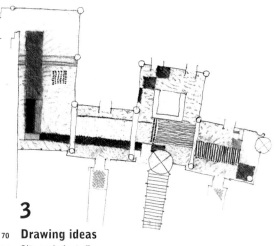

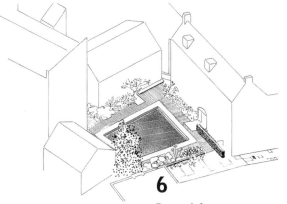

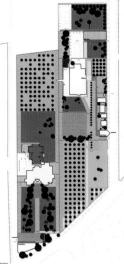

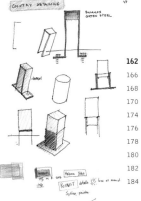
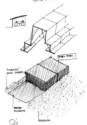

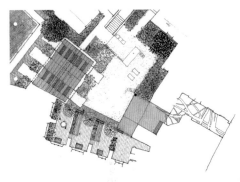

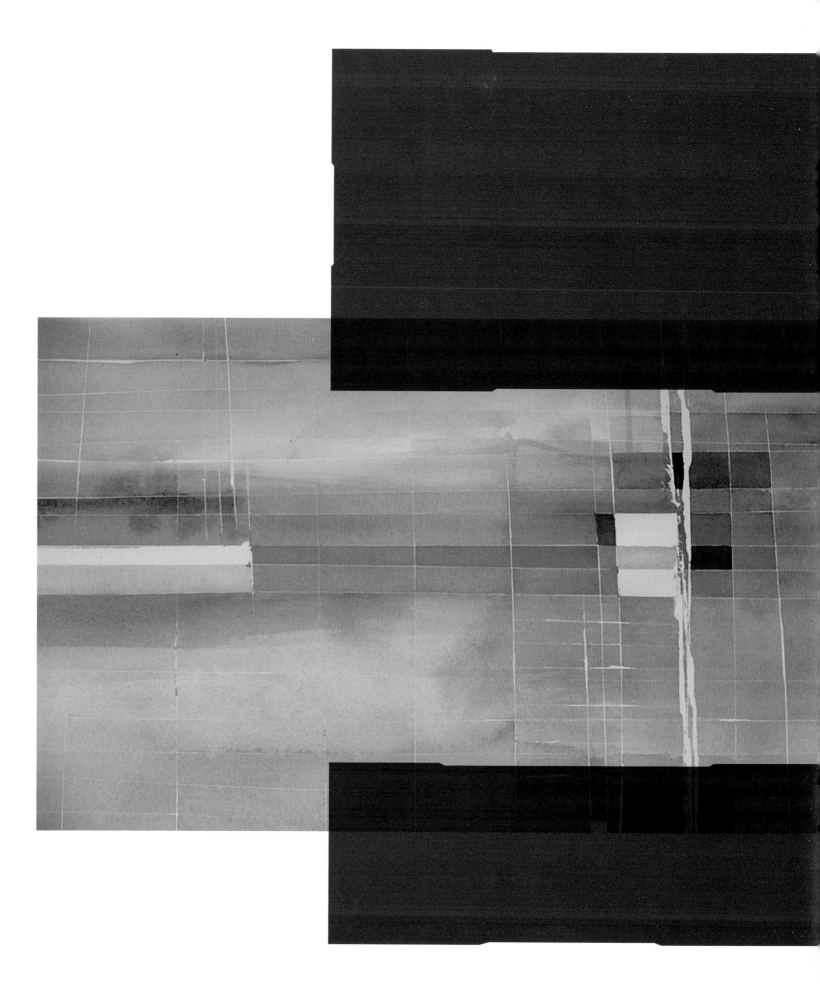

Introduction

Life drawing

The rhythmic discipline of
life drawing on a weekly basis
is indispensable for building
confidence and freedom in
observation and drawing.

6B, 2B and HB pencils and Staedtler
Ergosoft coloured pencils on A3 smooth
cartridge paper; 90 minutes.

Abstract in yellow

On p. 8: The medium of
watercolour allows chance to
play a major role in the final
image, which in this instance
can be interpreted as an
abstract landscape.

Winsor & Newton watercolours on
Arches Aquarelle hot-pressed paper;
over several days.

Everyone can draw, even if they think they can't. John Ruskin claimed in *The Elements of Drawing* (1857) that, with hours of irksome practice, he could teach even the least promising would-be artist to draw; indeed, that he had 'never met with a person who could not learn to draw at all'. But as with so many other disciplines, it is essential to develop the skill with rigour and determination (rather as learning to play a musical instrument requires constant practice). Henri Matisse, a consummate draughtsman, achieved his amazing fluidity of line through sheer hard work. For a period in the 1930s he spent every afternoon drawing a model, and throughout his life remained dismissive of those who tried to emulate his style without enduring the necessary graft. Life drawing is often considered the best way to learn to draw, as we all share an understanding of the subject – in its myriad different variations – in front of us. Drawing the naked form encourages careful observation, and leads to a greater understanding of the design essentials: light and shade, proportion, colour, movement and construction. There is, perhaps, no better way to develop 'a good eye'.

Keeping a sketchbook, too, is an invaluable discipline for a designer, and establishes drawing as an everyday activity. It does not matter if a particular drawing is good or bad; it is a reference, a memory jogger. Sketchbooks are wonderful playgrounds for ideas, lists, colour combinations to investigate, recording arresting patterns or capturing the view from a window. They are an insight into the thought process that led to a particular design solution. Receiving the appointment of a new job is always a pleasure, but it is also a responsibility. Irrespective of the size and nature of the commission, it is crucially important for the designer to get a feel for the site. While photographs are essential as records, sketches are a more immediate means of capturing a personal response to the locality, vital in the design process at a later stage. A new design should fit the site, both in dimensions and in spirit.

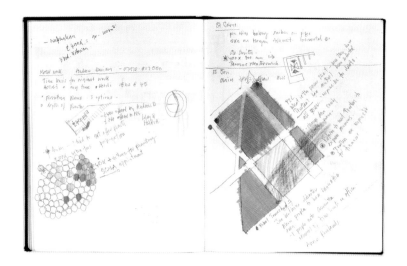

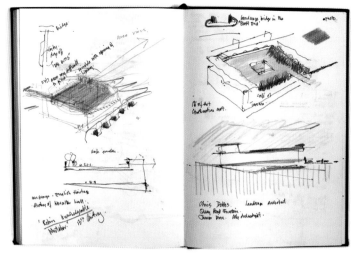

■

Sketching in journals
The results of doodling
during a conversation with
the project manager about
the Landscape Institute and
increased fees [above, left].
Concept sketches for the
Worcester library competition
[above, right].

Staedtler Ergosoft and Faber-Castell
Art Grip Aquarelle coloured pencils,
HB, 2B and 4B pencils, Staedtler
Pigment Liner 01 and Pilot G-Tec-C4
pen on smooth cartridge paper; 20–30
minutes each. Sketchbooks by
Dia Art Foundation, Ordning & Reda
and Paperchase.

The tension in the development of ideas can be quickly captured in a series of hand-sketches, and these unselfconscious freehand drawings used to tease out options for later discussion, which can then be more fully developed on a computer. The visual dialogue between digital and hand-drawings creates a dynamism for processing ideas, spaces and forms; the two contrasting media generate a valuable energy that drives the design along. The extraordinary accuracy of computer drawings legitimizes the initial ideas put down on paper, and shifting from hand-drawing to the precision of digital design underscores the designer's adeptness at solving problems. Software, skilfully used, can create images that are as sensitive and appealing as those earlier sketches. This book aims to demonstrate the enjoyment of weaving both of these processes together, and includes examples of design solutions — at St John's College, Cambridge (p.188) and Coventry Peace Garden (p.214) — that result from this pleasurable and economic way of working.

Recording ideas quickly

Ideas for gates in a private garden [below, left]; and paving
and step details [below, right]. A pre-Christmas timetable,
and experiments in grey [bottom].

10–15 minutes each.

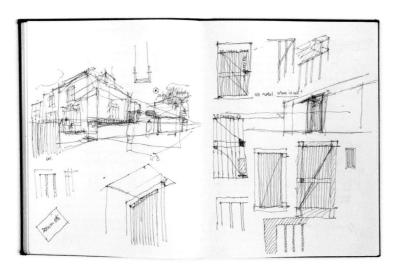

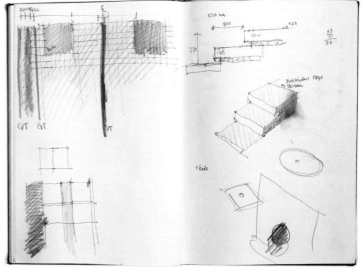

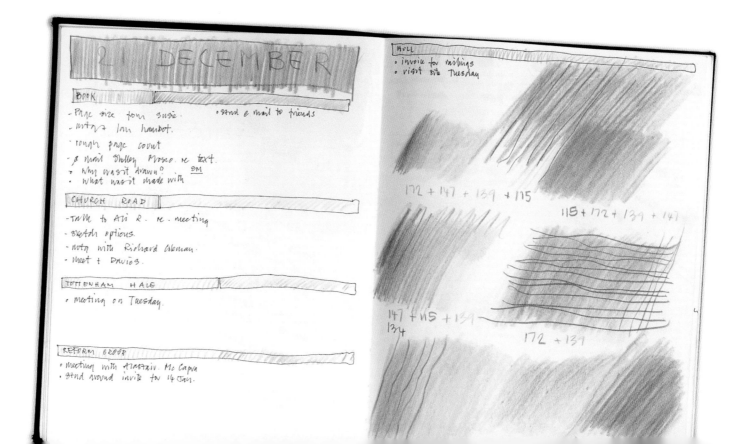

1

Absorbing the landscape

Spending several hours in intense concentration while drawing
a landscape adds immeasurably to the education of a designer.
The mind becomes freed from day-to-day thoughts, and is enabled
to formulate ideas that result directly from engagement with the
subject. These observations may not be original, but are a personal,
intuitive reaction that can be built on through further research.
The repeated discipline of drawing in the landscape helps build up a
portfolio of thoughts and forms a personal reference library of design
ideas, fostering a real knowledge in the subject of landscape design.
Such total engagement with a particular site sometimes verges on
an act of meditation. However indistinct the qualities of a landscape
may appear at first sight, one's senses become sharpened over time
to appreciate its unique merits and features, leading eventually to
an ability to assess an environment through critical and analytical
judgement – an invaluable tool in professional life.

    Unlike the lens of a camera, a designer's brain constantly
makes re-evaluations while drawing, often leading to new
perspectives on design. Through attempting to capture the qualities
of light in a drawing, one can begin to appreciate the varied
conditions over the course of a day, or a year, and the major impact
that light has on the appearance of a landscape. In the 1890s,
Claude Monet became so intrigued by the changing light conditions
across the façade of the cathedral at Rouen that he made over thirty
studies of the same subject. Similarly, the core natural materials in
landscape design (stone, water, pebbles, grasses, plants and trees)
are continually transformed by the changing light. To fully understand
and respect even half these qualities will distinguish one designer
from his or her competitors. Such insights, only understood through
close observation, prove invaluable in landscape design. One of
the great pleasures of drawing is the intellectual challenge inherent
in 'understanding' the subject, whether a landscape or a group
of buildings. Further research will reveal the underlying geology,
geography and individual microclimates of a site, and weave a

■

The sea, trees and houses
SAINTE MARINE, FRANCE
On p. 14: Maritime quaysides
are full of contrasts of scale,
both manmade and natural,
which respond to the demands
of the context and the
power of the sea.

Winsor & Newton watercolours on
hot-pressed paper (400 gms); 5 hours.

tapestry of facts and ideas into the initial discoveries made during the drawing process.

In an urban setting, questions begin to arise as to why the construction of a particular building – such as the Gothic cathedral in Burgos, Spain – took a certain path. Why, one might ask, did the stonemasons go to such extreme lengths to create the soaring, multi-perforated towers out of relatively soft limestone? What was the point of cross-lacing them with stone spheres adjacent to the pierced tracery? As the warm evening light turns increasingly orange, the sun appears to set in regular pulses, each lasting about ten minutes, emphasizing the pink of the limestone and enhancing the shadows of the perforations. The stone spheres and voids in the tracery seem to dance in complementary colours of purples and blues, like some Op Art light show of the 1960s. The climax comes at sunset, at the hour of evensong, and in the Middle Ages must have played an awesome and highly effective role in calling the faithful to worship, demonstrating the power and the glory of God with a pyrotechnic display on the west front of the cathedral.

More prosaically, while painting Cheyne Walk, just off the River Thames in London, it became clear that the white planes of the architecture of the International Modern Movement were inappropriate in a city redolent with pollution and traffic fumes; the implications of having to repaint every four years should be added to the sustainability of a project. The slow, intimate process of drawing helps to formulate these very basic questions, of such simplicity that they may under other circumstances be overlooked.

Drawing also allows a designer to experience the genius loci, or feng shui, of a site. Visiting remote Greek or Roman temples highlights the importance of this, as these temples were invariably built on the prime position in the landscape. Perhaps it is this early understanding of the magic of an individual site that is one of the reasons that travellers are still drawn to the same places today.

Cataloguing colours

LA PALMA, CANARY ISLANDS

The process of making marks with different coloured pencils is highly absorbing and enjoyable. The complexity of the various colour effects achievable is huge, and may be likened to the diversity of textiles. It is useful to record which colours were used to create a particular effect, thereby building up a reference system for future use.

Staedtler Ergosoft coloured pencils on A4 paper; 90 minutes.

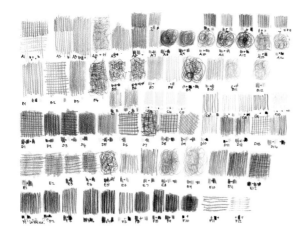

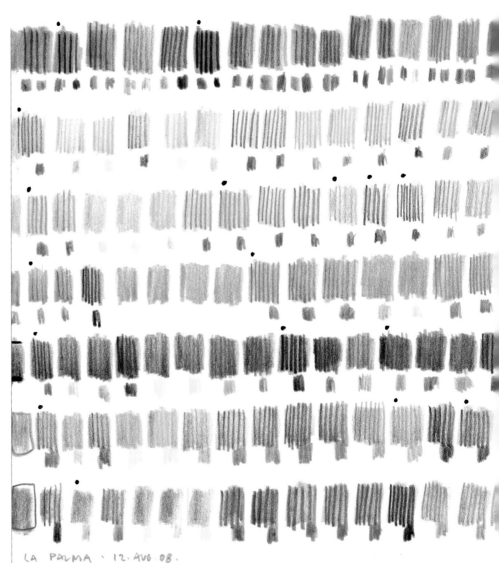

LA PALMA · 12· AUG·08.

Watercolour washes

It is possible to create hues with up to twelve separate watercolour washes. The basic colours should be light, and the water must be clean. The end results can be extremely pleasing, although memorizing the sequence of washes to create a particular colour is equally challenging. The choice of coloured media is personal to a designer: a skill in working with watercolour is highly valuable, but coloured pencils offer an easier and acceptable substitute.

Winsor & Newton watercolours on A3 Arches Aquarelle hot-pressed paper; 4 hours.

Time to draw

For a designer, the question 'When do you find time to draw?' could be put another way: 'When do you find time to think?' In the heat of the Caribbean, the pace of life is slow; spending a day drawing leaves seemed an appropriate use of time. The extraordinary linearity of the trunks of the Sea Grape tree exists in stark contrast to the circularity of its thousands of sparkling leaves.

Indian ink and Zebra Drafix pen on A3 paper; 1 day.

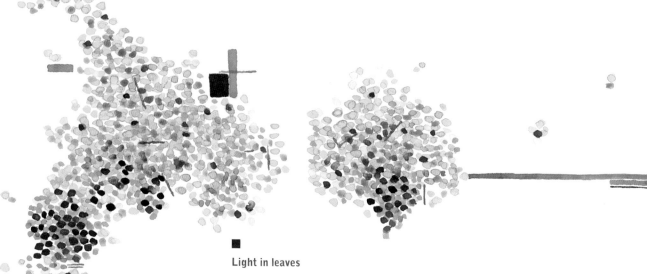

Light in leaves

BEQUIA, ST VINCENT & THE GRENADINES

Drying fast in the heat of the tropics, the pigment in a drop of watercolour will tend to migrate to the edge of the blob. This just so happens to coincide with the quality of the strong, luminous colours of the leaves when seen against the morning sunlight – one of those occasions when serendipity plays a part in the success of a painting.

Winsor & Newton Artists' watercolours, A3 Seawhite sketchbook; 60 minutes.

Coloured pencils and light

It is possible to make an astonishing range of marks with coloured pencils. Experimenting with media, independent of a subject, is both enjoyable and creatively liberating, but it is always helpful to record the sequence of each mix for later reference. The quality of manufacturers' pencils varies considerably, and it is worth exploring different brands to find the most sympathetic.

Staedtler Ergosoft coloured pencils on A4 paper; 60 minutes.

Pencil marks and plants

In order to draw plants convincingly, it is essential to try out several graphic approaches to sufficiently express their individual characteristics.

HB pencil, 2B graphite stick and 4mm B pencil on paper; 60 minutes.

'The spectacle of Djemaa el Fna is repeated daily and each day it is different. Everything changes: voices, sounds, gestures, the public which sees, listens, smells, tastes, touches. The oral tradition is framed by one much vaster, which we can call intangible. The square, as a physical space, shelters a rich oral and intangible tradition.'

Juan Goytisolo, in a speech at the opening meeting for UNESCO's Masterpieces of the Oral and Intangible Heritage of Humanity, 15 May 2001.

■

A space composed of people

DJEMAA EL FNA, MARRAKECH, MOROCCO

Spatially, this market square is an unremarkable area, but in the evening it is transformed. As the light begins to fade, it becomes an extraordinary theatre of colours, smoke, smells and sound, creating a hypnotic, dream-like vision. Crowds form around the storytellers, snake charmers and open-air food stalls. Since the light was changing fast, the scene was easier to record in coloured pencils than in watercolour.

Staedtler Ergosoft coloured pencils on A3 Bristol board; 75 minutes.

Cliffs and pebbles

SIDMOUTH, DEVON

In this section of world-heritage coastline at Sidmouth, the Triassic sandstone cliffs are an incredibly vivid colour. Frequent landslips expose fresh sections of unweathered red rock, the brightness of which contrasts with the duller quality of the beach pebbles, formed from an identical material but worn smooth over centuries of wave action. The sharp light qualities of the vertical cliffs and the more subdued beach differ dramatically.

Staedtler Ergosoft coloured pencils on A3 Bristol board; 60 minutes.

The first day of spring

CROWELL HILL WOOD, BUCKINGHAMSHIRE

The low angle of the sun cast multiple purple-blue shadows as it penetrated deep into the woodland, while young oak leaves added a dramatic colour contrast to the crop in the foreground.

Spring is an incredibly vital time of year: colours appear amazingly sharp, and bright sunlight enhances their clarity.

Staedtler Ergosoft coloured pencils on A3 Bristol board; 120 minutes.

Droxford Water meadows
July 02

Water meadows

DROXFORD, HAMPSHIRE

Landscape drawings can sometimes embody a powerful sense of nostalgia. Revisiting familiar surroundings can evoke feelings of déjà vu, and spark off a compulsion to capture the spirit of the place: in this case, water meadows in the English countryside.

Staedtler Ergosoft coloured pencils on A3 Bristol board; 45 minutes.

The Scottish colourists in the early 20th century practised the idea that it is possible, when looking hard enough at a sunlit landscape, to see the complementary colours of a subject in the shadows. The skill of training one's eye to be able to do this takes time to develop.

■

A chance encounter

AMIZMIZ, MOROCCO

Chance often plays a part in unexpectedly presenting an interesting subject, together with the time in which to draw it. I was sitting on a bus, waiting for the other passengers to arrive, when I noticed this large joint of meat hanging in a butcher's shop window. Although somewhat of a departure from the more usual landscape scene, it nevertheless made engrossing subject matter. One of my assistants, a vegan, chose this drawing as her leaving present!

Staedtler Ergosoft coloured pencils on A4 Bristol board; 15 minutes.

Industrial decay

MINIERA DI SAN GIOVANNI,
SARDINIA, ITALY

Searching for an exciting subject to draw can take an inordinate amount of time, but it is always worth striving to find something really stimulating. Everyone is inspired by different elements in the landscape, and it is this individual dialogue that sparks the necessary energy and enthusiasm for the creation of an interesting drawing. In this case, the extraordinary remnants of the Sardinian mining industry had been abandoned, left as memories of a bygone industrial age. How different from the English government's approach in the 1970s, when evidence of slag heaps in former coal-mining areas was removed and sanitized by 'polite' landscaping. This mine, with its rusting construction and doors swinging on their hinges, has an overwhelming sense of genius loci.

Faber-Castell Art Grip Aquarelle coloured pencils on A2 Bristol board; 3 hours.

Cartoon view

BARCELONA, SPAIN

This simple, almost cartoon-like drawing was made while on a day-trippers' boat that had just left the port of Barcelona. As the viewpoint was constantly, if gradually, changing over the course of the journey, one had to be highly selective, resulting in a surprisingly powerful drawing of the most important landmarks in the city.

HB pencil, A4 Seawhite sketchbook; 5 minutes.

Watercolour and line

SANTIAGO DE COMPOSTELA, SPAIN

The immense chimneys and general composition of this terrace, which forms one side of the Praza do Irmán Gómez, in Santiago de Compostela, has a strong De Stijl quality. Beginning by shaping simple blocks in watercolour and then drawing in line independently, creates an image with a certain tension between the two methods of observing and recording.

Winsor & Newton Artists' watercolours on A3 Arches Aquarelle hot-pressed paper; 90 minutes.

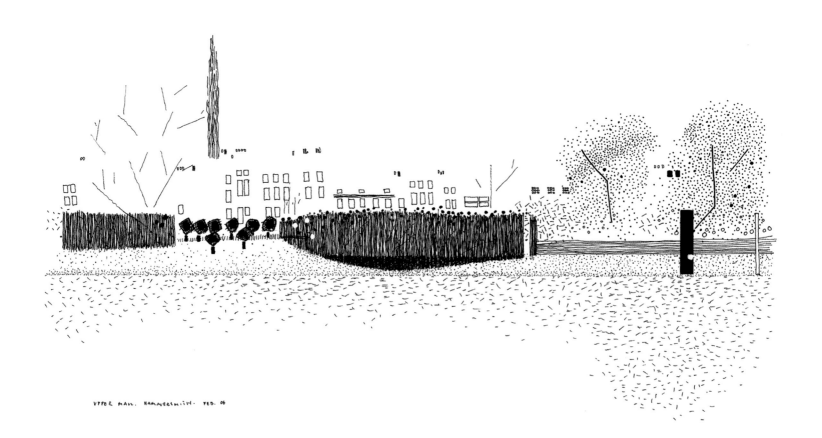

VPPER MALL. HAMMERSMITH. FEB. 06

■

Buildings as ghosts

HAMMERSMITH, LONDON
Not including the outlines
of the buildings along
Hammersmith's Upper Mall
helps to give emphasis to
the contrast created by the
planting in front of them.

Staedtler Pigment Liner and Staedtler
Lumocolor pen on A3 Arches Aquarelle
hot-pressed paper; 75 minutes.

Abstracting chosen elements of the context to create a convincing drawing enables one to focus on ideas generated by the subject and to learn from them, rather than to effect a more literal portrayal of the subject itself. Sometimes it is necessary to leave out extraneous detail to make a specific point.

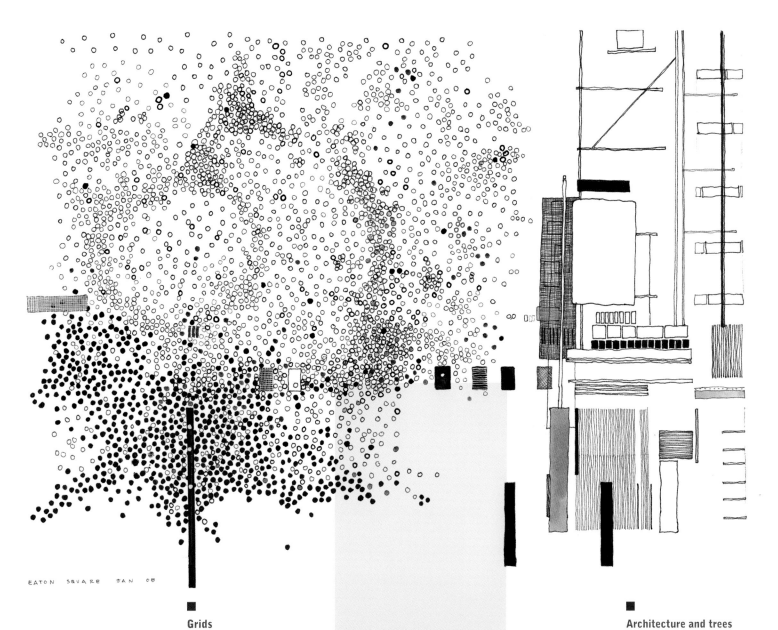

EATON SQUARE JAN 08

■

Grids

HYDE PARK SQUARE, LONDON

The superimposition of a
scaffold's grid over a
19th-century façade [right]
created an interesting and
geometrically complex
elevation. In some respects,
the free-functioning logic
of the scaffolding was
more interesting than the
constraints of the developer's
architecture. This was quite a
difficult drawing to make as
one's eyes kept straying from
the correct plane.

Staedtler Pigment Liner, Staedtler
Lumocolor pen and Winsor & Newton
grey ink on A3 Arches Aquarelle hot-
pressed paper; 2 hours.

■

Architecture and trees

EATON SQUARE, LONDON

Scaffolding erected over the
side elevation of another
19th-century façade [above]
created an interesting
Constructivist composition,
with the informality of the
trees reflecting a sense of
freedom against the repetitive
rhythm of the architectural
components. This relationship
between the trees and the
buildings is more dynamic
than trees planted regularly
along a grid would be.

Staedtler Pigment Liner and Staedtler
Lumocolor pen on A3 Arches Aquarelle
hot-pressed paper; 3 hours.

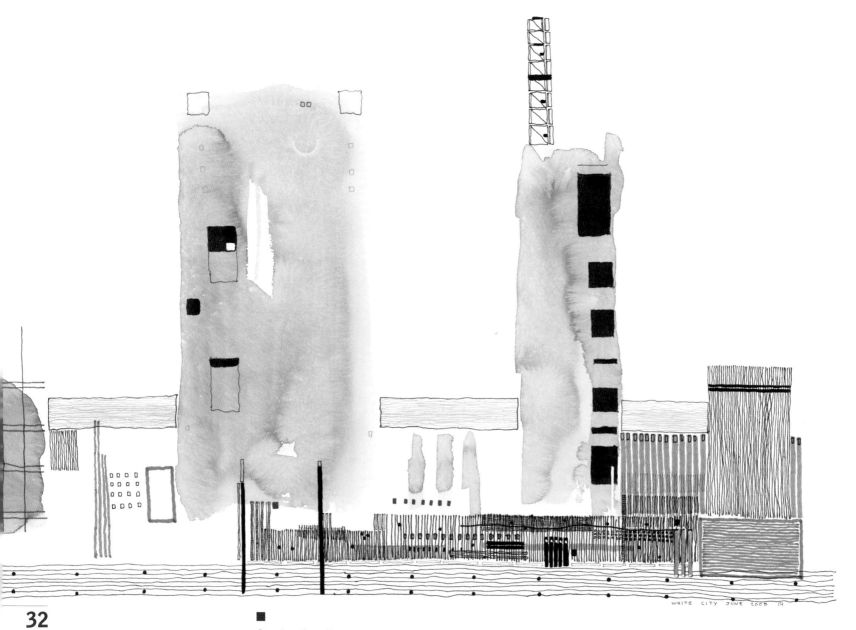

WHITE CITY JUNE 2008 14

Construction sites

WESTFIELD SHOPPING CENTRE, LONDON

A building under construction can be a more honest expression of our times than the eventual completed scheme. All too often, landmark buildings rely on external cladding to express a concept, masking the structural blood and bones of the project. Here, the liquidity of poured concrete against the linearity of reinforcing steel mesh gives a real insight into the raw guts of the building. It is always curious that security guards are so opposed to anyone recording this stage of construction, whether on film or in a drawing.

Winsor & Newton grey and black ink, Staedtler Pigment Liner and Tombow ABT felt-tip pens on A3 Bristol board; 2 hours.

Scales of buildings

THE THAMES AT MORTLAKE, LONDON

This drawing took twelve hours, over three sessions, to create. The risk was that it would go dead through being overworked. The incompatible juxtaposition of different scales of building appears to be compensated by the equally large changes of width in the tidal river.

Staedtler Pigment Liner 01/05, Faber-Castell Pitt Artists' pens, Winsor & Newton grey and black ink, and gold leaf on A2 Bristol board; 12 hours.

Rebuilding with a drawing

ST PETER-ON-THE-WALL, BRADWELL-ON-SEA, ESSEX

This tiny chapel was built in the 7th century from the remains of a Roman fort, which had previously occupied the site. The stonemasons clearly enjoyed constructing curious patterns in the walls with the mixture of materials at their disposal — a humour that still brings delight over a thousand years later.

Staedtler Pigment Liner 01/05, Zebra Drafix and Faber-Castell Pitt Artists' pens on A3 Bristol board; 90 minutes.

There can be something irresistible about a line drawing. The dynamic tension is often heightened by repetition, in particular the minor imperfections of a repeated element. Surprisingly, it remains important to concentrate on every mark to maintain the freshness of the drawing.

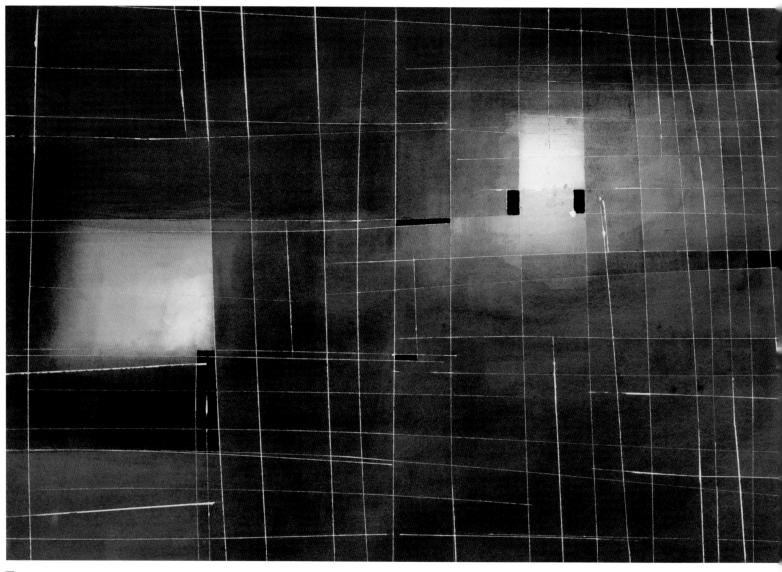

■
Abstract no. 1

Winsor & Newton Artists' watercolours
on Arches Aquarelle hot-pressed
paper (44cm × 70cm, 300 gms);
over several days.

These uncommissioned watercolours do not rely
on either logic or function for their success, and
serendipity played an important part in their
creation. I watched what happened on the paper
and learned from the behaviour of the materials,
unfettered by the limitations of a design project.

Abstract no. 2

Winsor & Newton Artists' watercolours
on Arches Aquarelle hot-pressed
paper (44cm × 44cm, 300 gms);
over several days.

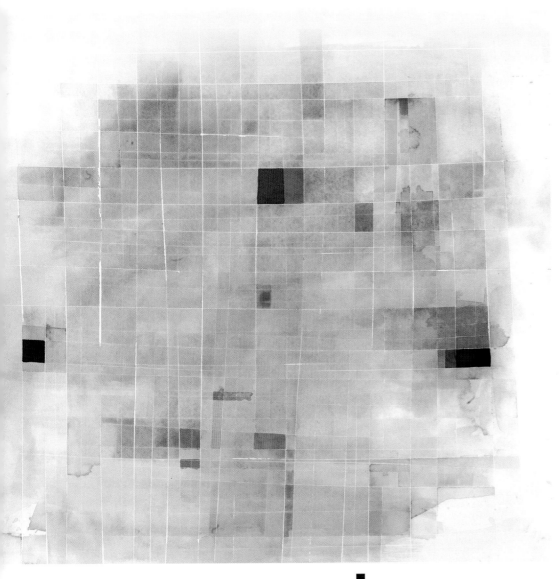

Abstract no. 3

Winsor & Newton Artists' watercolours
on Arches Aquarelle hot-pressed
paper (44cm × 44cm, 300 gms);
over several days.

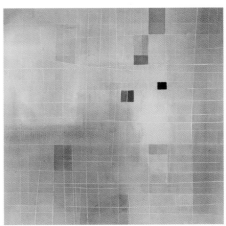

■

A quiet drawing

WEST SUSSEX

Drawing a sea mist in summer inevitably has a certain tension, as the sun
is always about to burn the mist away and spoil the quality of the light.

Winsor & Newton Artists' watercolours on A3 Arches Aquarelle hot-pressed paper (300 gms); 4 hours.

■
Creating highlights

GALICIA, SPAIN

When painting with watercolours, it is tempting to overstate highlights with white and black.
Using the background white paper as the accent is infinitely more powerful than white gouache.

Winsor & Newton Artists' watercolours on A3 Arches Aquarelle hot-pressed paper (300 gms); 2 hours.

■
The awesome scale of landscape

RIO GRANDE GORGE, NEW MEXICO

The immensity of landscapes such as this vast, flat plain,
fractured by the Rio Grande gorge, can be mind-boggling to
those unused to such massive dimensions of scale.
The phenomenal distances of the panorama are unsettling,
as are the magnificent skies, where several different weather
patterns can be seen to roll in from twenty or more miles
away. The constantly changing play of light makes the sky
an all-important feature of this natural setting, beloved of
painters over many years.

Winsor & Newton Artists' watercolours on A3 Arches Aquarelle hot-pressed paper
(300 gms); 6 hours.

To represent such abstract
qualities as scale, whether by
painting or drawing, can be a
dauntingly intellectual task.
The experience, however, helps
to inform and improve one's
conceptual abilities and skills.

■

Using different pencils

ROEHAMPTON, LONDON

The use of different widths and hardness of pencil, as well
as a rubber and smudging, can be a good way of expressing
the essential characteristics of plants. This type of image
is not competing with careful botanical drawings, but is instead
a crude method of helping to visualize the variations, always
useful when making planting plans.

HB, 3H and 4B 4mm pencils on A3 smooth cartridge paper; 45 minutes.

Caribbean plants

DOMINICA

The exuberant disparity of leaves found in a tropical rainforest encourages cartoon-like drawing. The effect of the extraordinary variety of naturally growing foliage can make planting plans appear somewhat irrelevant.

HB and 4B 4mm pencils on A3 smooth cartridge paper; 20 minutes.

Quick sketches often have a cartoon-like character, capturing the essence of the environment far more vividly than a photograph could.

Fist marks

LA GOMERA, CANARY ISLANDS

This beautiful California pepper tree has minute pinnate leaves that catch the slightest amount of breeze. In the extreme heat of the day, the microclimate inside the tree was appreciably cooler than out in the sunshine, due to the trembling of the leaves. Quick, jabbing marks, made while holding a pencil like a dagger, reflected the nervous quivering of the weeping tree.

Staedtler Ergosoft coloured pencils on A3 smooth cartridge paper; 6 hours.

The fury of the ocean

LA GOMERA, CANARY ISLANDS

Pencil and eraser were combined here to capture the
dynamics of the Atlantic Ocean. The dramatic breaking
of every seventh roller was mesmerizing; using a frozen image
of the breaking wave on the screen of a digital camera
helped while simultaneously drawing the scene from life.

2B and HB 3mm pencils on A3 smooth cartridge paper; 20 minutes.

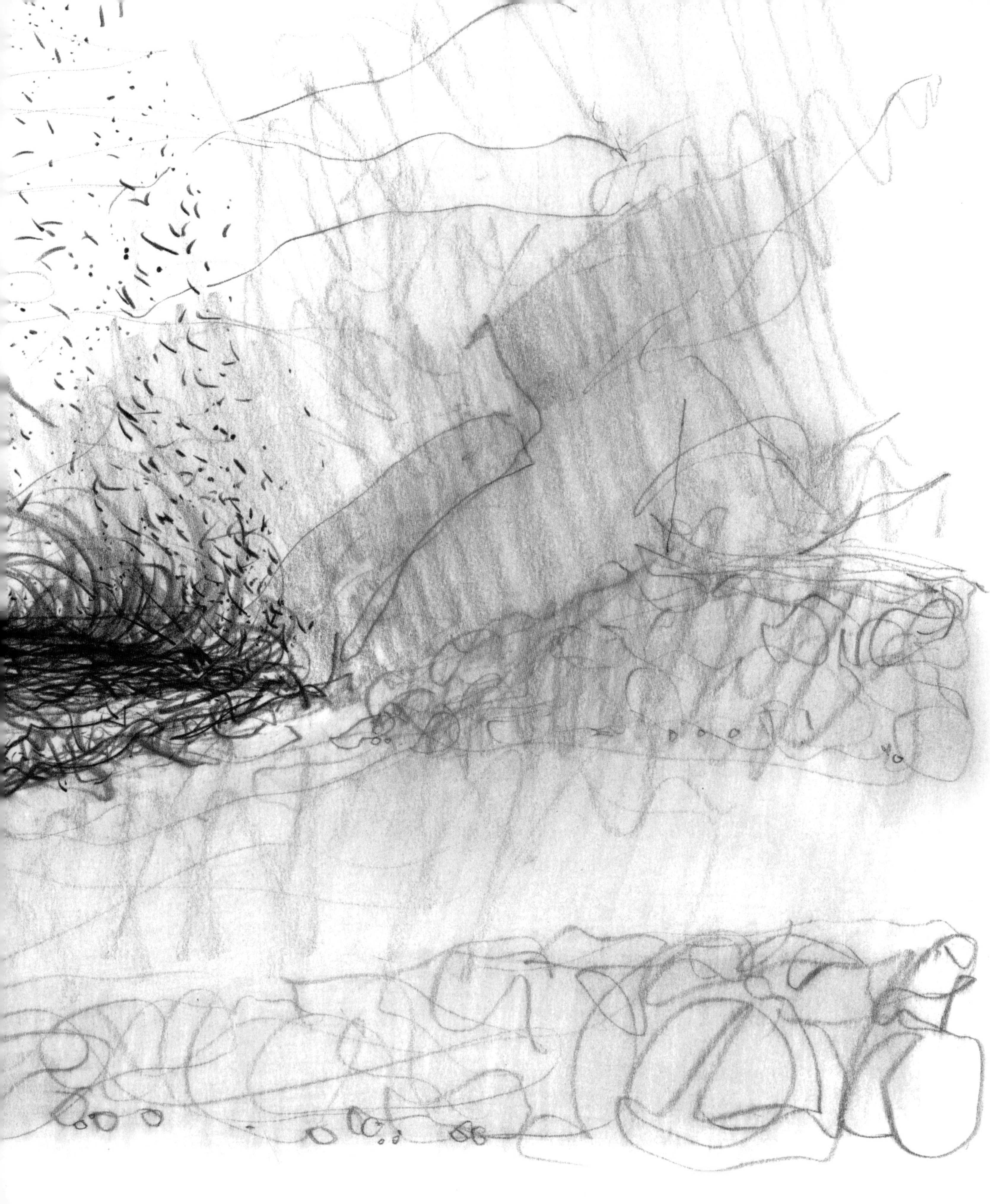

■

Abstract landscape

PORTO FLAVIA, SARDINIA, ITALY

Several centuries ago, the
Sardinian scrubland was
ravaged by fires, resulting in
widespread deforestation.
The subsequent regeneration
of the drought-tolerant plant
cover now forms the maquis
on the arid slopes of the island.

Faber-Castell Art Grip Aquarelle
coloured pencils on A2 Bristol board;
3 hours.

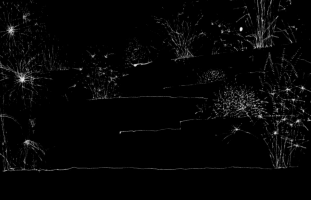

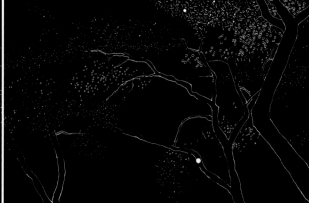

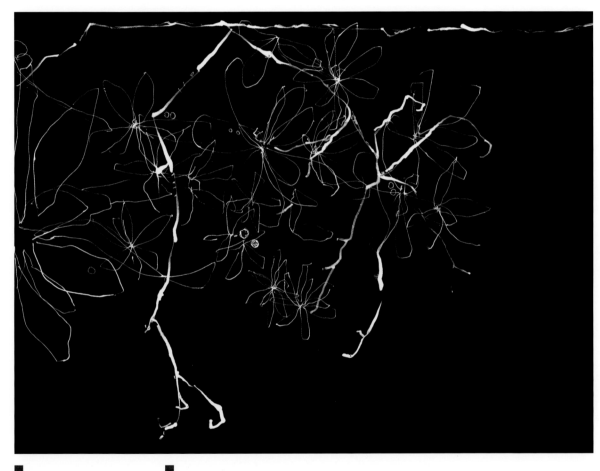

An ugly tree

ORTO BOTANICO CAGLIARI,
SARDINIA, ITALY

For a drawing to be dynamic,
it is important to abandon any
thought of beauty as a driving
force behind its creation. It
was fun to draw these crude,
somewhat grotesque leaves of
the kumquat tree, almost as
a personal attack on its thug-
like appearance.

White ink and dip pen on A3 black paper;
20 minutes.

A theatre of aquatic plants

ORTO BOTANICO CAGLIARI,
SARDINIA, ITALY

The terraces were designed by
a team who really understood
their subject [opposite, left].
The scheme used aquatic
plants sparingly, making the
most of their linear qualities,
with the overall effect
enhanced by the sound of a
waterfall in the background.

Wind-sculpted pine trees

ORTO BOTANICO CAGLIARI,
SARDINIA, ITALY

Japanese landscape art has
portrayed the vibrancy of
wind-blown pine trees over
many centuries. The subtlety
of their sculptural forms
[opposite, right], the sense of
movement in the trunk and
limbs of the tree, forces
an understanding of the
elemental power of wind.
In this environment, hot
breezes rising from the
Roman amphitheatre in
the south have driven the
prevailing wind currents.

White ink and dip pen on A3 black paper;
75 and 30 minutes.

2

Drawing on site

The world's longest pier
SOUTHEND-ON-SEA, ESSEX
On p. 44: An extraordinary
sense of infinity exists on
this pier, created by the
thin perspective of the
boardwalk and the flatness
of the surrounding estuarine
landscape. Its haunting
quality is mesmeric.

Staedtler Ergosoft coloured pencils,
A4 sketchbook; 20 minutes.

For thousands of years, the aborigines of Australia, surviving in
some of the earth's most inhospitable environments, have believed
that the land itself possesses the spirits of their ancestors.
Conversely, designers in our Western culture have become less
and less inclined to spend time on site, whether reflecting upon the
inherent power of the environment or understanding the past
from a creative perspective. Each site is unique, however, containing
both advantages and problematical complexities, and it is necessary
to experience its genius loci before beginning the design process.

In architecture, the design for a building may be new,
but the design of a landscape is always a conversion of an existing
place to something else. It is vital, therefore, to understand the
context in order to establish a genuine empathy with the site. This
real and sympathetic relationship, which fosters an understanding
of a location's latent energy and light qualities, invariably proves
essential during the later stages of a project. If, to paraphrase Paul
Theroux, the camera is the 'enemy of observation' – and photographs
are essential as factual records – the site is often best understood
during the act of drawing. At the start of a project, a few hours spent
'in' the site – drawing, listening, feeling and observing – are seldom
wasted. This is occasionally viewed as an ill-afforded whimsical
luxury, inferior in productivity to tasks carried out in the office, but
for landscape architects – who are selected, after all, for the unique
knowledge and skills that will lead to informed decision-making,
saving time and money – there is no substitute for drawing on site.

The practice of observing while on site, and the repeated
exercise of prolonged concentration, hones the ability to read a
landscape. The humility engendered by this process allows the
designer to have a balanced response that ultimately delivers a
huge amount of freedom; ideas are far more easily presented with
authority when backed up by a thorough knowledge of the site,
together with detailed points that previously escaped notice.

Drawings have an advantage over photographs in that they are highly selective in the information they contain. In a city environment, it makes sense to draw the essence of a context without the usual intrusion of road signs and traffic. This makes the task of presenting ideas to clients much easier; site drawings will only emphasize the elements that are of significance. Another bonus to be gained from drawing on site is the appreciation shown by a client for both the drawings themselves and the obvious extra effort a designer is prepared to make to understand the brief. On numerous occasions, the ensuing discussions have helped to establish a good relationship between the client and designer – an invaluable weapon when pitching for work.

While still on site, it is possible to test out new design ideas by drawing sketch views to incorporate the concept. This encourages the creation of relatively free and convincing images of the existing context, together with proposals that are drawn in the same manner. A quick impression of an idea, drawn with passion and excitement, and animated by people, light and shade, can be a powerful way of sharing a vision at a very early stage in a project. When these sketch designs complement more formal images, drawn to scale, they bring a breadth and depth to any presentation.

A client will have high expectations of his or her landscape architect, and a designer can easily feel daunted by the scope of work and breadth of design capability required to come up with an inspired solution. The process of spending time drawing on site, engaging with the issues and accustoming oneself to the project helps inestimably in generating the confidence to face these challenges. The obvious effort demonstrated by these site drawings is appreciated by the client and encourages a dialogue, usually only appropriate once a working relationship and mutual respect has been established. Sketches can also influence the method, format and presentation of a scheme to a client, and help convey a level of commitment to the project.

RUE DES CHASSAINES
∘ A CHAOTIC UNPLANNED
CORNER.
∘ CARS RULE NOT O.K.

• RAILINGS PROTECT MAISON
CARRÉE BUT MAKE A VERY
UNCOMFORTABLE SPACE.
∘ CARS BY RAILINGS RUIN
SPATIAL FLOW.

RUE MOLIÈRE.
UNDISTINGUISHED STREET.
ODD ARRANGEMENT OF TREES DO NOT ADD
MAISON CARRÉE JUST VISIBLE   CLARITY

○ PROGRESS   V.   KEEP ALL THAT IS OLD.

○ M. CARRÉE   V.G. EVERYTHING ELSE ✓.

○ SACRIFICE   THE LESSER FOR THE BETTER.

○ DO NOT BE   FRIGHTENED   OF THE PAST

WELL PROPORTIONED SPACE
CHANGE OF LEVEL INTERESTING
NASTY RAILINGS

WIDE PAVEMENTS ARE VERY GENEROUS BUT NOT FULLY USED
A BREAK IN THE AVENUE WOULD EMPHASISE THE SPACE
PRESENCE OF MAISON CARRÉE VERY/TOO RETICENT

■

Getting a feel for a place

PLACE DE CARRÉE D'ART, NÎMES, FRANCE

It was a wonderful experience to draw in Nîmes, when I was working at Foster Associates and they had just won the commission to design the main square adjacent to the new Bibliothèque. Spending a week drawing in that part of town was a terrific way to get the feel for both the place and the locals, and I like to think that the enjoyment experienced and the care taken to be sensitive to the context is reflected in the final design. On returning to London, however, my sunburnt face was evidence to some in the office that I had not been working when away, and had spent too much time outdoors 'having a nice time'.

Pentel felt-tip pen and Staedtler Pigment Liner 01, A4 Daler sketchbook; 30 minutes each.

13·MAY
ARCHIVES.   AREA THRU · THE AGES
MAISON CARREE
PHOTOS OF SITE + DEVELOP.
DRAFT : SURVEY   1:500.   (NURSERY SCHOOL)
4/5 SITE DRAWING.

PEDESTRIANS ON PAVEMENT.

Sometimes it can be an advantage to be an
outsider when designing in different parts of the
world. Immersion into an unfamiliar culture is
stimulating, and can result in the development of
a landscape that is appropriate, not simply one
with a generic, 'one-style-fits-all' stamp on it.

Anticipating the completed scheme

PLACE DE CARRÉE D'ART, NÎMES, FRANCE

These conceptual sketches [above and right] were made on site
and illustrate proposals to surround the historic Maison Carrée
with water and a line of trees, and to re-establish the qualities
of the former peristyle. The scheme was presented to the
mayor, but failed to find favour. The photographs (top) show
the scheme on completion in 1992.

Zebra Drafix 01 pen on A4 paper; 20 minutes.

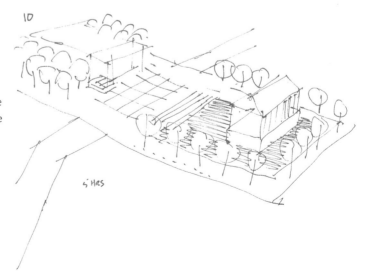

Shopfronts

MARYLEBONE HIGH STREET AND BOW LANE, LONDON

Modern shop design places a physical and psychological barrier – the ubiquitous plate-glass window – between the casual passerby and the shopkeeper's wares. The pavement directly outside – seen here in Marylebone High Street [left, top] and Bow Lane [left, bottom] – constitutes a potentially dynamic commercial zone; in this 'commercial forecourt', one is neither inside the shop nor outside it. The zone reflects both the character of the shopkeeper and the products on sale, and creates an environment rich with incidental engagements.

HB pencil on A3 smooth cartridge paper; 70 minutes each.

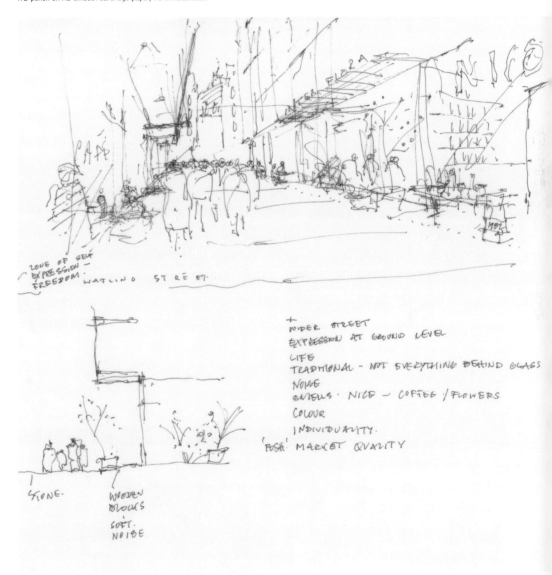

Proposals for new shop frontage

WATLING STREET, LONDON

These designs for Watling Street [above], an ancient road that dates to Roman times, stress the need for colour and activity.

Pilot G-Tec-C4 pen on A3 tracing paper; 60 minutes.

Upon leaving the residence,
the departing view of the
drive is framed by rows of
plants growing in terracotta
pots [left].

Faber-Castell Art Grip Aquarelle
coloured pencils on paper; 10 minutes.

The landscape design of an
embassy residence may be
constrained by the need to
reflect a correct impression of
'Britishness' to visitors.

Arriving

BRITISH EMBASSY,
DAMASCUS, SYRIA
An unpretentious drive leads
directly to the front door.
The existing layout, with its
central reservation of palm
trees, takes up much of the
road and disarticulates
the space [above].

Faber-Castell Art Grip Aquarelle
coloured pencils on paper; 15 minutes.

The Queen's Lawn

BRITISH EMBASSY,
DAMASCUS, SYRIA
The Queen's birthday is
an important date in the
diplomatic calendar. The
occasion is celebrated with a
champagne party in June on
the traditionally British grass
lawn [above, right].

Faber-Castell Art Grip Aquarelle
coloured pencils on paper; 15 minutes.

An embassy garden

Pool courtyard

BRITISH EMBASSY,
DAMASCUS, SYRIA

The most informal entertaining
area in the complex, where
the ambassador's guests are
made to feel 'part of the family'.

Faber-Castell Art Grip Aquarelle coloured
pencils on paper; 15 minutes.

■

Understanding places

DUISBURG, GERMANY

These drawings are all about gaining an understanding of the various streets that surround a site.

Staedtler Pigment Liner 01, A4 Daler sketchbook; 20 minutes each.

PAPPENSTRASSE
STRANGELY PROPORTIONED STREET - TOO WIDE - VACUOUS.
BIRCH. HORNBEAM. PLANE TREES

Creating minimal, elemental line drawings is a good discipline, as the process encourages an understanding of the essential mood of a city. The drawings do not attempt to portray realism, but are cartoons of the streets and spaces.

MULHEIMER STRASSE
A STRANGE UNDESIGNED SPACE - LARGE TREES
HAVE AN ODD QUALITY - GHOSTLY?

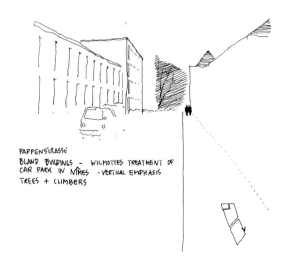

PAPPENSTRASSE
BLAND BUILDINGS - WILMOTTES TREATMENT OF
CAR PARK IN NÎMES - VERTICAL EMPHASIS
TREES + CLIMBERS

PAPPENSTRASSE
WHITE / GREY BUILDINGS CONTRAST PERHAPS POORLY
TO OTHER POST WAR BUILDINGS DUE TO LACK OF
INTEREST IN DETAILS: WONDERFUL IF CLAD IN VIRGINIA CREEPER!
IF LANDSCAPE PROPOSAL IS ACCEPTED CORNER
BUILDING SHOULD GO

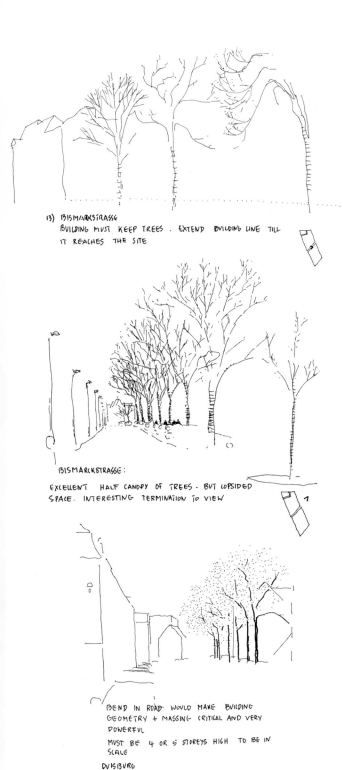

13) BISMARKSTRASSE
BUILDING MUST KEEP TREES. EXTEND BUILDING LINE TILL
IT REACHES THE SITE

BISMARCKSTRASSE:

EXCELLENT HALF CANOPY OF TREES. BUT LOPSIDED
SPACE. INTERESTING TERMINATION TO VIEW

BEND IN ROAD WOULD MAKE BUILDING
GEOMETRY + MASSING CRITICAL AND VERY
POWERFUL
MUST BE 4 OR 5 STOREYS HIGH TO BE IN
SCALE
DUISBURG

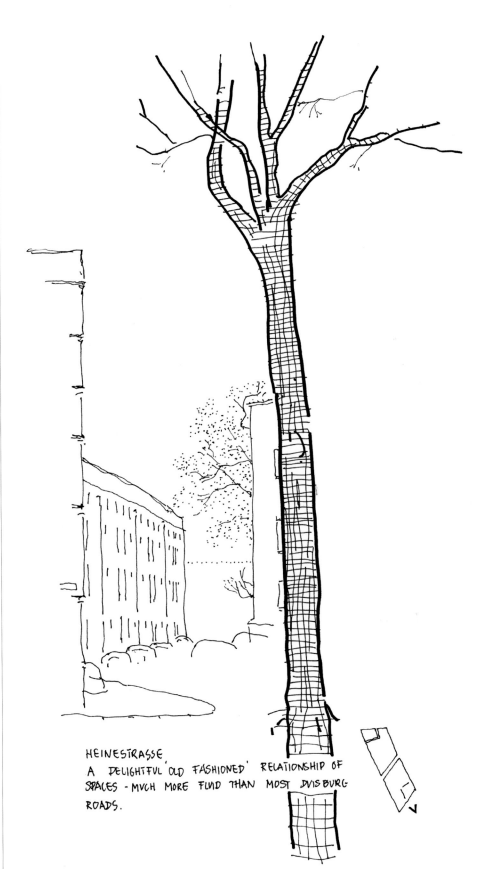

HEINESTRASSE.
A DELIGHTFUL 'OLD FASHIONED' RELATIONSHIP OF
SPACES - MUCH MORE FLUID THAN MOST DUISBURG
ROADS.

The practice of design, whether at home or abroad, has historically involved the designer in a process of investigation and analysis, driven by observation. Nowadays, with technology the buzzword, site recordings are often made on camera and hand-drawn sketches have become a rarity. This emphasis on speed and efficiency loses sight of the intellectual journey undergone in reaching a design solution.

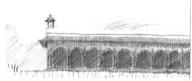

■ **Movement and colour**

THE RED FORT, NEW DELHI, INDIA

Silk drapes, hung from metal hooks between stone columns, seem to dance in the breeze and increase the movement of the air [above]. The colours of the sandstone and shadows in the evening light were magical. The drawbridge and moat at this gated entrance [top, right] offer security to the 17th-century fort (security at the entrance to an embassy is an issue that often poses severe design challenges).

Faber-Castell Art Grip Aquarelle coloured pencils on A4 paper; 35 minutes each.

■ **Creating microclimates**

LODI GARDENS, NEW DELHI, INDIA

Because of the modern reliance on air conditioning to solve internal air-temperature problems, architects no longer need to understand the principles of microclimate or turn to more traditional design solutions. In India, the intense heat and light has influenced a style of building that reflects the importance of courtyards, verandahs and pierced stone lattices to create microclimates of cool air.

Faber-Castell Art Grip Aquarelle coloured pencils on A4 paper; 25 minutes.

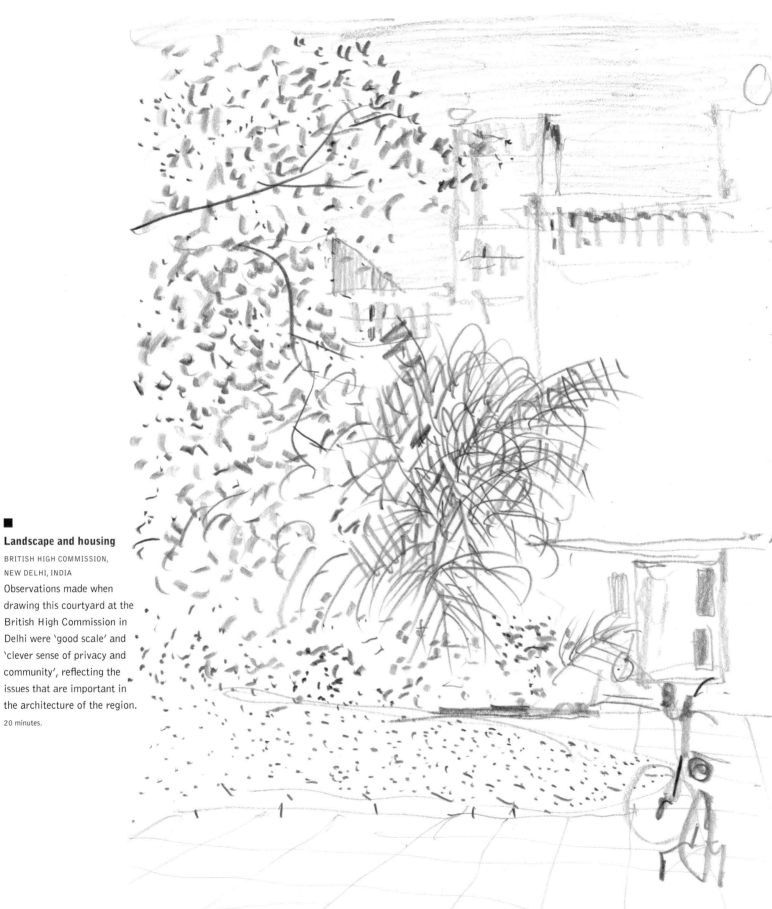

Landscape and housing

BRITISH HIGH COMMISSION,
NEW DELHI, INDIA

Observations made when
drawing this courtyard at the
British High Commission in
Delhi were 'good scale' and
'clever sense of privacy and
community', reflecting the
issues that are important in
the architecture of the region.
20 minutes.

LANARK. VERY GOOD RELATIONSHIP BETWEEN ARCHITECTURE
+ PLANTING DESIGN.

ROAD WITH NO FOCUS/PURPOSE. FIDDLY STONE DETAILS. VERY WIDE.

GARRISON/MAINTENANCE. YARD ROAD. VISUAL LINK TO OUTSIDE

No 1 BUNGALOW - NOT A BUNGALOW! HUGE GARDENS. IS THIS THE BEST USE OF
GARDEN SPACE. + LAWNS

■

Analysing the grounds

BRITISH HIGH COMMISSION,
NEW DELHI, INDIA

This series of drawings [left]
notes the existing relationship
between the architecture and
the planting design.

Faber-Castell Art Grip Aquarelle
coloured pencils on A4 paper;
35 minutes each.

■

Gurkha quarters

BRITISH HIGH COMMISSION,
NEW DELHI, INDIA

Unlike the rest of the
compound, the soldiers'
quarters are lively places;
notices posted by officers
regarding tidiness seemed
to be healthily ignored
[opposite, below left].
Drawing other people's
private spaces must always
be done quickly and discreetly.

Faber-Castell Art Grip Aquarelle
coloured pencils on A4 tracing paper;
5 minutes.

MAIN ENTRANCE "GROSVENOR HOUSE" ORIGINAL AVENUE OPPOSITE FRONT DOOR ? HSH TO MAKE SECURITY ELEGANT. MUDDLED FIRST IMPRESSION

Seemingly naïve site-survey plans that reflect a designer's experience and memory may in fact be more informative than formal, polished graphics. In the same way, a farmer might describe his land in rough drawings that are nonetheless rich with a latent understanding of the soil.

B29
MORE LIFE · PEOPLE · FUN.

■

A muddled first impression

BRITISH HIGH COMMISSION, NEW DELHI, INDIA

The existing main entrance [left] provides a drab public face to the British presence in India, in marked contrast to Sir Edwin Lutyens's designs with Herbert Baker in the 1920s. This drawing was useful when making a point to the British High Commissioner.

2B and HB pencils, rubbed and smudged, on A4 paper; 15 minutes.

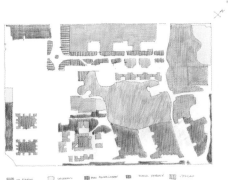

■

Paths and circulation

BRITISH HIGH COMMISSION, NEW DELHI, INDIA

The choice of colours helps to make a point in a subliminal way [right, top]. The act of tracing over the outlines of the buildings fosters an understanding of the spaces between them [right, middle]. Informal paths created during recent landscape improvements are in marked contrast to the highly formal layout of the 1950s [right, bottom].

Faber-Castell Art Grip Aquarelle coloured pencils on A3 tracing paper (laid over site plan); 90 minutes each.

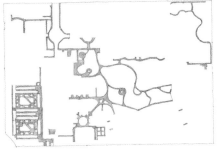

Analysis sketches

Past, present and future

PITZHANGER MANOR, EALING, LONDON

These preliminary sketches draw on historical and contemporary research of the area, and, although free in form, sum up the spirit and direction of the design proposal. The architect Sir John Soane bought Pitzhanger Manor in 1800 as a country house for entertaining guests, and remodelled the existing building using ideas developed by Giorgio Vasari, the 16th-century art historian and architect, in Arezzo. In 1804, Soane commissioned John Haverfield to redesign the landscape to suit the new style of the house. These three coloured drawings represent a new landscape based on Haverfield's ideas. The purpose of the design was to screen the historic house from the modern context of the neighbouring medium-rise buildings. The landscape architect Geoffrey Jellicoe called this design attitude 'creative conservation', an approach that does not simply restore and replant an original design, but reinterprets it to fit and enhance the modern context.

Staedtler Ergosoft coloured pencils on A4 paper; 35 minutes each.

Drawing on site

■
Aerial view

PITZHANGER MANOR,
EALING, LONDON

The landscape concept in context [below].

Faber-Castell Art Grip Aquarelle coloured pencils and Pilot G-Tec-C4 pen on A4 paper; 45 minutes.

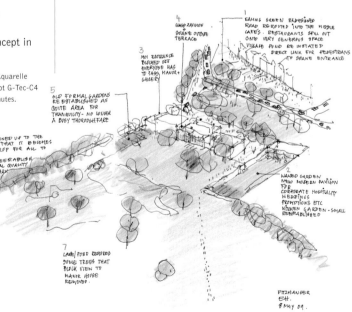

■
A change in perspective

WALPOLE PARK, EALING, LONDON

Recording the landscape with white ink on black paper (rather than black on white) helps to emphasize certain features of the design [opposite]. The result is slightly more awkward, and the image appears unfamiliar, challenging our normal way of looking at a landscape.

Winsor & Newton white ink and Pentel Hybrid Gel white pen on A3 Daler black paper; 45 minutes each.

1746

CLEARLY DEFINED LANDSCAPE SPACES
EALING VILLAGE GREEN + POND
MANOR HOUSE WITH A FORMAL
GARDEN, FIELDS BEYOND

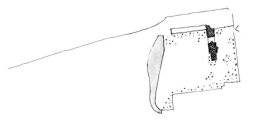

1800

JOHN HAVERFIELD - ASSYMETRICAL
ENTRANCE OFF EALING GREEN,
OPEN LANDSCAPE TO THE WEST
OF THE HOUSE. EDGES OF THE
ESTATE SOFTENED + BLURRED
WITH PLANTING

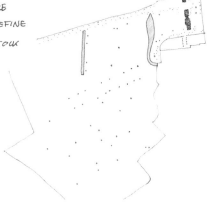

The use of historic maps

PITZHANGER MANOR, EALING, LONDON

This series of drawings, based on three hundred years of
historic maps, show the site from 1746 to 2009 and illustrate
the changes over the centuries to the landscape design,
including Sir John Soane's addition of trees to the grounds
in 1801, the removal of the lake in 1865, and the addition
of a war memorial in 1934.

Faber-Castell TG1 0.25 technical pen and HB pencil on A3 tracing paper;
45 minutes each.

1832

THE PLAN PREPARED FOR THE SALE
OF THE ESTATE.
THE FISH POND WAS MADE TO DEFINE
THE EDGE OF THE ESTATE.
SHRUB PLANTING ADDED BY MATTOCK
LANE

1865

THE LAKE BY THE HOUSE IS
REMOVED. THE LINK TO THE
WALLED GARDEN IS REMOVED
KITCHEN GARDEN WALL IS
SCREENED.
THE AVENUE IS PLANTED DEFINING
THE EDGE OF THE SPACE TO THE
FISH POND

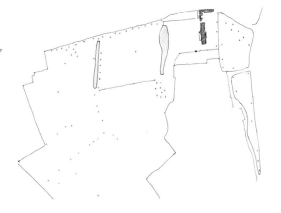

1896
STRANGELY THE LAKE BY THE HOUSE
RE APPEARS, BUT THE AVENUE OF
TREES LEADING TO THE FISH POND
IS NOT SHOWN.
A NUMBER OF TREES ARE NOT RECORDED

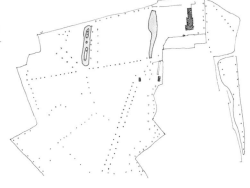

1915
THE NEW AVENUE LEADING TO THE SOUTH
ENTRANCE GATE IS PLANTED, THIS
CUTS THROUGH THE OPEN QUALITY
OF THE PARK, LATER TO BE FURTHER
DESTROYED BY THE MAYORS' AVENUE
THE FISH POND AVENUE IS SHOWN AS
A SINGLE LINE + EXTENDED EAST-
INTRODUCING MORE STRAIGHT LINES

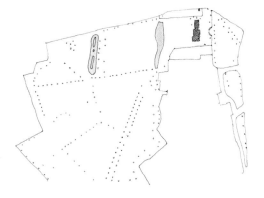

1934
THE WAR MEMORIAL INTRODUCES MORE
INAPPROPRIATE FORMALITY TO THE
FRONT OF THE HOUSE, DESTROYING SCENES
OBLIQUE ENTRANCE AND SIDE VIEW
WHICH HIGHLIGHTS THE TILE FLOATING
COLUMNS.
THE MEMORIAL DESTROYS THE INTIMACY
OF THE FRONT GARDEN. THE REMAINING
LANDSCAPE IS UNCHANGED.

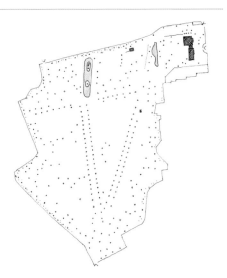

2009
A LARGE LOCAL PARK LACKING IDENTITY
OR CHARACTER. THE BEST IS NOT MADE
OF THE HOUSE AS A BACKDROP TO
THE LANDSCAPE. THE AVENUES, NICE AS
THEY ARE, CUTS UP THE SPACE. THE
WATER BODIES ARE WEAK

Old maps provide a wealth of information for the initial research of a new site. It is often a good exercise to trace over them in the process of making a new drawing; this promotes thought as to why changes were made in the past, and whether or not those alterations were improvements. A new set of drawings, in the same style, both equalizes the graphics and emphasizes the design improvements.

In design competitions, sketches
that convey a highly personal
reaction to a site often help to
distinguish one's own submission
from those of the competitors.

■

Site view

WORTHING, WEST SUSSEX

This sketch of the raised
walkway and changing huts was
one of a series of drawings
made on site that demonstrated
an analytical understanding of
the project.

Faber-Castell Art Grip Aquarelle coloured
pencils on A4 smooth cartridge paper;
30 minutes.

■

Seaside competition

WORTHING, WEST SUSSEX

This group of drawings
formed part of a competition
submission for a new swimming
pool. The judges responded
favourably to the the proposal:
'This was a landscape-driven
solution that delivered an
excellent landscape concept.
This was the strongest scheme
in terms of its relationship
to the environment and to
Beach House.' The house
in its original 19th-century
context [above].

Faber-Castell Art Grip Aquarelle coloured
pencils on A4 smooth cartridge paper;
30 minutes.

Site view

WORTHING, WEST SUSSEX

The view back towards
the centre of town, along the
shingle beach.

Faber-Castell Art Grip Aquarelle
coloured pencils on A4 smooth cartridge
paper; 30 minutes.

Concept sketches

WORTHING, WEST SUSSEX

These quick sketches were
important to our visualization
of the project. Because
the beach's pebbles were
uncomfortable to walk upon,
we proposed decking that
would link a swimming jetty
from the new pool to the sea.

Faber-Castell Art Grip Aquarelle
coloured pencils on A4 paper;
25 minutes each.

East Grafton.
Do you adnven the field
sitter with us or against us 'Bush'. check out planning. development plan
Old limes. Are the dominate the landscape

View from the back garden

EAST GRAFTON, WILTSHIRE

The location of the modern cottage at this site is an ancient one, and the genius loci deserves respect and inclusion in the new landscape proposals [above].

Staedtler Ergosoft coloured pencils on A3 smooth cartridge paper; 30 minutes.

The village green

EAST GRAFTON, WILTSHIRE

As seen in this site drawing [top], the cottages and their gardens that overlook the village green establish the gentle character of the settlement, but the relatively recent introduction of non-indigenous evergreen hedges erodes the sense of community. The design exploits the idea of 'borrowed landscape', incorporating the line of old lime trees to make the garden feel larger. These old trees exude a huge personality that the residents of the village respond to. A proposal for a small, complex patio [right], intended to contrast with the scale of the lime trees.

Staedtler Ergosoft coloured pencils on A3 smooth cartridge paper, 60 minutes; HB 0.5mm pencil on A4 paper, 15 minutes.

Having just six hours to become acquainted with the site, half the time was spent drawing and absorbing. Afterwards, over lunch, discussions with the client led to further design ideas.

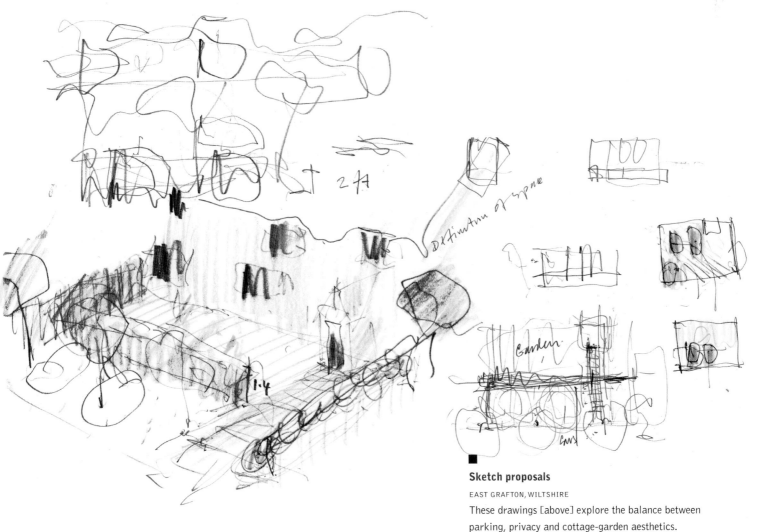

■ **Sketch proposals**

EAST GRAFTON, WILTSHIRE

These drawings [above] explore the balance between parking, privacy and cottage-garden aesthetics.

Faber-Castell Art Grip Aquarelle coloured pencils on A3 tracing paper; 10–15 minutes each.

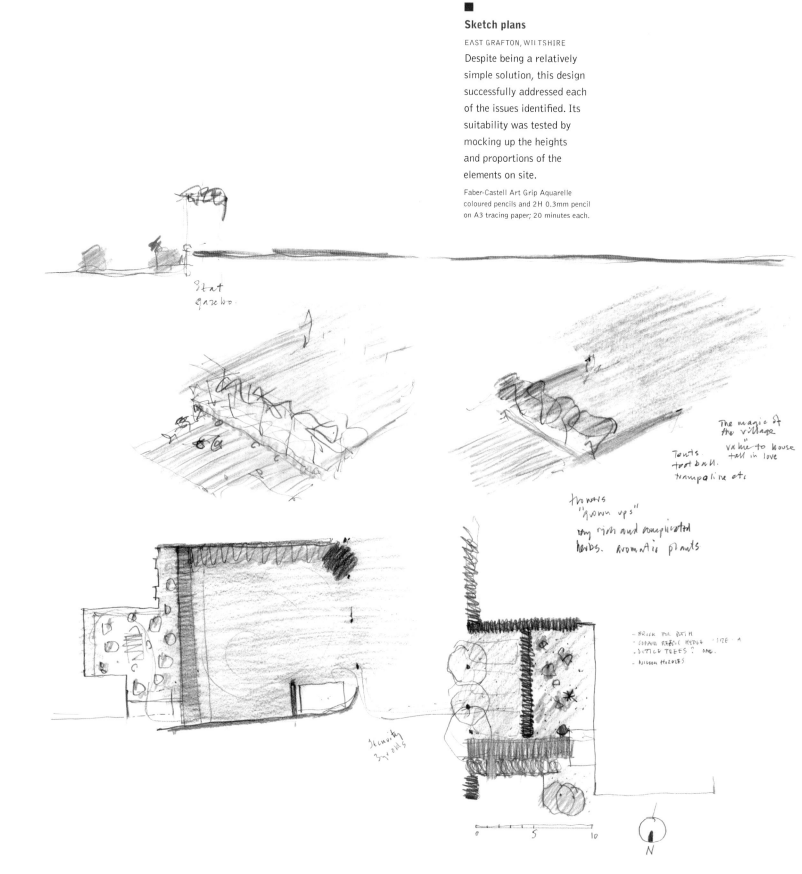

■

Sketch plans

EAST GRAFTON, WILTSHIRE

Despite being a relatively
simple solution, this design
successfully addressed each
of the issues identified. Its
suitability was tested by
mocking up the heights
and proportions of the
elements on site.

Faber-Castell Art Grip Aquarelle
coloured pencils and 2H 0.3mm pencil
on A3 tracing paper; 20 minutes each.

flat
gazebo.

The magic of
the village
value to house
fall in love

Tents
football.
trampoline etc.

flowers
"grown ups"
very rich and complicated
herbs. aromatic plants

- BRICK FOR PATH
- COPPER REBAR HEDDLE : SIZE A
- LITTLE TREES ? ONE.
- WILLOW HURDLES

security
3 years

0   5   10

N

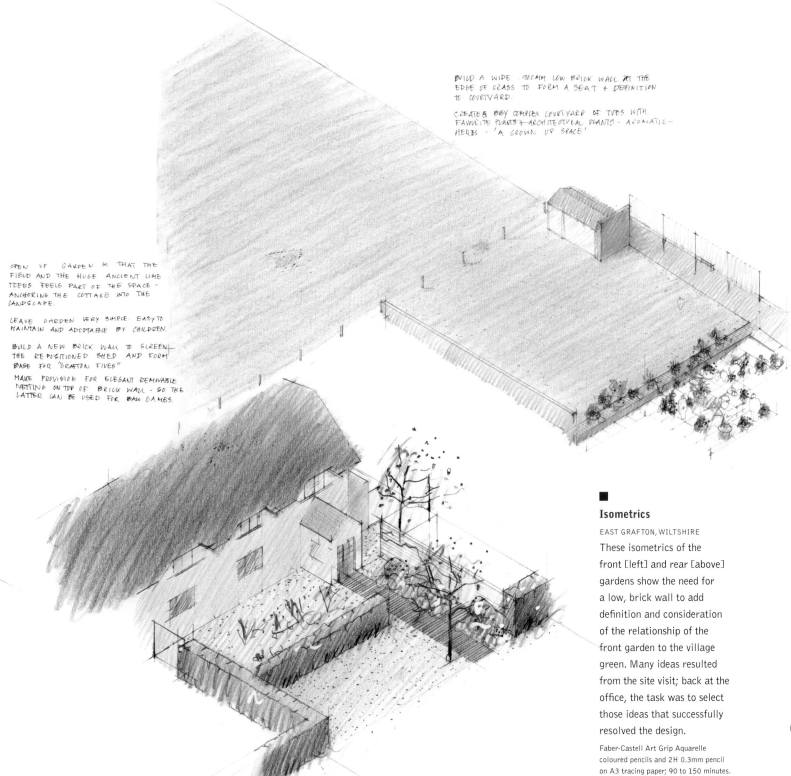

BUILD A WIDE .900MM LOW BRICK WALL AT THE
EDGE OF GRASS TO FORM A SEAT + DEFINITION
TO COURTYARD.

CREATE A BUSY COMPLEX COURTYARD OF TUBS WITH
FAVOURITE PLANTS + ARCHITECTURAL PLANTS - AROMATIC -
HERBS . 'A GROWN UP SPACE'

OPEN UP GARDEN SO THAT THE
FIELD AND THE HUGE ANCIENT LIME
TREES FEELS PART OF THE SPACE -
ANCHORING THE COTTAGE INTO THE
LANDSCAPE.

LEAVE GARDEN VERY SIMPLE. EASY TO
MAINTAIN AND ADOPTABLE BY CHILDREN.

BUILD A NEW BRICK WALL TO SCREEN
THE REPOSITIONED SHED AND FORM
BASE FOR "GRAFTON FIVES"

MAKE PROVISION FOR ELEGANT REMOVABLE
NETTING ON TOP OF BRICK WALL - SO THE
LATTER CAN BE USED FOR BALL GAMES.

Isometrics

EAST GRAFTON, WILTSHIRE

These isometrics of the
front [left] and rear [above]
gardens show the need for
a low, brick wall to add
definition and consideration
of the relationship of the
front garden to the village
green. Many ideas resulted
from the site visit; back at the
office, the task was to select
those ideas that successfully
resolved the design.

Faber-Castell Art Grip Aquarelle
coloured pencils and 2H 0.3mm pencil
on A3 tracing paper; 90 to 150 minutes.

69

A village garden

CONSIDER THE RELATIONSHIP OF THE FRONT GARDEN TO THE
GREEN - SUITABILITY OF PLANTS ESPECIALLY HEDGES.

CARS NOT TO PENETRATE THE GARDEN .
NEW COPPER BEECH HEDGE 1.4 CMS TALL TO SCREEN
CARS FROM THE HOUSE.

NEW RURAL WATTLE FENCE IN FRONT OF OIL TANK
FENCE + HERBACEOUS PLANTING (SOUTH FACING).
BRICK PATH TO THE FRONT DOOR .

TWO SMALL TREES PLANTED TO SOFTEN VIEW OF THE
GABLE END OF THE VILLAGE HALL

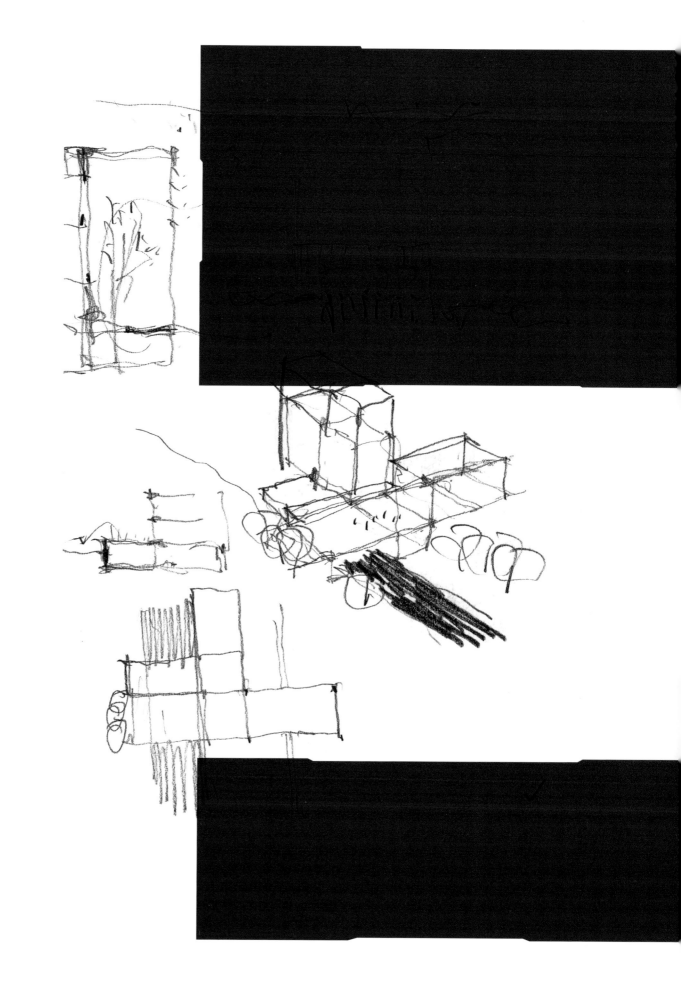

3

Drawing ideas

■

■

Putting an initial concept down on paper has to be one of the most
exciting moments for any designer, architect or landscape architect.
But where do ideas come from? Landscape architects, unlike many
other design professionals, never start with a blank canvas, as any
commission involves converting an already existing space. Adequate
time and full concentration are needed to communicate successfully
with a site and draw inspiration from it; here is the opportunity to
make a mass of notes that will help to form the eventual design,
and notebooks are soon filled with rapid sketches and observations
as the hand and brain interpret thoughts and concepts in quick-fire
succession. These drawings are informal, and probably quite messy,
but will later stimulate ideas through reinterpretation and lead to
other design solutions. This creative period is difficult to recreate
convincingly at a later stage in the project, when the design is more
definite. Walking the site with another person also fosters discussion,
and ideas seem to flow more easily from the triangular dialogue
created between two people and the existing landscape.

A design can sometimes suffer from being too respectful or
'safe', and consequently can seem rather dull. When a fresh approach
is needed, an invaluable perspective can be gained by viewing the
site from an aeroplane, creating a balance with the physical, tactile
and spatial impressions previously experienced on the ground. Large
elements in the landscape appear smaller and less intractable, and
the overall context becomes all-important, forcing a rethink of the
suitability of the design. Aerial photographs are no substitute for
seeing the site for oneself from the sky, although oblique aerial
photographs, which carry some degree of perspective, are often useful
when it is necessary to insert and test a new design idea. Drawing a
series of ideas in a loose, even chaotic way at the start of a project
is similarly advantageous. This free approach encourages discussions
with no predetermined outcome, and allows a designer to engage
other people in the creative process, which is always important in

winning people over to support a concept, particularly when a scheme has been developed by a team, rather than a committee. A certain amount of confidence is required in these circumstances to prevent the designer losing all control of the process.

The excitement surrounding an important project is infectious, and embraces the landscape design itself. While it is flattering to be appointed to design new external space, the landscape architect needs to retain authority over his or her area of responsibility, as other members of a multidisciplinary design team may want to become overinvolved in the process. The ability to draw ideas freely, conveying the poetry of landscape, is an important skill with which to retain the team's respect. The resulting sketches, accompanied by written or verbal descriptions, should be capable of transmitting the three-dimensional reality of the design.

Drawings that explore ideas for planting are an attempt to make sense of abstract concepts. The elements of movement, sparkle, smell and seasonal change are not easy to convey on paper, but are nonetheless important in a planting scheme. Disassociating the appearance of plants from a strictly realistic portrayal can be a good method of rendering them in a more symbolic way, and suggests their many other attributes. Inevitably, this approach is formed by an extremely personal vocabulary that needs explanation and to be supplemented by more conventional graphics. Preparing actual planting plans can be daunting, due to the huge choice of plants available, but the task is enlivened by portraying plants unrealistically, using bright colours. It is even more challenging to evoke the dynamics of a variety of plants by using only a range of greens.

■
Diagrammatic analysis

HULL HISTORY CENTRE,
EAST YORKSHIRE

Analytical drawings, based
on Ordnance Survey maps,
of the circulation routes and
main landmarks of the site.

1. Noise generated by traffic
   on the surrounding roads.
2. Main vehicular routes.
3. Principal pedestrian routes.
4. Location of local cafés and
   public houses.
5. Main views into the site.
6. Location of nearby public
   open spaces.

Ordnance survey maps, adjusted with
Photoshop; drawing by Claudia Corcilius.

A set of careful site-analysis studies can bring a
potential landscape project to life, and often prove
influential in persuading local decision-makers
and politicians to support a scheme.

■

Microclimate studies

HULL HISTORY CENTRE,
EAST YORKSHIRE

The studies demonstrate how
much sunshine the new 'pocket
park' and covered walkway
would receive during the day,
throughout the year.

1. 21 March and 21 September,
at 10 am: the entrance and
the north side of the park
are in sun.

2. 21 March and 21 September,
at noon: the pocket park
and terrace are in sun,
and the trees cast some
welcome shade.

3. Afternoon in midsummer:
the pocket park is in the
afternoon sunlight.

Ordnance survey map, adjusted with
Photoshop; drawing by Claudia Corcilius.

1

N

2

3

When walking in the countryside
we are constantly aware of
levels, from rolling hills to the
gradual incline of a river valley,
but in cities we tend to ignore
such changes in the contours of
the landscape.

■

Colour-coding levels

WALBROOK SQUARE, LONDON

Changes of level can be difficult to communicate visually. Whereas a dimension line clearly reflects a horizontal length, two spot-heights do not convey information with the same impact. In an attempt to address this issue, we tried several different methods. The site is by the historic River Walbrook, one of the most important rivers in Roman London. Although now invisible, its presence is apparent in the inclined river valley, which still exhibits a 3m change of level across the site.

In order to understand the slopes and their significance, each 20cm change in level was coloured differently, much like a topographic map. This unconventional approach and intense concentration on levels eventually led to a savings of £750,000 on the design of the ground-floor slab.

Berol Karismacolor coloured pencils over a photocopy of the site plan; A3 drawing by Heidi Hundley, 1 day.

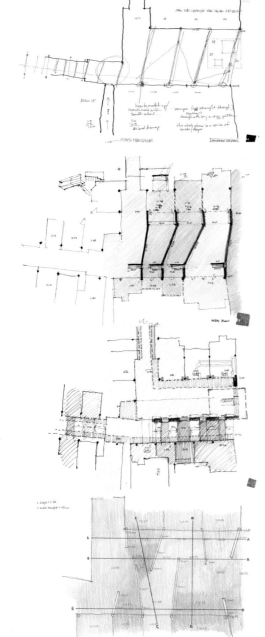

A puddle in a newly constructed landscape indicates a design failure.

Levels and drainage studies

WALBROOK SQUARE, LONDON

Although working out levels and designing falls for drainage takes quite a long time, this is the crux of a designer's skill and the process should be enjoyable. Sometimes it can be helpful to engage with the site levels by imagining oneself as a drop of water, as it will always take the shortest route downwards, effectively illustrating the natural lie of the land. It is better to veer towards stronger gradients, such as 1:30 or 1:35. Very shallow gradients can be difficult to achieve successfully.

Pilot G-Tec-C4 pen and Staedtler Ergosoft coloured pencils on paper (30cm × 42cm); 3 hours each.

Designing on site

AMBASSADOR'S RESIDENCE,
DAMASCUS, SYRIA

This drawing [right] was
made on site while walking
and talking with a local
nurseryman from Beirut.
Discussing both the existing
and proposed planting with
a local expert, conversant
with regional conditions and
availability of stock, saved
a huge amount of time. The
drawing is a record of our
conversation. This could have
been kept in an electronic
notebook; on paper, however,
it captures the spirit of the
moment in visual form.

Pilot G-Tec-C4 pen and Staedtler
Ergosoft coloured pencils on A3 tracing
paper; 4 hours.

Sketch plan

AMBASSADOR'S RESIDENCE,
DAMASCUS, SYRIA

The plan [opposite, top] was
drawn in the aeroplane on the
way home from Syria. It is
important to complete a
design stage, however roughly,
before losing the atmosphere
of a foreign country; once
back in the studio, the frisson
of the site lessens. A section
through the landscape
[opposite, bottom right]
illustrates the relationship
between the elements in
the design.

Pilot G-Tec-C4 pen and Staedtler
Ergosoft coloured pencils on A3 tracing
paper; 6 hours.

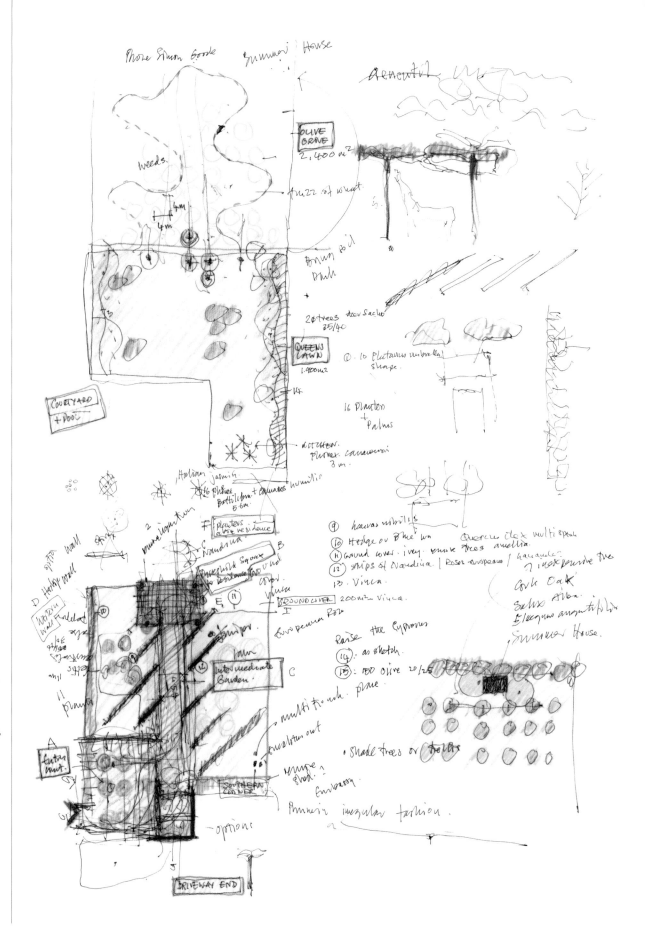

TENNIS COURT

CUT DOWN EXISTING STEEL POLES + NET 6 TO 3.5M
TALL. PLANT JASMINE TO COVER THE WIRE MESH.
REBUILD STEPS IN NEW ALIGNMENT.

POOL AREA

CONSTRUCT RETAINING WALL + PERGOLA BETWEEN POOL +
THE EMBASSY TERRACE. 2.5 M TALL FROM POOL LEVEL
CONSTRUCT RETAINING WALLS BETWEEN POOL AREA + CLUB
GARDENS. PLANT POOLSIDE OF WALL. MAKE WIRE
PERGOLA BY POOL TO CREATE SHADE. PLANT THE WEST
SIDE OF THE POOL WITH GROVE OF TREES.

CLUBHOUSE + GARDENS

CONSTRUCT CLUB HOUSE WITH FLAT ROOF (VISIBLE) INTEGRATED
WITH GUARDHOUSE 25 M LONG MAX. CREATE PERGOLA
WALK BY CLUBHOUSE. NEW PATH. STEPS + LAWN
BUILD 2.5M CONCRETE WALL THROUGH CLUB HOUSE @
90°. CREATE GARDENS + TREES, SHRUBS. ALLOW FOR
PLAY EQUIPMENT.

BOUNDARY TREATMENT.

CONSTRUCT BLAST WALLS AS REQUIRED. LIFT UP ALL THE
NEW PLANTING. ITALIAN CYPRESS + ROSEMARY +
PLACE IN A TEMPORARY NURSERY. DESIGN BRACKETS FOR
ELECTRIC WIRES SO THAT THEY ARE CONSIDERED
PLANT SEMI MATURE PINES RANDOMLY

ENTRY COURTYARD

REPAVE WITH A DARK BASALT STONE. TAKE DOWN
ENTRY GATE + CART AWAY. BLOCK UP OPENING WITH CONCRETE
BLOCKS. REBUILD STEPS TO FACE ARRIVAL
PLANT A GROVE OF OLIVE TREES +
ONE ANCIENT TREE. BUILD A
RETAINING WALL BETWEEN TERRACE
+ COURTYARD.

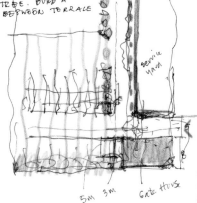

5M 3M   GATE HOUSE

35m =
14 SPACES
14
14
———
42

SERVICE YARD GATE HOUSE

CONSTRUCT GATE HOUSE 8M DEEP X 2M LONG. FLAT ROOF
BUILD CONCRETE BLOCK WALL 3M HIGH TO ENCLOSE EXISTING
X RAY BUILDING STORE ETC — RENDER + PAINT WALL A
STRONG COLOUR.

CAR PARK

CONSTRUCT WALL 2.2M TALL BETWEEN CAR PARK +
STAFF RECREATIONAL AREA. PAVE CAR PARK WITH
DARK MATERIAL - NOT STONE. CONSTRUCT STAINLESS
STEEL PERGOLA OVER - TRAIN PLANTS OVER.
CABLE

0.0

+2.45

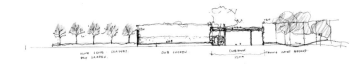

POOL LEVEL GRASSES CLUB GARDEN CLUBHOUSE SERVICE YARD GROUND
PLAY GARDEN

SERVICE YARD

BRITISH EMBASSY DAMASCUS. 12 NOV 08

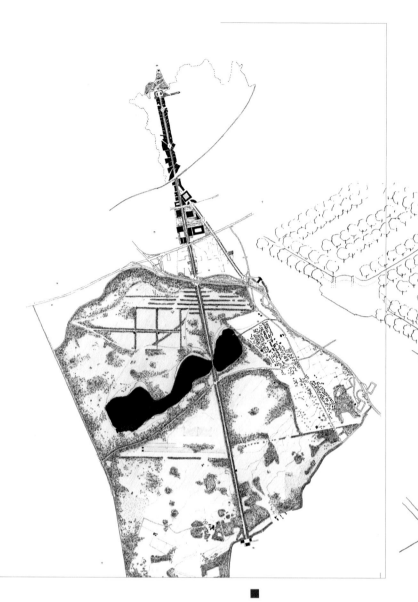

Freehand masterplan

PLACE DE CARRÉE D'ART,
NÎMES, FRANCE

This drawing [above], which
only took three hours to make,
explores the possibility of
creating a new formal avenue
into Nîmes from the airport,
through a new public park.
Although the scheme was
not realized, the idea carried
considerable plausibility; the
line of track planned for
the TGV in this part of France
was to be rerouted to avoid
clashing with the concept.

Zebra Drafix pen, coloured pens
and lake-coloured acetate on A1 tracing
paper, printed on smooth cartridge
paper; 3 hours.

Context of the scheme

PLACE DE CARRÉE D'ART,
NÎMES, FRANCE

This isometric view [below]
shows the proposal for the
Place de Carrée d'Art in the
larger city context.

2H pencil on A1 tracing paper and
Mylar film; 20 hours.

Looking out onto the world
below from an aeroplane window
gives a broader perspective,
and encourages bold thinking
and drawing.

Conceptual design ideas

These freehand sketches were made while flying back to London from Glasgow, and illustrate proposals for the Building Schools for the Future scheme. The level of the playing fields is sunk below the surrounding ground level, forming an amphitheatre, and the resultant spoil used to enhance the ground modelling of the remainder of the flat site. When enlarged for presentation, the original vigour of the drawing was not lost. Moreover, the graphic quality of the lines was exaggerated and emboldened via the enlargement process.

Lamy fountain pen on A3 paper, enlarged to A0; 90 minutes.

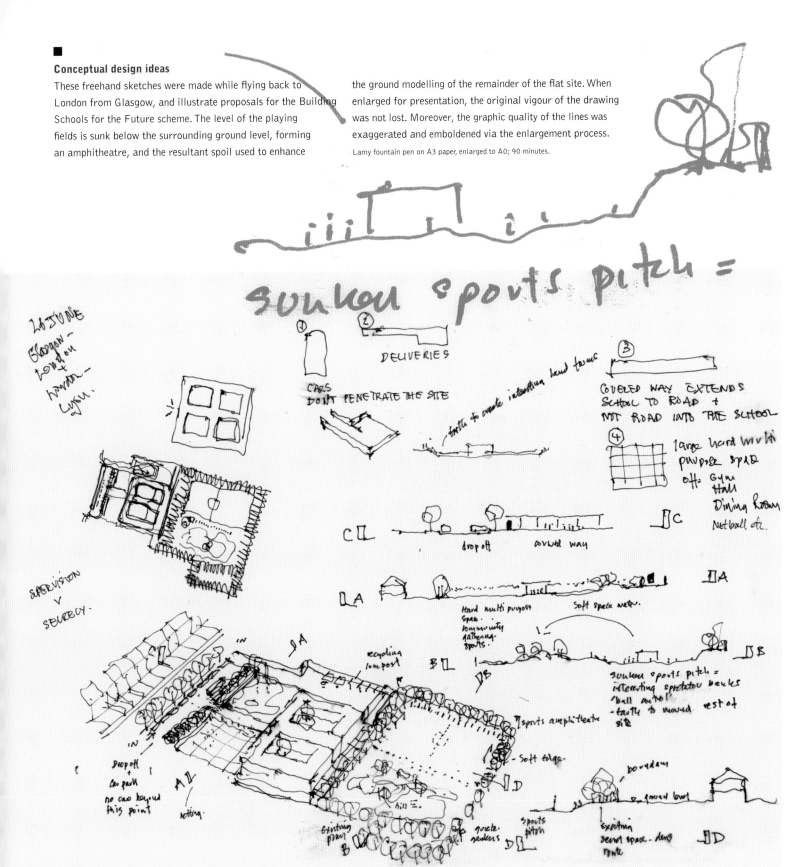

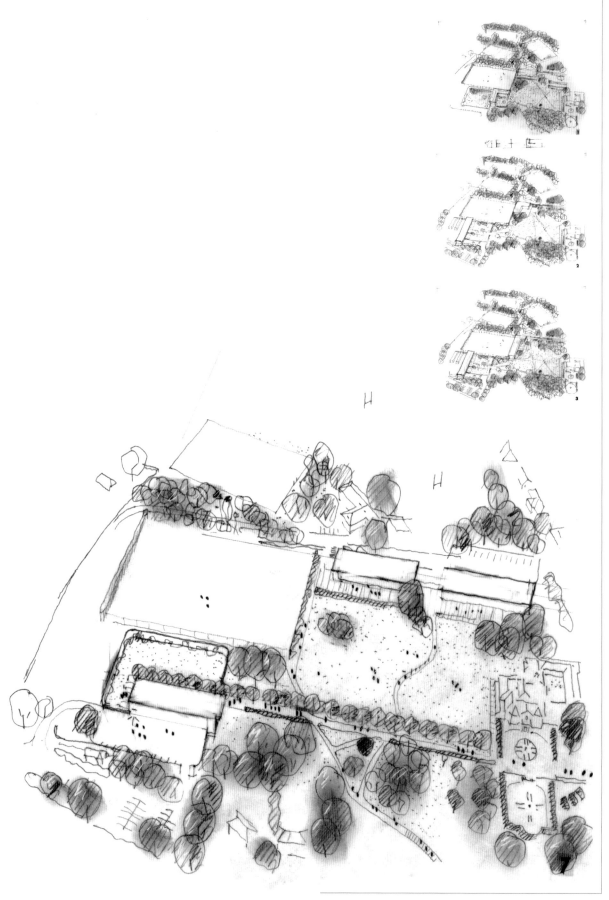

Spatial planning studies

SEVENOAKS SCHOOL, KENT

These fairly scruffy pencil sketches were made to explore the landscape spaces created by a series of architectural options for new dormitory blocks. Drawings made on tracing paper over an oblique aerial photograph give a detached, godlike view of a site, which can encourage imaginative ideas while still being rooted in three dimensions (unlike drawing over a two-dimensional plan). Employing a rubber for smudging and Tipp-Ex for highlights produces a vision of a somewhat imperfect world, which is ultimately closer to reality than many more polished methods of presentation. They are also quick to do, and therefore are cost-effective.

HB pencil on tracing paper (30cm × 42cm), with Tipp-Ex highlights; 60 minutes each.

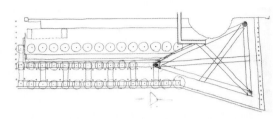

Working towards a dream

THE LONDON EYE,
SOUTH BANK, LONDON

These plans [right] were drawn three years prior to the eventual construction of the London Eye on the city's South Bank. The drawings for the surrounding landscape were made during that heady period when the improbabilities of the structure ever winning planning approval were gradually being replaced by a growing sense of confidence in the project. They explore different configurations of an avenue leading up to the 'Millennium Wheel'.

HB 5mm pencil on A0 tracing paper, reduced to one-third; 2 hours each.

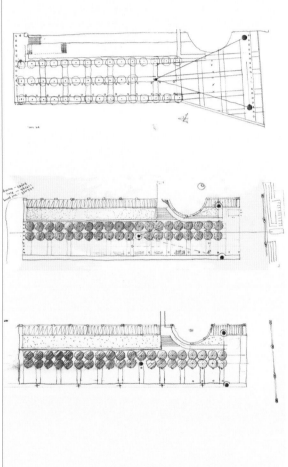

83

The final scheme

THE LONDON EYE,
SOUTH BANK, LONDON

Rows of double-white cherry trees [above] that would create a climax of frothy, ebullient blossom in springtime were eventually chosen to frame the roadside approach to this iconic and innovative structure.

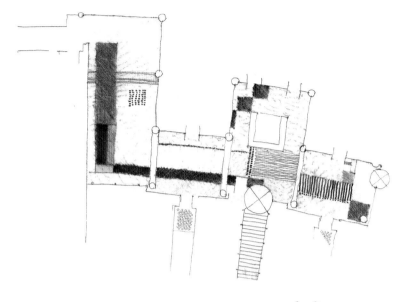

Paving and planting ideas

LLOYD'S REGISTER GROUP, FENCHURCH STREET, LONDON

The design idea for a deconsecrated city churchyard was based on the Islamic concept of recreating paradise on earth via a garden, or carpet. This 'carpet' was based on a gobelin Bauhaus textile, made by Gunta Stölzl in 1932 using cotton, wool, linen and metal threads; the resulting pattern dictated the organization of the planting and paving. It is important that landscape drawings sparkle to reflect the dynamics of an exciting project. The tracing paper was coloured on both sides to increase the density and richness of the finished drawing.

HB pencil on A2 tracing paper, with highlights in felt-tip pen and Tipp-Ex; 4 hours.

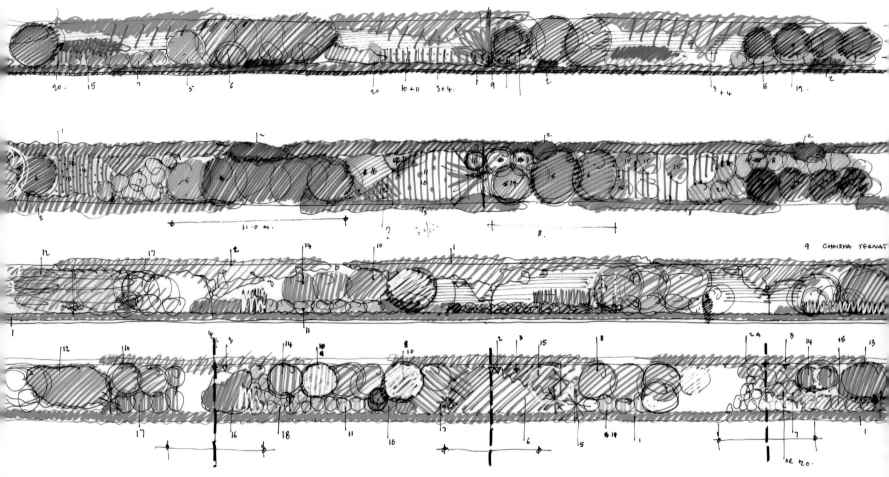

■
Planting for a cricket ground

LORD'S CRICKET GROUND, ST JOHN'S WOOD, LONDON

These planting options of white flowering plants were made
after the selection was approved by a committee of eight.
Pattern, repetition and proportion become the dominant
elements, so that the drawing portrays the abstract concept
behind the planting. It is essential to back up these drawings
with technical information, including planting profiles
(such as the one on p. 87).

Tombow ABT felt-tip pens and Rotring 0.18 technical pen on
A1 tracing paper, reduced to one-third; 2 days.

Using bright, unrealistic
colours to represent different
plants can give a lift to the
design process, so that it is not
simply a horticultural exercise.

Plants for a college

IMPERIAL COLLEGE LONDON

A bold planting scheme [right] was created to capture the attention of the students upon entering the campus.

Gaining inspiration

LORD'S CRICKET GROUND, ST JOHN'S WOOD, LONDON

Although it is tempting to draw inspiration from works of art, the result will be disappointing as the changing nature of plants means that they will not reflect the constancy of a painting.

Tombow ABT felt-tip pens on A3 tracing paper; 45 minutes each.

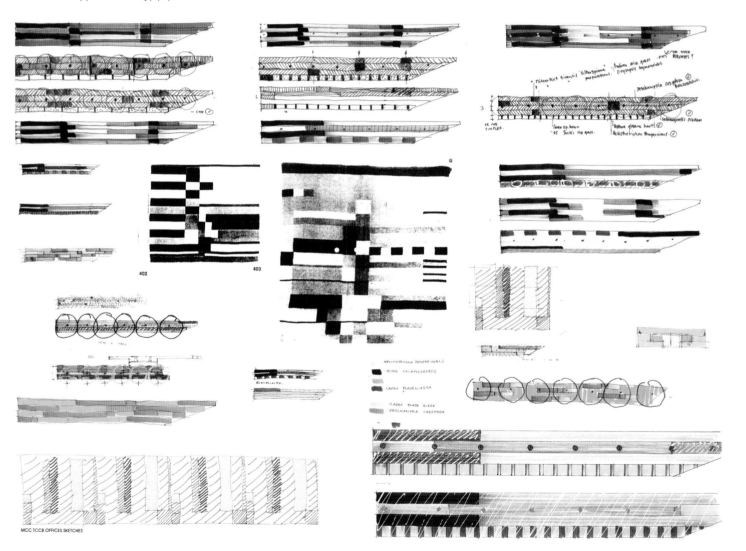

MCC TCCB OFFICES SKETCHES

Representing plants realistically on paper is difficult, as they can change dramatically throughout the year. The use of hot, intense colours when drawing planting plans is a personal response to the huge choice available.

Dryopteris affinis

Dryopteris affinis fronds

■ Planting profile

ST JOHN'S COLLEGE, CAMBRIDGE

A catalogue of planting profiles [left], generated for each design project, builds into an important source of horticultural information. Each plant profile – this one is for Dryopteris affinis, or Golden male fern – contains botanical and technical information obtained from a wide range of professional sources, and is useful when presenting a planting plan to a client.

■ Plan and elevation

IMPERIAL COLLEGE LONDON

These two drawings were made to challenge and test a concept for the new planting at the entrance to Imperial College London, in South Kensington. The sketchplan [above] reflects the atmosphere created by the proposed plants.

Tombow ABT felt-tip pens on tracing paper; 1–2 hours.

Name	**DRYOPTERIS AFFINIS**	Golden male fern
Size	H 1-1.2m x S 90cm	

Description Evergreen fern. Lance shaped pinnate fronds dark green with golden brown scaly stems. Likely to break in winter after gales or snow. Tolerant of some sun and more wind resistant than other ferns. Stunning ginger brown coziers unfurl in spring

Maintenance Cut back any brown or old fronds in winter to allow new growth to emerge.

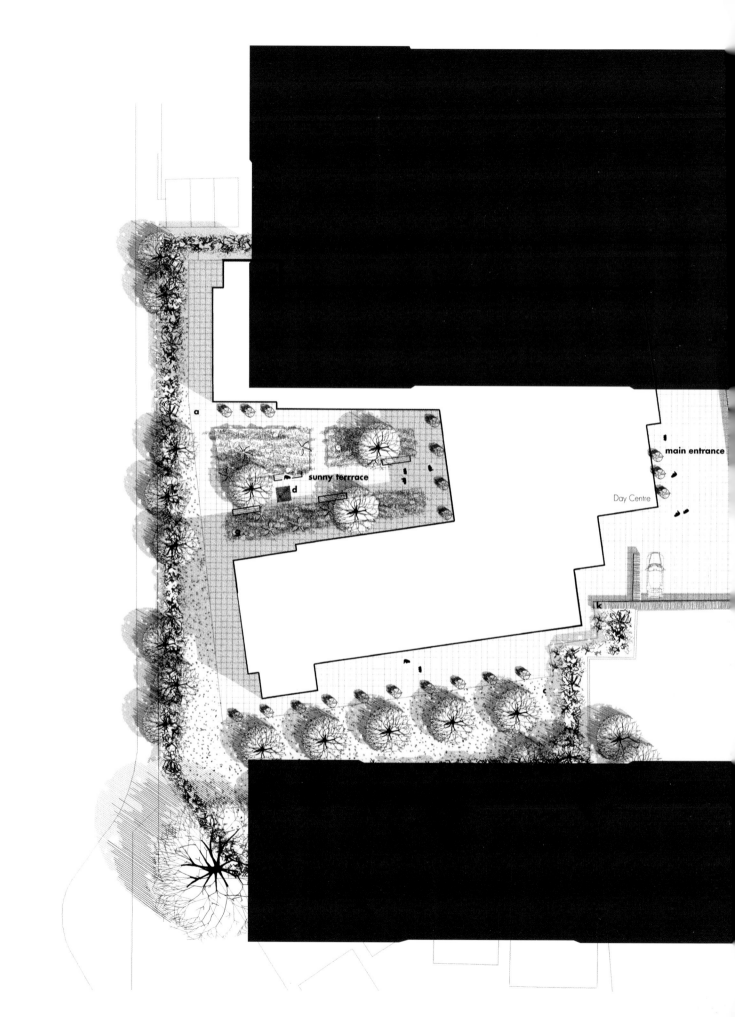

main entrance

sunny terrrace

Day Centre

4

Plans, sections + elevations

■

Landscape for a care home
WEALDEN, EAST SUSSEX
On p. 88: Part of a submission
for a design-and-build
competition for Agewell,
this drawing was intended
to illustrate the delight an
English garden setting could
bring to a new care home.
Vectorworks software program;
drawing by Matilda Jones, 3 days.

■

In creating a new landscape design, landscape architects take on a great responsibility: to find a solution that redefines and regenerates a site. To fully describe the outline proposals, plans that will communicate a designer's vision need careful preparation. At the conceptual stage, these plans can be more exacting to construct than the equivalent architectural drawings. They need to gain credibility by demonstrating good planning, and by conveying a range of qualities that sum up both the overall mood of the design and the skills of the designer. The drawings need to show the balance between a rational approach and a genuine emotional commitment, and require no little skill in committing them successfully to paper.

A catalogue of marks and textures is very useful when making a drawing that reflects a sense of individuality. It is a good idea to be continually on the lookout for ways to convey ideas visually, ensuring that one's developing portfolio of drawings remains fresh. Shadows are highly efficient at portraying space on a plan. They also imply a mood regarding the time of day or year by the quality of the shadow cast, its density and length. Working out the contrasts between light and dark – a technique called chiaroscuro – helps a designer to understand, on plan, the design in three dimensions. Some degree of thought is necessary when transferring these freely drawn marks and impressions to computer to avoid the resulting digital images from becoming impractically heavy. Generally, original hand-drawings will need to be traced over on screen with different line thicknesses to create a cell that can be placed anywhere.

A well-drawn landscape plan allows one to become absorbed in the richness of the image. The drawing conveys a life of its own instead of being just a dry diagram, and stimulates the client's imagination to draw on experiences of a similar place and to 'fill in the gaps'. This ability to encourage cross-referencing of experience is a powerful skill that is worth developing. By the same token, black-and-white drawings are sometimes more evocative than coloured plans, as more is left to the imagination. The tradition of etching and engraving has left a legacy of beautiful tonal drawings that rely on the medium itself to create extraordinary richness and highlights through hatching. These images can inspire contemporary interpretation. It is possible to make fine digital drawings that have some of the richness of engravings by ordering the line qualities and hatchings appropriately. While the culture of digital imagery is constantly looking forward, there is nothing retrogressive in finding inspiration from the past.

There are also situations when a direct approach to presenting an idea is better than a formal plan layout. This could be due to various factors, from a limited period of time available, to the landscape playing only a small part of the total project, to the client being unused to reading plans. In these instances, simple but sensitively drawn cartoon plans have a useful role. This type of drawing can distil the landscape down to no more than six basic elements to concentrate the discussion. The plans are usually drawn quickly, in freehand, and then scanned and coloured. They accentuate what is most important about the scheme, reflecting a balance between the freedom of sketched design ideas and the lithographic quality of perfectly flat colours. They are also easy to reproduce, and thus are frequently useful in reports or projected onto screens. It is important to be controlled in the use of colour so that the drawing is able to breathe. A library of carefully selected colours ensures constant identity, even when a series of drawings have been created by several different people in the studio.

Landscape images are by nature random and organic. They do not naturally lend themselves to being drawn on a rigid X:Y axis. There is a huge margin of opportunity available to create dynamic plans and elevations, combining the precision of computer drawings with the freedom of marks made by hand.

Man has been creating images with tools and colouring them with pigment far back into the distant past. Using radio-carbon dating, we know that the famous cave paintings in Lascaux, in southwestern France, can be traced back to the Paleolithic era, over 17,000 years ago.

Colour tests
This page was sent out to an external printing service in order to make a comparison between the original and returned prints.

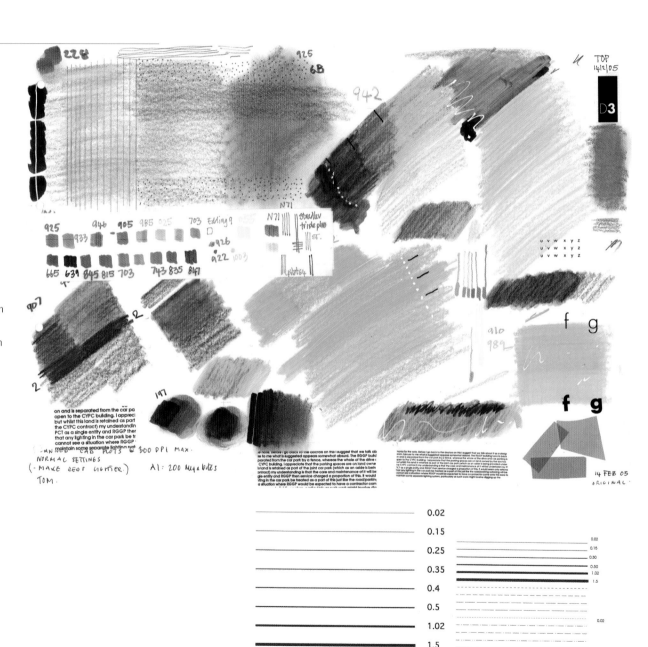

Hatchmarks

These hatchmarks [above] were inspired by Albrecht Dürer's engravings of the 16th century. The wide range of lead weights, thicknesses and applied pressure makes drawing in pencil an enjoyable process, albeit often a messy one. Other experiments [above, right] explored the possibility of transferring pencil marks into digital images.

The process of designing by hand underwent a revolution when, in 1959, car manufacturer General Motors launched an investigation into the use of computers in designing automobiles. IBM joined the project a year later, and in 1963 developed the first computer-aided design program. The age of digital drawing had arrived.

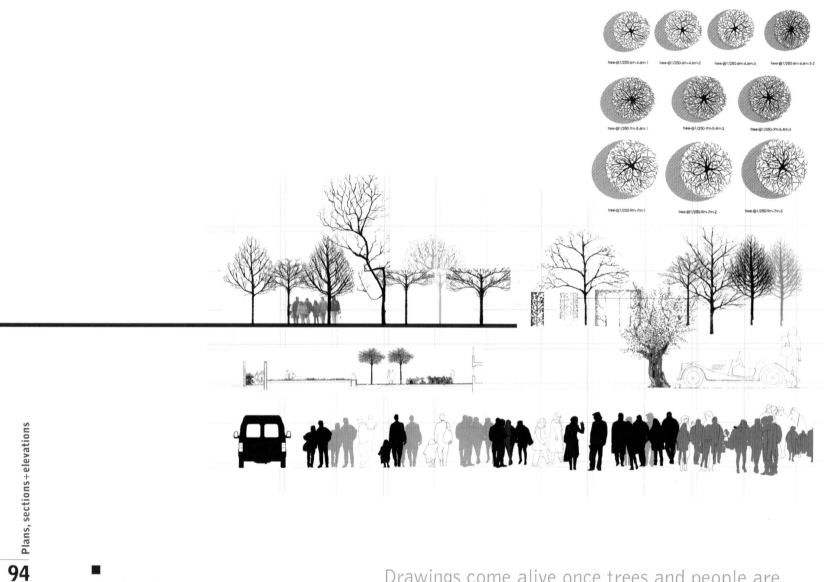

94

■
Elevations of trees

MITRE SQUARE, LONDON

When designing a new scheme that is to be knitted into
an existing landscape, incorporating the silhouettes of existing
trees introduces an air of credibility into a drawing. This
is a time-consuming process, but has often proved to be a
worthwhile exercise.

Drawings come alive once trees and people are
added to elevations and sections. It is useful to
build up a collection of photographs of members
of the public walking, sitting, talking. Outlines
of these images then begin to form the basis of a
library of graphics, available for insertion into
a drawing at a later stage.

Printing textures

An understanding of the limitations of commercial
printing machines avoids both disappointing results and
arguments with the printers.

Edding Brilliant paper marker, Faber-Castell TG1.S technical pen, 0.3mm pencil
and Tombow ABT felt-tip pen on A3 tracing paper.

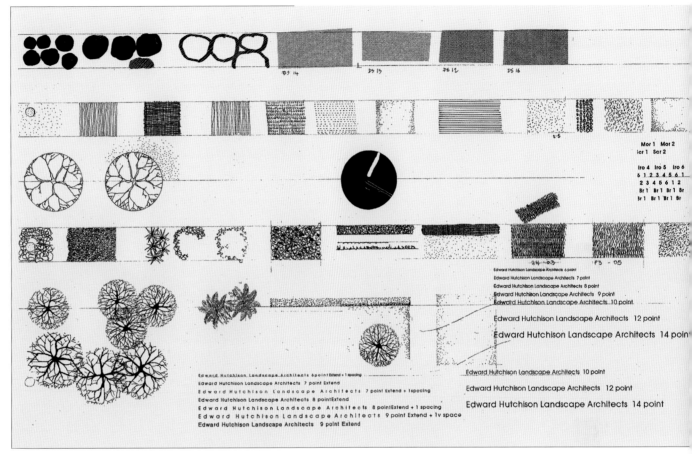

Digitizing freehand marks

Experiments with a variety of scanned marks, with a view
to creating digital drawings. In reality, this proved to be a
cumbersome process, with few true benefits over a hand-drawn
planting plan.

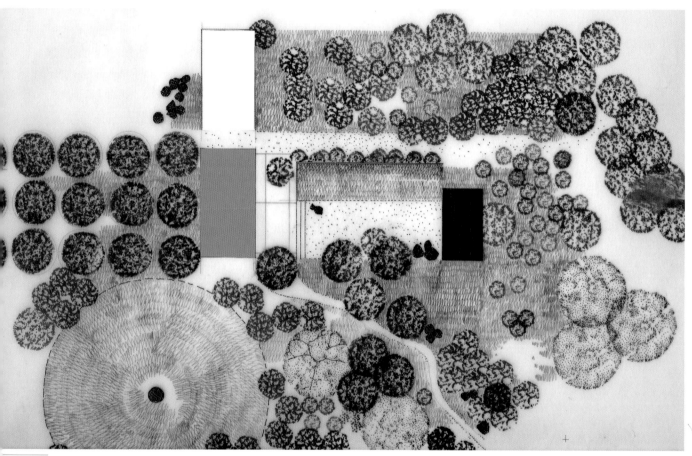

Using rubber stamps
Bespoke rubber stamps [left],
based on careful drawings
of different trees, pick up
ink from the stamp pad with
varying intensities, giving the
trees a sense of individuality.
Pencil and ink tests [below] of
graphics were also produced.

Ink, pencil and rubber stamps on
A3 tracing paper; 3 hours.

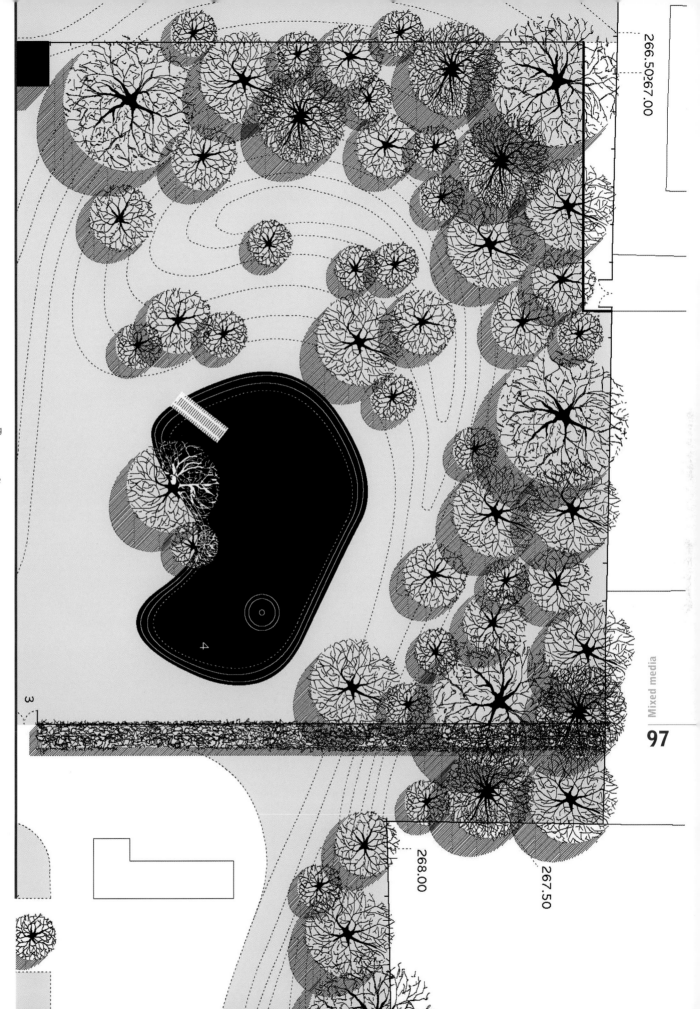

Printing digital plans

Achieving satisfactory printing results required considerable dialogue with the printers. Initial problems concerned the massive size of the drawings, which could be up to 30 megabytes for an A0 print.

Vectorworks software program; drawing by Claudia Corcilius.

266.50 267.00

268.00

267.50

3

4

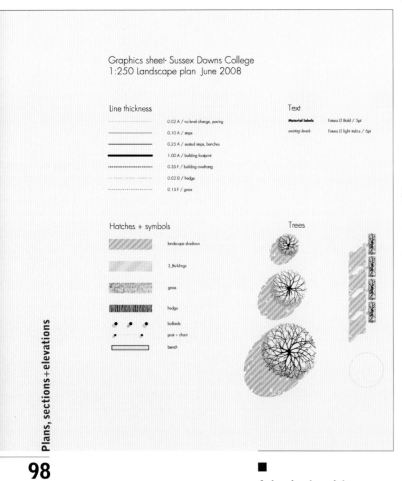

Graphics sheet- Sussex Downs College
1:250 Landscape plan June 2008

Line thickness

0.02 A / no level change, paving
0.10 A / steps
0.25 A / seated steps, benches
1.00 A / building footprint
0.35 F / building overhang
0.02 D / hedge
0.15 F / grass

Text

Material labels   Futura LT Bold / 5pt
existing levels   Futura LT Light Italics / 6pt

Hatches + symbols

landscape shadows
3_Buildings
grass
hedge
bollards
post + chain
bench

Trees

■
A drawing template

SUSSEX DOWNS COLLEGE,
EAST SUSSEX
Drawings at different scales
require different graphic
weights for the image to
be read and understood.
Balancing the line weights
can be a lengthy process,
so a record is essential.

Vectorworks software program;
A0 drawing by Matilda Jones.

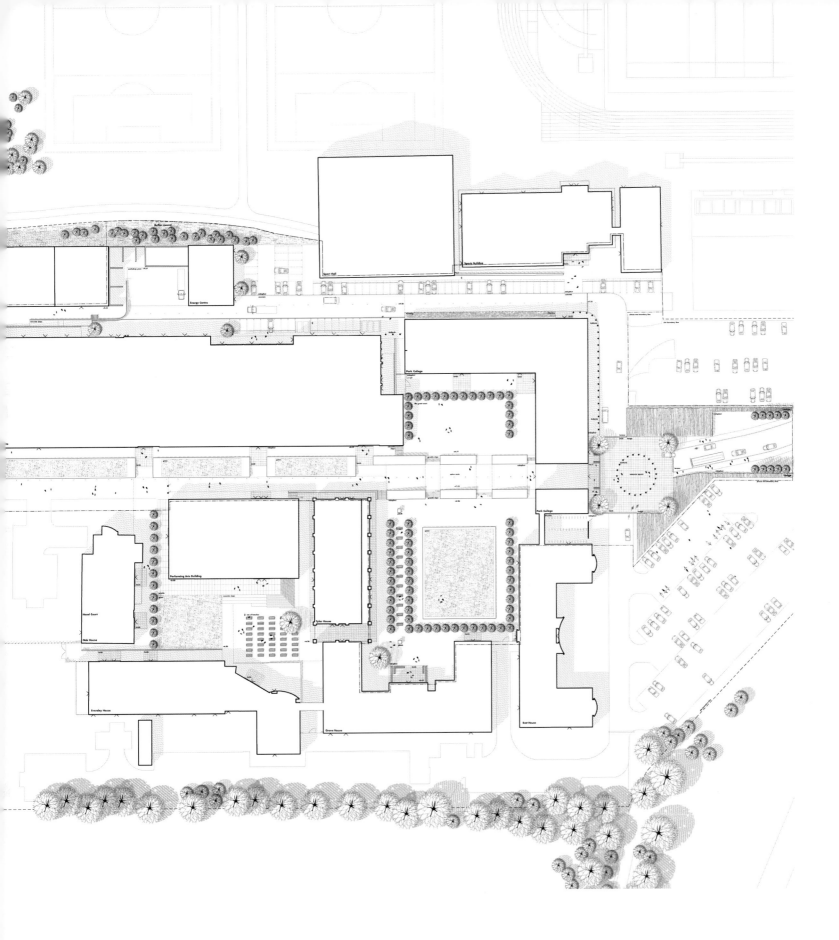

Computer-generated proposals

WALBROOK SQUARE, LONDON

It took over two hundred hours to make this drawing of Walbrook Square, but when compared to Giambattista Nolli's mapping of Rome in the 18th century, which took over forty years to complete, this is no time at all. The importance of the drawing was that it clarified the context and scale of the streets, shops and churches surrounding the Norman Foster/ Jean Nouvel proposal on Cannon Street. This was achieved by first walking around the area and noting the bollards, trees, and so on, and taking measurements of the shops. Through the drawing, a comparison could be made of the scale of the new against the old. Respect for the site is reflected in the sensitivity of the drawing, which, despite being computer-generated, is similar in spirit to the earlier hand-drawings.

Vectorworks software program; drawing by Heidi Hundley.

Fill explorations

WALBROOK SQUARE, LONDON

Once the drawing is vectorized, the digital result provides the opportunity to experiment with different line thicknesses and tones in the solid areas.

Vectorworks software program; drawing by Heidi Hundley.

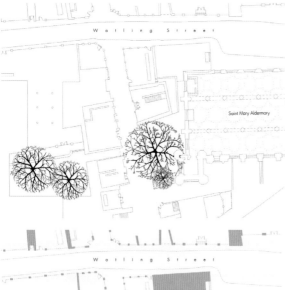

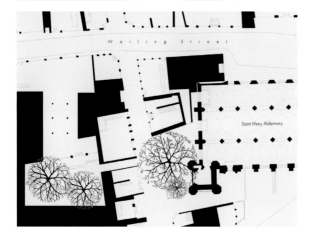

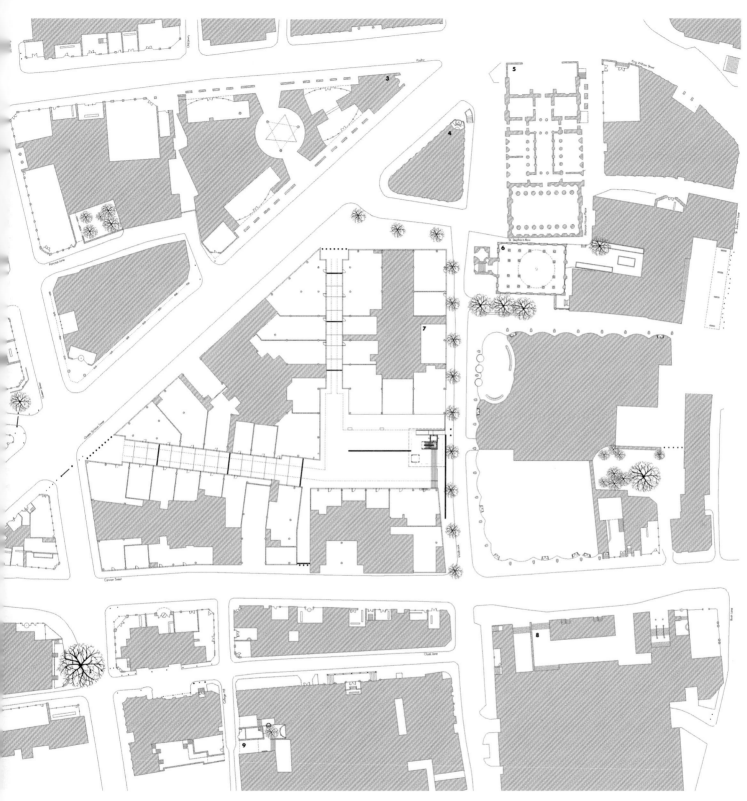

The accuracy achieved through drawing with a
computer gives it authority. In this case, drawing
by hand would have been impractical.

Towing Path

Basingstoke Canal

Walled Garden

Entrance

The use of mixed media in a drawing helps enormously in bringing an image to life. Digital drawings on their own can appear somewhat lifeless and technical, but the addition of pencil and ink can highlight and enhance the important ideas, ultimately creating a better drawing.

Bridge Road

Victoria Way

■

Site plan for an art gallery

THE LIGHTBOX, WOKING, SURREY

This drawing was made for a planning submission, and its aim
was to convey the context: a highly problematic site for an art
gallery. The site's awkward shape was formed by a triangle,
wedged between an 18th-century canal and a six-lane ring road.
The entrance to the gallery is via a canalside garden, shielded
from the road by a substantial gabion wall. The drawing shows
in some detail the road, art gallery, new landscape and the
richness of the canalside planting.

Vectorworks software program; with Faber-Castell technical pen, Transtext
and razor blade on A1 tracing paper.

■

Ideas for housing and a school

AXTON CHASE SCHOOL, KENT

This drawing was made for a public consultation meeting to describe proposals to develop part of the school grounds for housing. It was drawn on tracing paper, laid over an Ordnance Survey map and an aerial photograph, a combination that enabled the graphics to convey the most important points of the landscape. Each tree was drawn to approximately the correct scale, and included many small trees that were not featured on the map. The richness of the residential development was shown in a simplified manner.

Faber-Castell 0.13, 0.18 and 0.5 technical pens and Berol Karismacolor pencils on A1 tracing paper, reduced to one-third; 2 days.

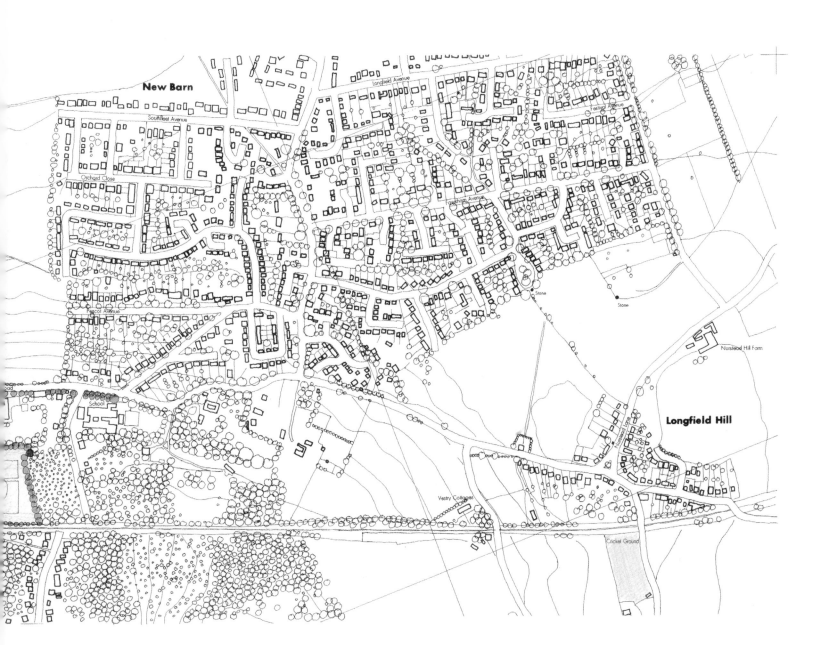

New Barn

Longfield Hill

Nurstead Hill Farm

Vestry Cottages

Crickel Ground

■

Site plans for care homes

HASTINGS AND ROTHER,
EAST SUSSEX

These drawings formed
part of the design-and-build
competition bid for Agewell.
The trees were drawn first by
hand, and then redrawn on
computer, using different line
thicknesses to create cells.
The grass was drawn with a
hard pencil and pen, and then
scanned. When working in a
multidisciplinary team, it is
vital that the most important
site drawings are made by
the landscape architect,
obviating the danger of the
design being misinterpreted
or compromised by another
member of the team.

Vectorworks software program;
A3 drawing by Matilda Jones;
3 days each.

Meticulous black-and-white
drawings of a landscape subject
are often astoundingly lively,
triggering an important role for
the imagination. These drawings
attempt to capture digitally some
of this precision and vigour.

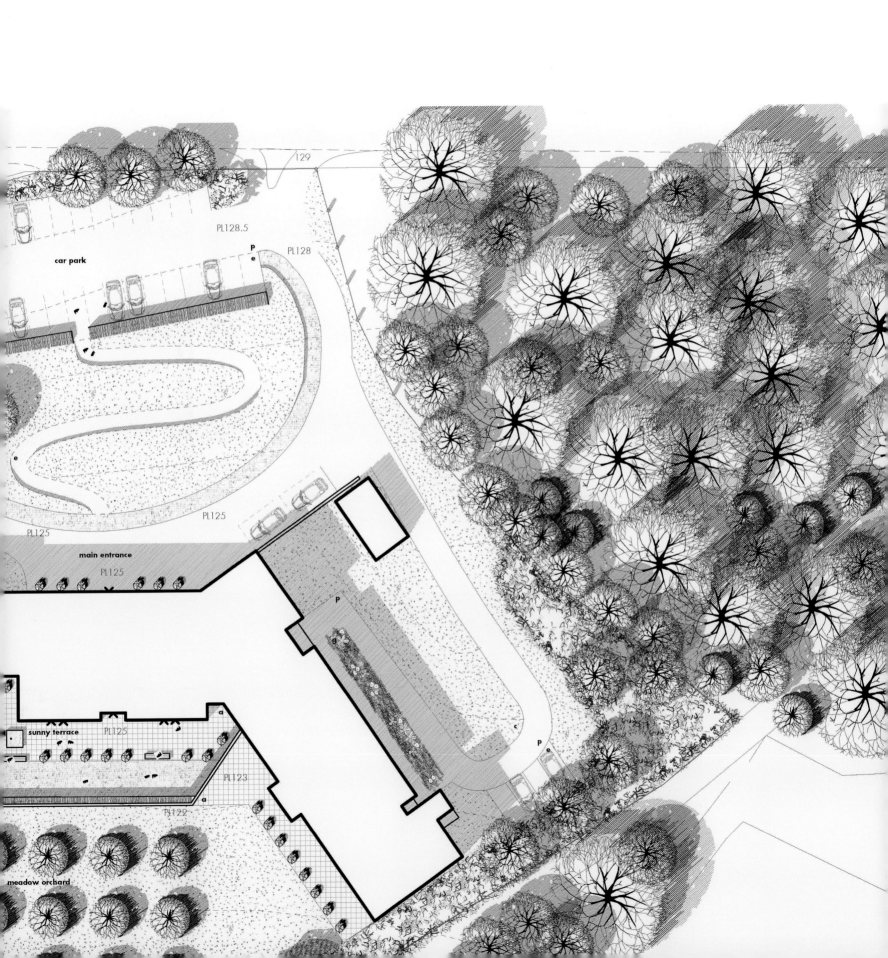

car park

PL128.5

PL128

P
e

129

PL125

e

PL125

PL125

main entrance

PL125

P

g

sunny terrace

PL125

a

a

c

P
e

PL123

PL122

meadow orchard

A landscape proposal for a
car park [below], to suit the
new landscape masterplan
for the Dunhurst (ages 7–13)
and Dunnannie (ages 3–7)
schools, part of the larger
Bedales campus.

Faber-Castell TG1.S 0.13, 0.18 and 0.5
technical pens on A3 tracing paper.

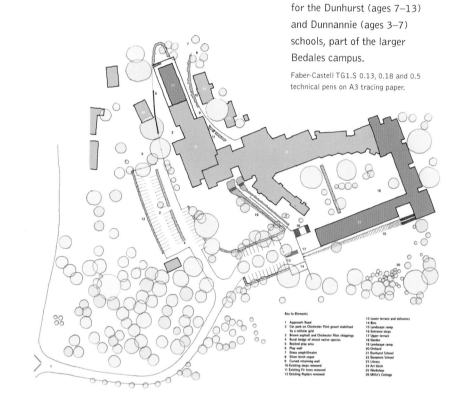

It is helpful to keep to a muted
palette of carefully selected
colours, so as not to overpower
the line quality of the drawing.
This also allows the remaining
white paper to become a
dynamic plane, which can be
read in a variety of ways – grass,
a road, a path – introducing a
degree of sensitivity to the image.

Key to Elements

1 Approach Road	13 Lower terrace and deliveries
2 Car park on Chichester Flint gravel stabilised by a cellular grid	14 Bins
	15 Landscape ramp
3 Brown asphalt and Chichester Flint chippings	16 Entrance steps
4 Rural hedge of mixed native species	17 Upper terrace
5 Resited play area	18 Garden
6 Play wall	19 Landscape ramp
7 Grass amphitheatre	20 Orchard
8 Silver birch copse	21 Dunhurst School
9 Curved retaining wall	22 Dunannie School
10 Existing steps removed	23 Library
11 Existing Fir trees removed	24 Art block
12 Existing Poplars removed	25 Workshop
	26 Millie's Cottage

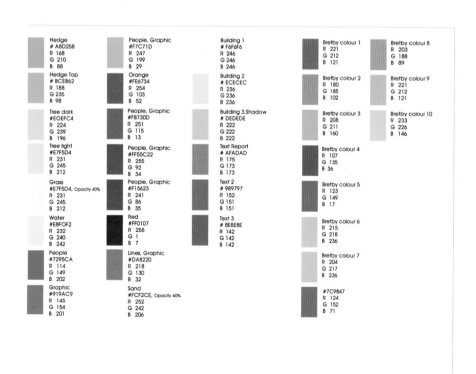

Hedge # A8D258 R 168 G 210 B 88	People, Graphic #F7C71D R 247 G 199 B 29	Building 1 # F6F6F6 R 246 G 246 B 246	Bretby colour 1 R 221 G 212 B 121	Bretby colour 8 R 203 G 188 B 89	
Hedge Top #BCEB62 R 188 G 235 B 98	Orange #FE6734 R 254 G 103 B 52	Building 2 # ECECEC R 236 G 236 B 236	Bretby colour 2 R 180 G 185 B 102	Bretby colour 9 R 221 G 212 B 121	
Tree dark #E0EFC4 R 224 G 239 B 196	People, Graphic #FB730D R 251 G 115 B 13	Building 3,Shadow # DEDEDE R 222 G 222 B 222	Bretby colour 3 R 208 G 211 B 160	Bretby colour 10 R 233 G 226 B 146	
Tree light #E7F5D4 R 231 G 245 B 212	People, Graphic #FF55C22 R 255 G 92 B 34	Text Report # AFADAD R 175 G 173 B 173	Bretby colour 4 R 107 G 135 B 36		
Grass #E7F5D4, Opacity 40% R 231 G 245 B 212	People, Graphic #F15623 R 241 G 86 B 35	Text 2 # 989797 R 152 G 151 B 151	Bretby colour 5 R 123 G 149 B 17		
Water #E8F0F2 R 232 G 240 B 242	Red #FF0107 R 255 G 1 B 7	Text 3 # 8E8E8E R 142 G 142 B 142	Bretby colour 6 R 215 G 218 B 236		
People #7295CA R 114 G 149 B 202	Lines, Graphic #DA8220 R 218 G 130 B 32		Bretby colour 7 R 204 G 217 B 236		
Graphic #919AC9 R 145 G 154 B 201	Sand #FCF2CE, Opacity 40% R 252 G 242 B 206		#7C9847 R 124 G 152 B 71		

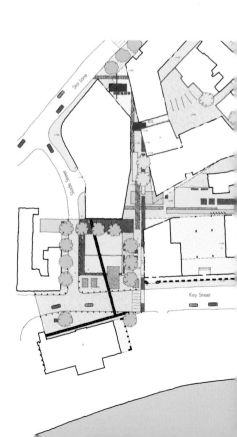

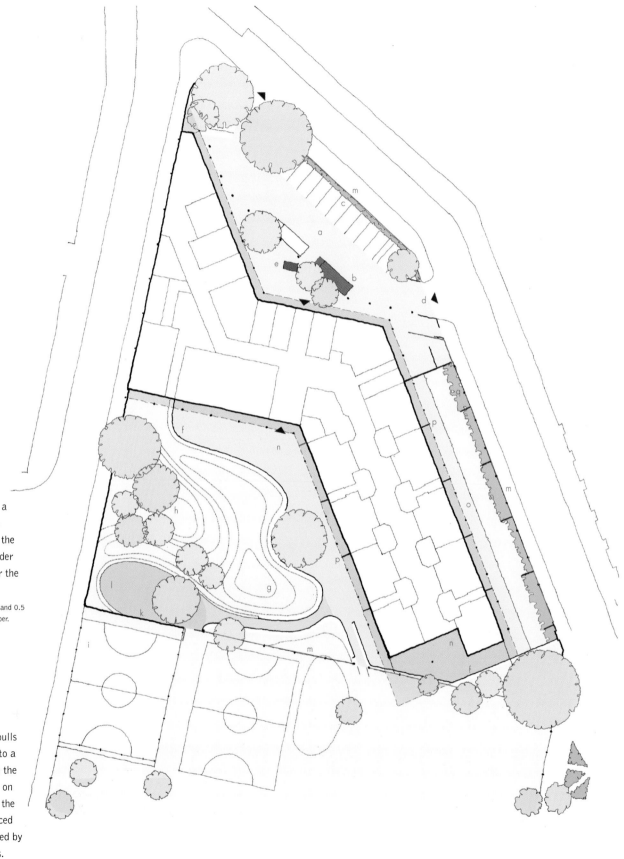

■
Ideas for a school

MICHAEL TIPPETT SCHOOL,
LAMBETH, LONDON
Landscape proposal for a
school for special needs
[right]. This school was the
first to be completed under
the Building Schools for the
Future scheme.

Faber-Castell TG1.S 0.13, 0.18 and 0.5
technical pens on A3 tracing paper.

■
**Landscape for a
development site**

IPSWICH, SUFFOLK
This design [opposite] pulls
the new development into a
strong relationship with the
historic Customs House on
the quayside. Currently, the
grain of the site is divorced
from its context, enclosed by
a network of busy roads.

Faber-Castell TG1.S 0.13, 0.18 and 0.5
technical pens on A3 tracing paper.

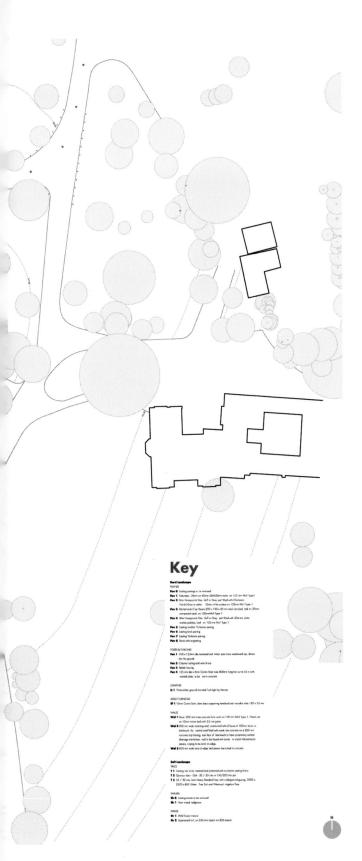

Key

Hard Landscape

PAVING
Pav 0 Existing paving to be removed
Pav 1 Natural stone - 25mm on 60mm LBM/20mm sand on 150 mm Mot Type I
Pav 2 Bitta Honeycomb Tiles - Buff or Grey part filled with Chichester Flint & Silver to within 10mm of the surface on 100mm Mot Type 1
Pav 3 Marshmesh Clay Pavers 200 x 100 x 50 mm stack bonded, laid on 30mm compacted sand on 100mmMot Type 1
Pav 4 Bitta Honeycomb Tiles - Buff or Grey part filled with 20mm or white marble pebbles, laid on 150 mm Mot Type 1
Pav 5 Existing random Yorkstone paving
Pav 6 Existing brick paving
Pav 7 Existing Yorkstone paving
Pav 8 Stone sett engraving

POSTS & FENCING
Fen 1 700 x 125mm dia tanalised oak timber post once weathered top, driven into the ground
Fen 2 Chestnut paling and wire fence
Fen 3 Rabbit fencing
Fen 4 125 mm dia x 6mm Corten Steel tube 800mm long tree cut at 45 o with welded plate, to be set in concrete

LIGHTING
Lt 1 Flameselect ground mounted flush light by Artcote

STREET FURNITURE
Sf 1 10mm Corten Steel plate base supporting tanalised oak wooden slats 120 x 55 mm

WALLS
Wal 1 Stone 300 mm mass concrete form work on 150 mm Mot Type 1. Pavers set on 10mm mortar bed with 3:5 mix joints
Wal 2 900 mm wide retaining wall, constructed with 2 faces of 100mm brick or brickwork, the central void filled with weak mix concrete on a 200 mm concrete strip footing, top face of blockwork to have proprietary vertical drainage membrane, wall to be faced with bricks to match Michelmersh pavers, coping to be brick on edge
Wal 3 600 mm wide kerb of edge laid pavers haunched in concrete

Soft Landscape

TREES
Tr 1 Existing tree to be retained and protected with a chestnut paling fence
Tr 2 Quercus robur - Oak - 20 / 25 cms = 150/200 lrts pot
Tr 3 25 / 30 cms Extra Heavy Standard tree, with cellgrow root pruning, 3500 x 2500 x 850 LNmn. Tree Tool and Watersoil irrigation Pipe

SHRUBS
Sh 0 Existing shrubs to be removed
Sh 1 New mixed hedgerow

GRASS
Gr 1 Wild flower mixture
Gr 2 Supersward turf, on 230 mm topsoil on 200 subsoil

N

Unless carefully balanced, digital landscape plans can sometimes convey the same amount of excitement as a wiring diagram. The selection of one element for emphasis – in this case, choosing to present the existing and proposed trees in colour – lifts the communicative powers of the drawing to a higher level.

■

Partial redevelopment

BEDALES SCHOOL, HAMPSHIRE
The proposed masterplan
for the Orchard Building,
the heart of the school.

Vectorworks software program;
A0 drawing by Claudia Corcilius.

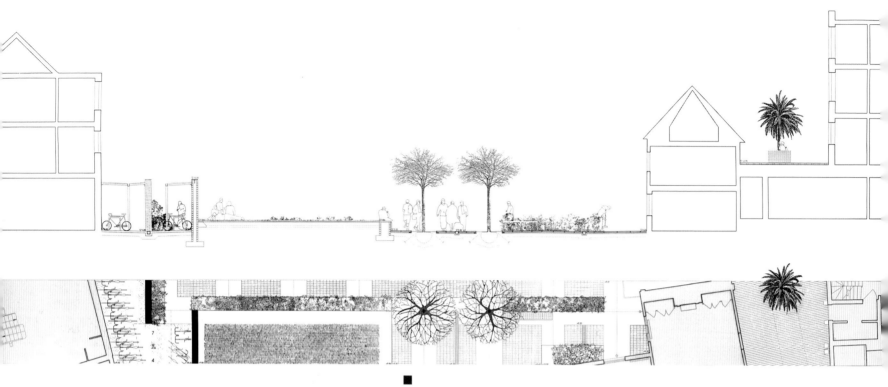

■

Sections

ST JOHN'S COLLEGE, CAMBRIDGE

The development over a five-year period of the landscape design for this project was an enjoyable collaboration between the architects and landscape designers, and this is perhaps reflected in the drawings. The architectural sections formed the basis for the space and landscape design. Sections and 'strip plans' can be a good way of conveying the three-dimensional quality of a proposal. The basic drawing of the intricate hard landscape [top] was printed on tracing paper, and the soft landscape was then added in a variety of media. The proposal for developing a formal design for the courtyard [above] was later abandoned.

Vectorworks software program, with Faber-Castell 0.18 technical pen, 3H 3mm pencil and Transtext; A0 drawing by Claudia Corcilius, 3 days.

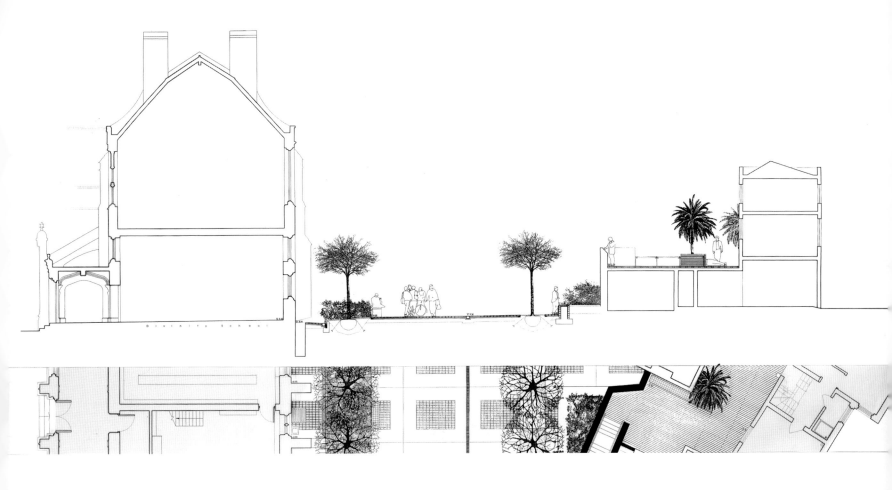

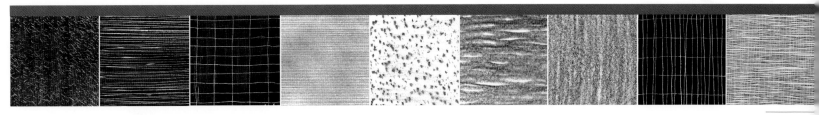

Paving palette

There are endless opportunities to create beautiful
textures. Considerable skill is required, however, to avoid
making the drawings look like a series of hard-edged tiles.

B 5mm and 2H 3mm pencils and felt-tip pen, with a Swann-Morton scalpel blade.

Although the process is time-consuming, it
is always worth carefully working out sections.
The drawings are invaluable in conveying the
qualities of spatial design, and are useful when
explaining the richness of a scheme to clients
who may find difficulty in reading plans.
In addition, sections illustrate the successful
integration of the landscape with the architecture
by demonstrating a skilful resolution of
changes of level, reinforcing the importance
of the role played by the landscape designer in
a multidisciplinary project. It is occasionally
necessary to exaggerate some aspects of
the design and simplify others, thus effectively
communicating the proposal through an
enhanced image.

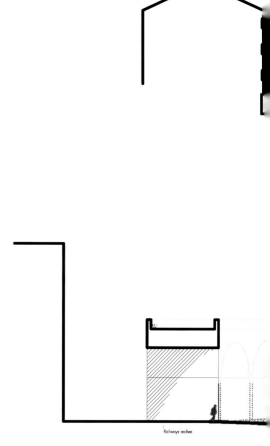

Railways arches

Competition drawings

WORCESTER, WORCESTERSHIRE

These drawings for a competition for a library and history
centre illustrate a section through the proposed library above
the critical flood level, showing its integration with the
small pocket park to the south, the hotel, terrace and car
parking [top]; a long section of the pocket park, with the
elevation of the library shown three dimensionally [middle];
and a cross-section through the park, café and terrace to
the north with the railway arches beyond [bottom].

Vectorworks software program; A0 drawing by Angela Oña de la Blanca.

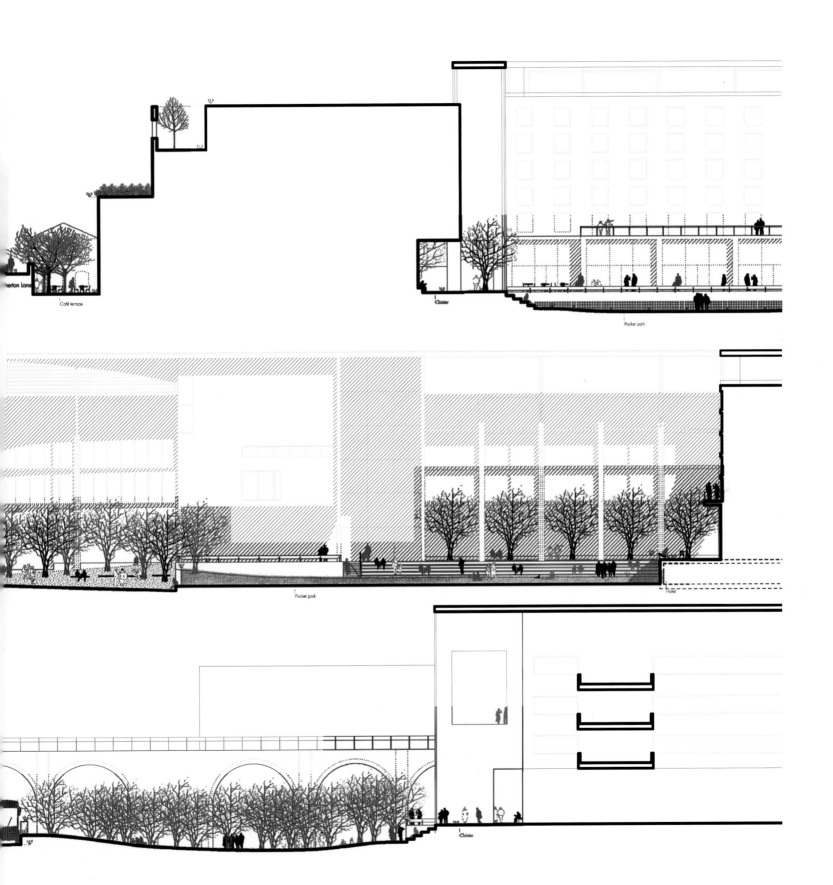

Café terrace

Cloister

Pocket park

Pocket park

Hotel

Cloister

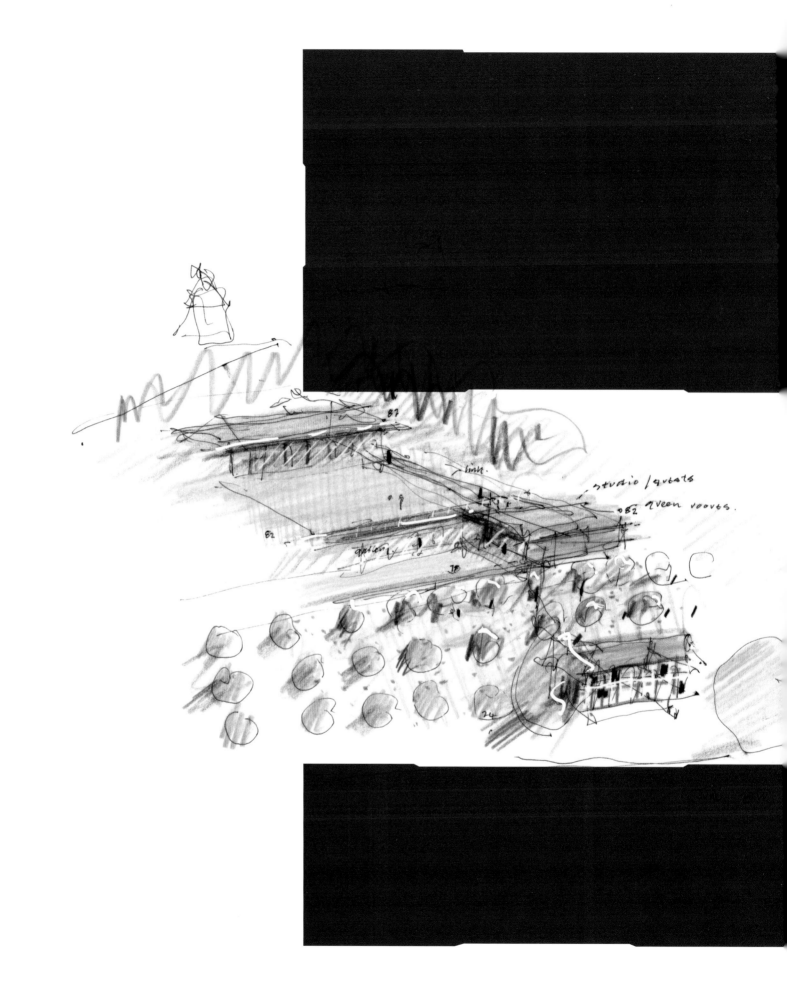

studio / artats

082 green roofs.

studio / artats

5

Perspectives

■ **A country house on a hill**
SCARLETTS, FURNACE LANE, KENT
On p. 116: An exploratory
sketch for the construction
of two new houses behind a
16th-century listed building.
The concept maintains the
openness of the countryside,
while emphasizing the
importance of the old house.

Pilot G-Tec-C4 pen and Faber-Castell
Art Grip Aquarelle coloured pencils on
A3 smooth cartridge paper; 30 minutes.

■

It is only too easy to draw perspectives badly. In our modern society,
we become less and less critical of this type of drawing, taking
computer-generated perspectives for granted as the default method
of architectural illustration. Too often these images do not stand up
to scrutiny, and are constructed with insufficient attention paid to
vanishing points and sightlines. In the past, the majority of important
commissions relied heavily on a designer's skills to show the proposed
scheme to a client in an accessible and convincing format. These
delicate works take considerable skill and sensitive collaboration to
translate the concept into a polished presentation, often by someone
outside the design team. But the continuing development of computer
software has changed this method of working, and it is now relatively
easy to create in-house perspectives, or 'fly-throughs', of a scheme.

But an important communication role remains for perspectives
drawn by the designer, rather than by a third party. The benefits
of being able to produce a freehand perspective should not be
underestimated. It is intellectually dynamic to watch an idea drawn
up quickly in three dimensions, and semi-realistic views often help
steer the concept at a fast pace in the early stages of a project
when the ideas under formation are fragile and can be subject to
misunderstanding. The explosive enthusiasm of the designer at this
critical evolutionary point in the design process can help convey the
essence of those ideas through a series of lightening-quick sketch
perspectives. It is surprising how often these fleeting images later
become important visual anchors, holding the initial design concept
steady through the extended life of a project.

Nowadays architectural perspectives are often presented to
the client through the means of photorealism. This method requires
a very high degree of technical information at an early stage in the
scheme – software, no matter how sophisticated, can only produce an
image if it is supplied with detailed instructions on a complete range
of design decisions. This requirement can force the team to make

choices about every visible component of the scheme at a premature stage, often resulting in compromise. There is also the temptation to show a utopian vision of the scheme: the sky an azure blue; the people universally beautiful; and everything ideally suited to the environment. Of course, it is difficult to justify the expense of creating an image of anything less than the ideal, but, alas, these visions of future perfection generally fall short of reality.

The majority of people are only able to focus on a relatively limited amount of information. The amount they take in is scaled in importance, dependant on their personal interests. It is thought that after gazing at a view, a person retains a maximum of only six elements. On this basis, it is possible to construct a perspective drawing that is direct and powerful in its message, but is actually limited in information (regarding the detailing or choice of materials used in construction, for example). In the past, some of the most successful presentation drawings were created as fleeting impressions, enabling the designer to concentrate on the essence of the scheme: mood, scale, light qualities, and how the public would use the space, allowing the client's imagination to fill in the blanks.

The format of the picture plane is important. Horizontal drawings with a ratio of 3:8 are generally best used to convey a landscape design. This shape, as well as being a dynamic proportion, tends to concentrate the mind on the design by reducing the amount of paper dedicated to foreground and sky. It cannot be over-emphasized that the constant practice of drawing in a sketchbook is vital in helping to build up confidence in one's drawing abilities. Once he or she is able to draw spontaneously in front of other people, the designer achieves a respect from clients, colleagues and technicians. It becomes possible to communicate ideas verbally and visually, ensuring accuracy of both design and vision.

Slag-heap regeneration

SPENNYMOOR, CO. DURHAM

These three drawings were made for the Art into Landscape competition, and subsequently exhibited among the prizewinners at the Serpentine Gallery in London. The brief was to regenerate a slag heap outside Spennymoor, so the design proposal incorporated a football pitch into the erstwhile industrial landscape. Extensive ecological research into pioneer plant species, together with a site visit with an ecologist, enabled a far greater understanding of the issues involved.

HB, 2B and 3H pencils on A1 tracing paper, reduced to one-third; 12 hours each.

The transient nature of a sketch
often makes a quick perspective
more engaging than a perfectly
set-up drawing. It is important
to capture a spirit and sense
of excitement, at the possible
cost of accuracy, to create a
persuasive drawing.

lombardy poplar windbreak

121

■
Screen railings
ALL SAINTS' COLLEGE,
CAMBRIDGE
A simple line drawing,
constructed over a collage of
coloured photographs. The
drawing tests the quality
of transparency of the screen
railings, which link the
College courtyards to the
small public space.

Pilot G-Tec-C4 pen on A4 tracing paper;
60 minutes.

The power of a sketch
perspective is its ability to
express a number of points
clearly. Effective communication
is critical when working in
a multidisciplinary team, and
these quick drawings are
useful to complement the more
detailed information contained
in plans and sections.

■

Visual barriers

BRITISH HIGH COMMISSION,
NEW DELHI, INDIA

Hedges, in addition to the
existing trees, form an
invaluable visual barrier
to screen a new car park.

Pilot G-Tec-C4 pen and Faber-Castell
Art Grip Aquarelle coloured pencils
on A4 paper, with Tipp-Ex highlights;
30 minutes.

■

Embassy approach

BRITISH EMBASSY, DAMASCUS, SYRIA

This sketch illustrates how tree-planting could improve the
approach road, framing the view to the hills in the distance.

Pilot G-Tec-C4 pen and Faber-Castell Art Grip Aquarelle coloured pencils on
A4 paper, with Tipp-Ex highlights; 30 minutes.

TOTTENHAM HALE STF
ALL VERY SEVERE

A pedestrian bridge

TOTTENHAM HALE STATION, LONDON

The initial design sketches for a competition investigated a
500m-long 'green bridge' in North London that would enable
pedestrians to cross a dual carriageway and railway track.
Sloping green walls would create an enclosed garden
environment, helping to mask the uncompromising, somewhat
bleak surroundings. The judges deemed the proposal to be
too prescriptive.

Staedtler Ergosoft coloured pencils on A4 paper; 30 minutes.

Bright, sun-drenched colours
can help promote the overall mood
of a landscape design.

Competition bid

LEWES, WEALDEN, ROTHER AND
HASTINGS, EAST SUSSEX
These four drawings formed
part of a competition bid
for designing, building and
maintaining a series of
Agewell care homes for the
elderly in East Sussex. As
first impressions are critical
in the success of a design,
the entrance drives and
courtyards were carefully
considered to create a non-
institutional welcome, set in
the context of a traditional
English garden. This mood
would have been far more
difficult to convey using
conventional sections and
elevations. Clockwise from
top left: designs for sites in
Rother, Hastings, Wealden
and Lewes.

Faber-Castell Art Grip Aquarelle
coloured pencils on A4 paper;
15 minutes each.

With practice, impromptu perspectives become quicker and easier to construct, along with the ability to explore a design idea speedily and to pursue or abandon a train of thought.

2003 LEICESTER CATHEDRAL PRECINCT

126

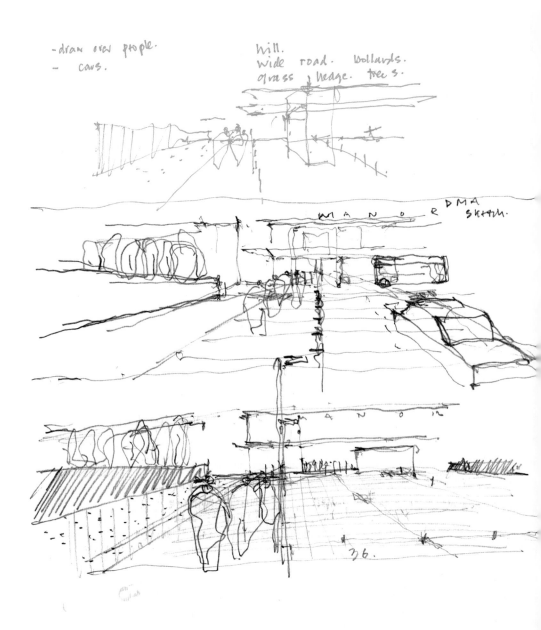

- draw over people.
- cars.

hill.
wide road. bollards.
grass hedge. trees.

MANOR DMA sketch.

MANOR

36.

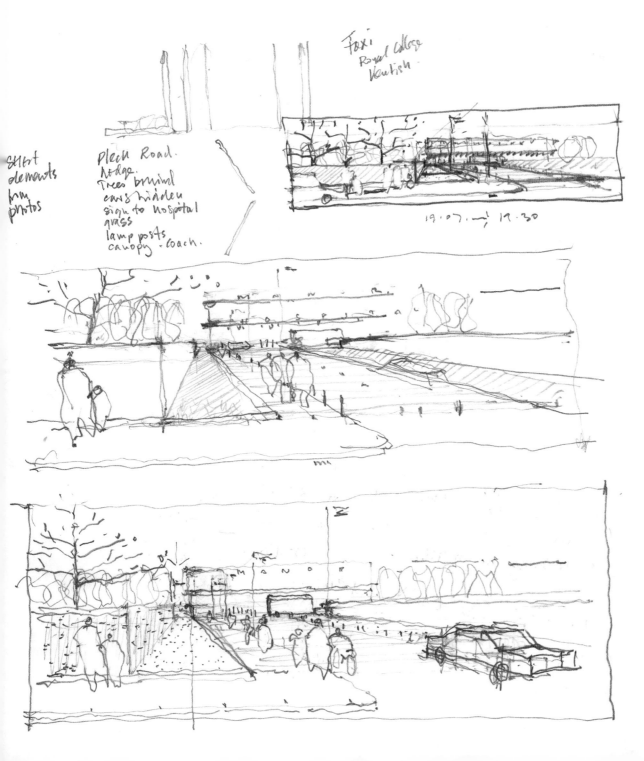

Taxi
Royal College
Kentish.

Street
elements
from
photos

Plech Road.
hedge.
Trees behind
cars hidden
sign to hospital
grass
lamp posts
canopy - coach.

19.07. 19.30

Approach to a hospital

WALSALL MANOR HOSPITAL,
WEST MIDLANDS
These drawings [left]
investigate different
approaches to a National
Health Service hospital,
forming part of an exemplar
design exercise instigated by
the Government. The intention
was to create a simple, direct
access, easily understood by
pedestrians and drivers, which
would help to reduce the
stress of a hospital visit.

HB 5mm pencil on A4 paper;
20 minutes each.

Drawing on the train

LEICESTER CATHEDRAL,
LEICESTERSHIRE
Sharing a train journey with
the design team will often
prompt informal drawings.
As the movement of the
train makes it impossible
to draw a straight line, the
perspectives possess a naïve
quality [opposite, far left].
Creative discussions, as yet
unrefined by more detailed
consideration, are well served
by this type of drawing –
a quick impression of
animated conversation.

Staedtler Ergosoft coloured pencils on
paper; 45 minutes.

Impromptu sketches

127

49

Public Lighting:
Lanterns:

Aesthetics committee

■
Preliminary drawings

HULL HISTORY CENTRE,
EAST YORKSHIRE

These three drawings were
made at an early stage of the
project. Although tenuous,
the sketches are remarkably
similar to the finished scheme,
seen in the photograph.

Pilot G-Tec-C4 pen and Staedtler
Ergosoft coloured pencils on A4 paper;
10 minutes each.

Sketches for a library

WORCESTER LIBRARY,
WORCESTERSHIRE

These quick sketches explore
the relationship between the
library and landscape. A new
colonnade embedded into the
south façade of the library
links into the pedestrian route,
used by students going from
the new university campus
to the city. A small, south-
facing 'pocket park' helps
to reinforce the library as a
destination point, linking it
to the network of public open
spaces within the city.

Staedtler Ergosoft coloured pencils on
paper; 20 minutes each.

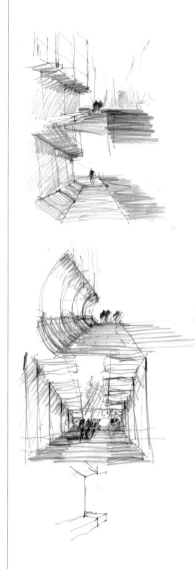

■
Design for a conservatory

GLASGOW, SCOTLAND

This competition proposal
uses photographs of tropical
plants, collaged onto
a computer perspective
of the conservatory, to
portray the contrast between
mathematical engineering
and the exuberance of
the vegetation.

A1 tracing paper overlaid on a
photocopy; 12 hours.

■
Anti-terrorist façades

WALBROOK SQUARE, LONDON

A series of quick sketches
that explore the junction
detail between the pavement
and shopfront or office
façade, designed to withstand
vehicular attack.

Pilot G-Tec-C4 pen and Faber-Castell
Art Grip Aquarelle coloured pencils on
A4 paper; 4 minutes each.

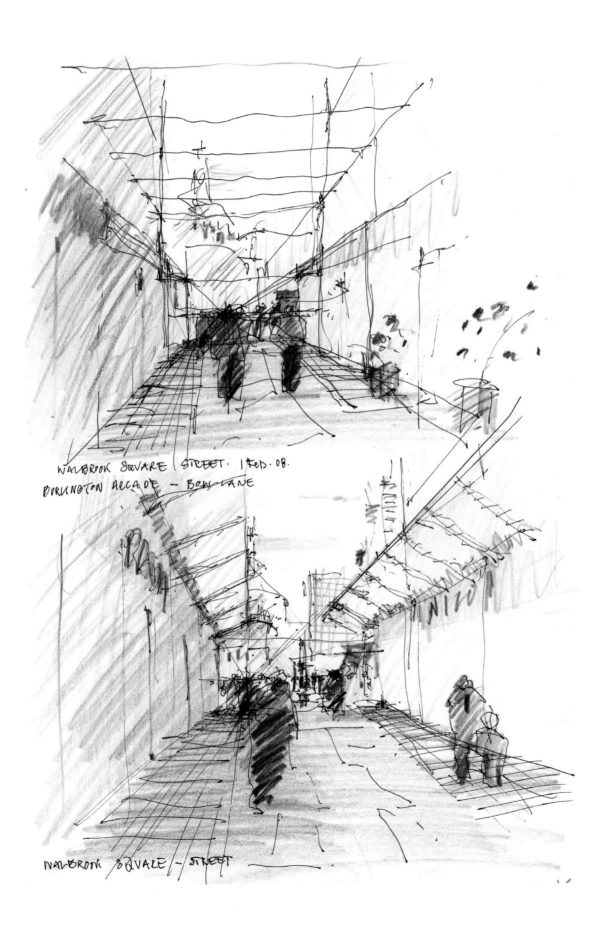

WALBROOK SQUARE STREET. 1 FEB. 08.
BURLINGTON ARCADE — BOW LANE

WALBROOK SQUARE — STREET

Office solutions

WALBROOK SQUARE, LONDON

In an attempt to ameliorate the canyon-like quality of streets in areas of a large concentration of offices, these perspective sketches investigated the addition of several experimental lightweight structures. Although St Paul's Cathedral is not visible from this point, including it in the drawing helps to locate the view in the City of London.

Pilot G-Tec-C4 pen and Faber-Castell Art Grip Aquarelle coloured pencils on A4 paper; 10 minutes each.

131

Streets and public places

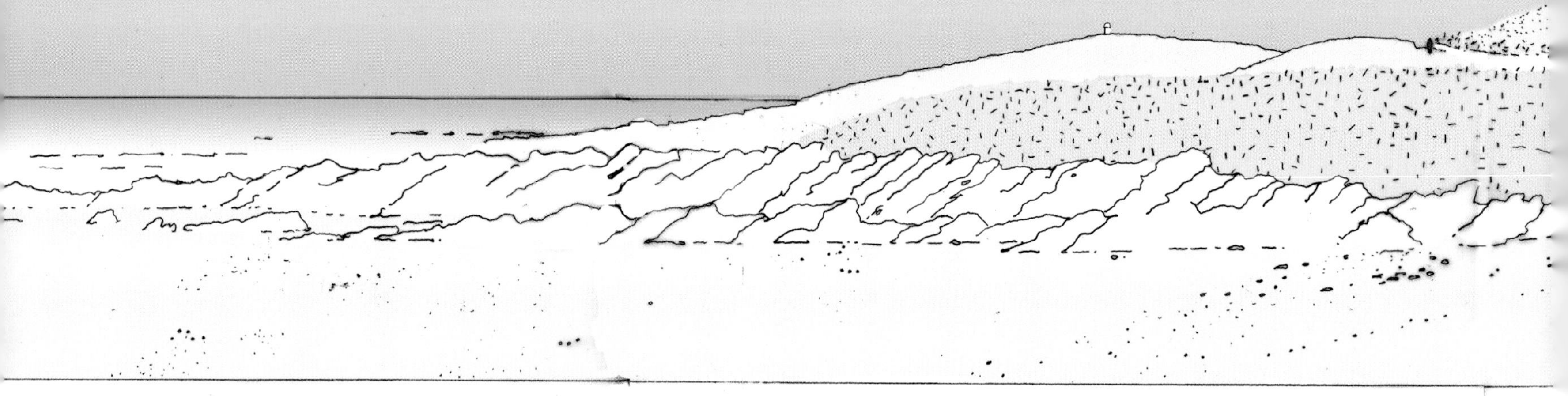

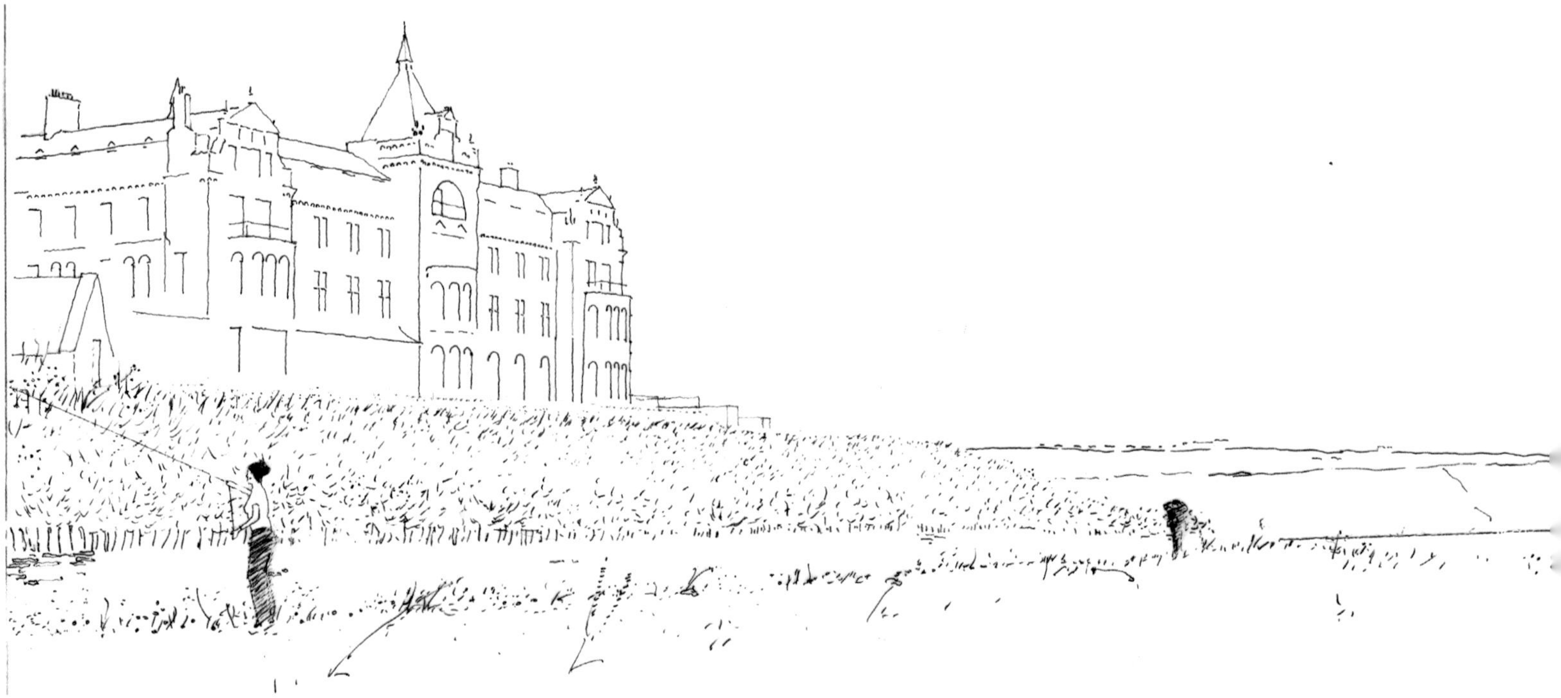

Perspectives

The information in perspective drawings can be selective. If extraneous details are omitted, attention is focused on the design's most important points. These sparse sketches can be surprisingly effective in communicating the essence of a design.

Coastal redevelopment

HEADLAND HOTEL,
NEWQUAY, CORNWALL

This fine coastal site demanded respect. The client wished to double the footprint of the hotel, and, because of the sensitive nature of the landscape, it was decided to build the new facilities underground. The quality of the development proposal and the full set of drawings won planning approval without being presented to the committee. The client, realizing the difficulty of the task that had been set, promised a trip in his hot-air balloon as a reward.

2H pencil on A1 tracing paper, reduced to one-third, scanned and coloured in Photoshop; 16 hours each.

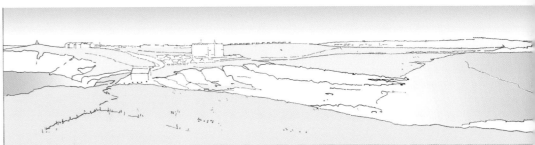

133

6

Isometrics

■

Transferring a plan to an isometric drawing at a different scale is a tricky business. It involves constructing a numbered orthogonal grid over the plan; another sheet of paper bears a corresponding numbered 30°/60° grid, the datum on which the isometric will be constructed. Vertical projections relating to the plan (the corresponding sections and elevations) are then measured above and below the horizontal on the skewed 30°/60° grid, and slowly the three-dimensional design emerges onto the paper as if by magic, even though the mathematical process used to create the image is exacting, with little left to chance. The system becomes complicated when the angles of the initial setting-out (of a building, for example) are not at 90°, and a degree of license is needed to minimize the distortion that inevitably follows.

Isometric drawings can take quite a long time to complete, but the creative process of redrawing the design forces one to engage three-dimensionally with the project. The clarity of an isometric image allows the whole team to understand the proposal from the designer's viewpoint. Moreover, the struggle involved in creating complex isometrics fosters a basic understanding of three-dimensionality at an early stage, which can then be built upon with complete confidence as the scheme develops. Axonometric projections at 45°/90° are considerably easier to create than isometrics, but, since they do not carry the same implied perspective, are generally less useful in describing a scheme.

Another advantage of an isometric drawing is that it can be tailored to concentrate attention specifically on certain principles of the design. A selective process is often useful in choosing to omit irrelevant information, allowing the designer to emphasize instead, for example, how the general public are likely to use the proposed new landscape spaces. In this case, the isometric can illustrate people who do not merely 'fill' the space, but are actively engaged in using it. These images help to engage the client with the design in a

■

Garden for a town house

HORNTON STREET,
KENSINGTON, LONDON

On p. 134: Isometric views of the proposed planting strategy for a town garden beneath mature plane trees.

Rotring 0.18 technical pen on A1 tracing paper; 3 days.

meaningful dialogue, as a result of direct understanding of the scheme. Clients are not always able to fully understand plans, but find an isometric instantly comprehensible, which helps to refine the brief. Early concentration on broad principles enables the discussion of details to take place at a much later stage, avoiding the design becoming choked with minor fault-finding during the initial period.

Drawings within the construction industry are often legal documents, articulating the requirements of the parties in a contract and involving large expenditure of funds, with potentially serious implications. The gravitas underscored in an architectural drawing fosters substantial conversations; the meetings in which these occur can be lengthy and ponderous. It is possible, however, to introduce a lightness of tone when presenting an isometric drawing of the same scheme. This is a useful device for a designer: the ability to present a scheme with a variety of different types of drawing, incorporating a few humorous touches within an isometric projection, and helping the team to relax and remain open to new ideas and concepts. Isometric drawings clearly set out the principles of space, with supporting details of the design (such as materials) of secondary importance. This feature is useful in design development, allowing a whole range of options to be presented to support the main three-dimensional proposal, without the latter becoming compromised.

Discussion of these options also allows a client to engage creatively in the decision-making process without endangering the main idea. It is important to keep a record of all projects undertaken during one's career, regardless of whether they were built or only reached the design stage. These records can be useful in many ways, one of the most important being a ready source of experience when compiling a pitch for new work. A back catalogue of isometric drawings clearly describes the progress and range of past work in a lighthearted and simple-to-understand manner, easily accessible to a new client.

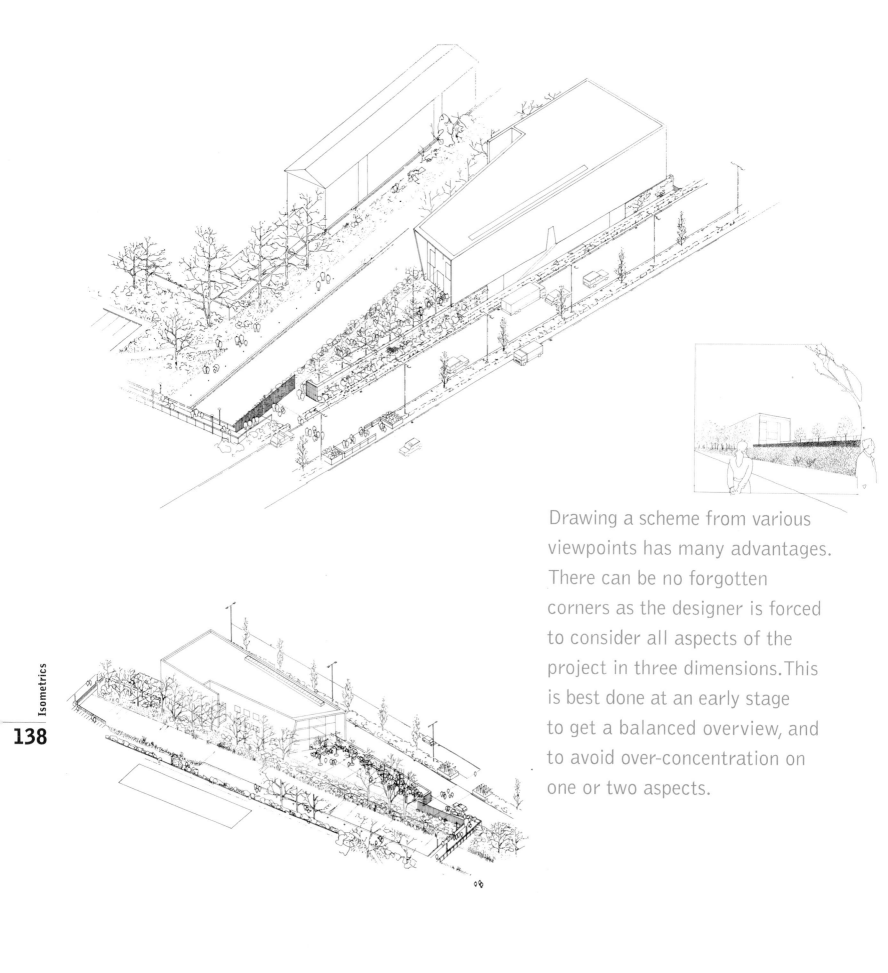

Drawing a scheme from various viewpoints has many advantages. There can be no forgotten corners as the designer is forced to consider all aspects of the project in three dimensions. This is best done at an early stage to get a balanced overview, and to avoid over-concentration on one or two aspects.

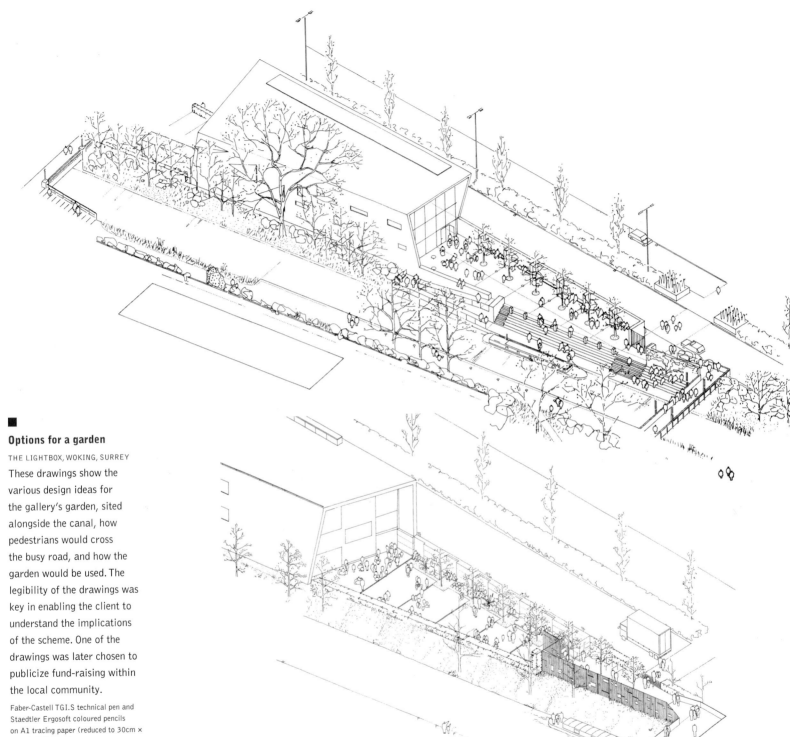

Options for a garden

THE LIGHTBOX, WOKING, SURREY

These drawings show the various design ideas for the gallery's garden, sited alongside the canal, how pedestrians would cross the busy road, and how the garden would be used. The legibility of the drawings was key in enabling the client to understand the implications of the scheme. One of the drawings was later chosen to publicize fund-raising within the local community.

Faber-Castell TGI.S technical pen and Staedtler Ergosoft coloured pencils on A1 tracing paper (reduced to 30cm × 42cm); 2 days each.

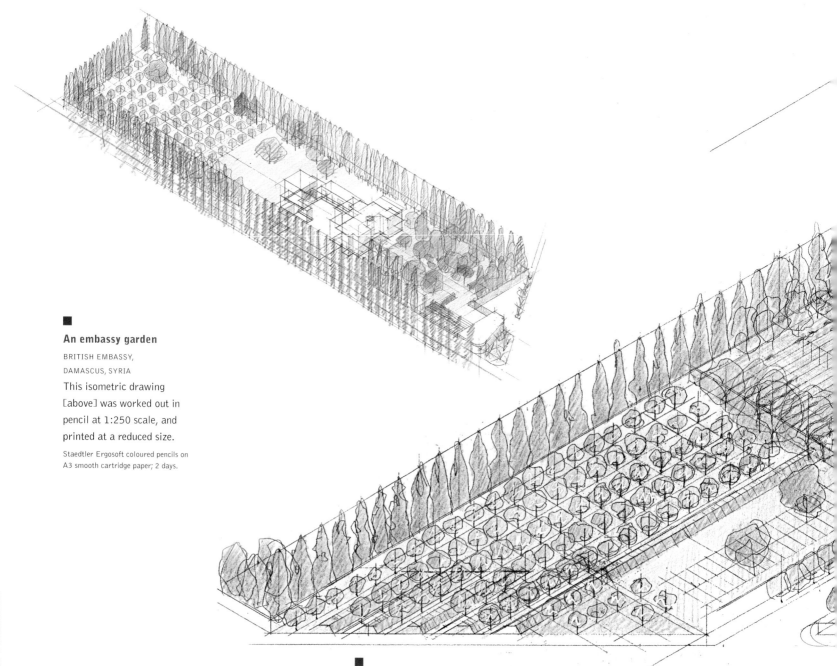

■

An embassy garden

BRITISH EMBASSY,
DAMASCUS, SYRIA

This isometric drawing
[above] was worked out in
pencil at 1:250 scale, and
printed at a reduced size.

Staedtler Ergosoft coloured pencils on
A3 smooth cartridge paper; 2 days.

■

A clear, bold planting plan

BRITISH EMBASSY, DAMASCUS, SYRIA

An isometric demonstrating how an unexciting modern villa could be converted, via strong
landscape design, into the British Embassy. The existing spaces were remodelled with a bold
planting plan, while a line of Italian cypress trees emphasized the profile of the distant hills,
simultaneously screening the building from view until the last moment. As water extraction in
the area is now limited, plants were chosen that would require minimal irrigation for their first
three years in situ; after this period, they should be sufficiently well established to cope with
the extremely arid climate. The original pencil workings were kept to show the history of the
drawing in a ghost-like form; this also prevents the image from appearing too 'perfect'.

Tombow ABT felt-tip pens on tracing paper, with Tipp-Ex highlights; 2 days.

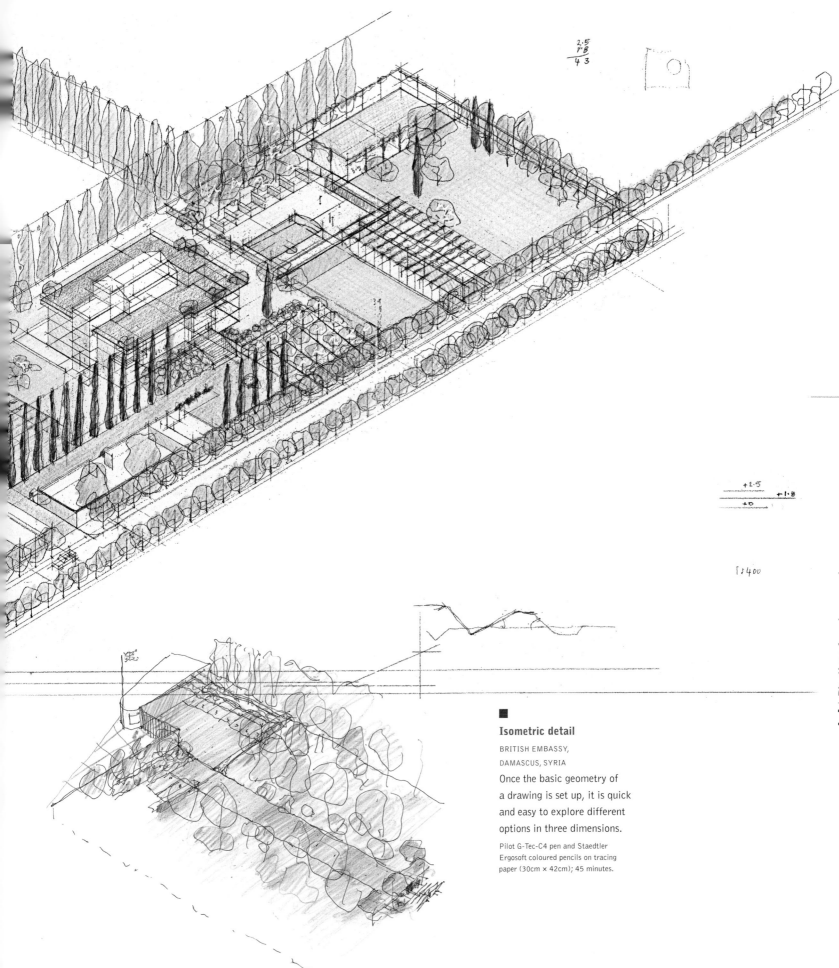

141

■

Isometric detail

BRITISH EMBASSY,
DAMASCUS, SYRIA

Once the basic geometry of
a drawing is set up, it is quick
and easy to explore different
options in three dimensions.

Pilot G-Tec-C4 pen and Staedtler
Ergosoft coloured pencils on tracing
paper (30cm × 42cm); 45 minutes.

A prototype primary school

This hypothetical isometric for the Building Schools for the Future programme illustrates innovative external spaces surrounding a primary school. The large plaza in front is conceived as both a drop-off point for the children and, when the school is closed, an amenity for the local community. Traditional playing fields, so often characterless landscapes, are here embedded at a lower level to create a sunken sports amphitheatre and a centre for outdoor productions; the resulting earth spoil is used to remodel the site. A very fine pen was used to reflect the scale of the children. It was drawn in memory of Jenny Adey, an inspiring head teacher in Croydon, who advised us on the design.

Faber-Castell 0.13 technical pen on A0 paper, scanned and coloured in Photoshop; 6 days.

Clarifying spaces

BEDALES SCHOOL, HAMPSHIRE

Isometric drawings can be
complicated to set up. At
Bedales, the ground sloped
and the buildings were not
at right angles to each other.
This particular drawing
proved to be very useful in the
design process, and clarified
the validity of the spaces
generated between the new
buildings. The area created
between buildings to the right
of the drawing, for example,
appears as an awkward and
unsatisfactory space, and
proved to be so when built.

Rotring 0.18 technical pen and Berol
Karismacolor pencils on A0 paper;
4 days.

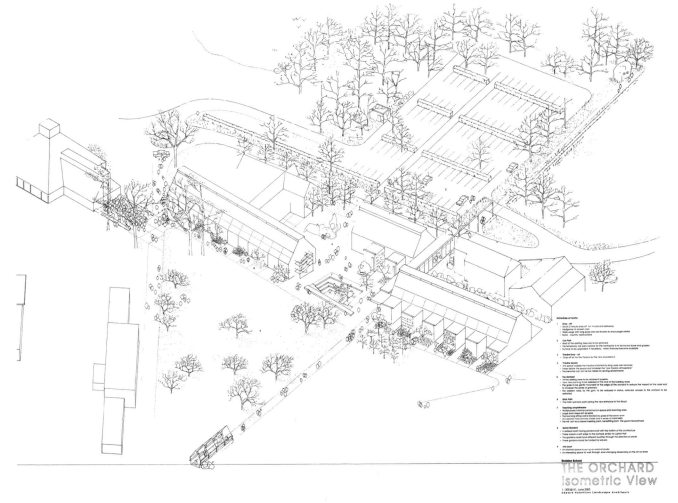

THE ORCHARD
Isometric View

Planting solutions

ROYAL ACADEMY OF MUSIC, LONDON + IMPERIAL COLLEGE LONDON

Two new planting beds were proposed at the west entrance
to the Royal Academy of Music [below, left]. This mainly
monochromatic drawing for Imperial College London
emphasizes the importance of the green planting [below].

Rotring 0.18 technical pen and Berol Karismacolor pencils on A1 paper; 2 days each.

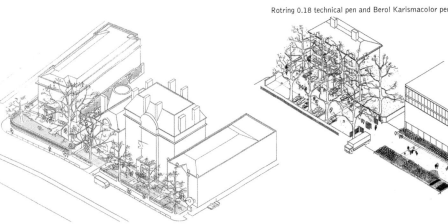

Landscape for education

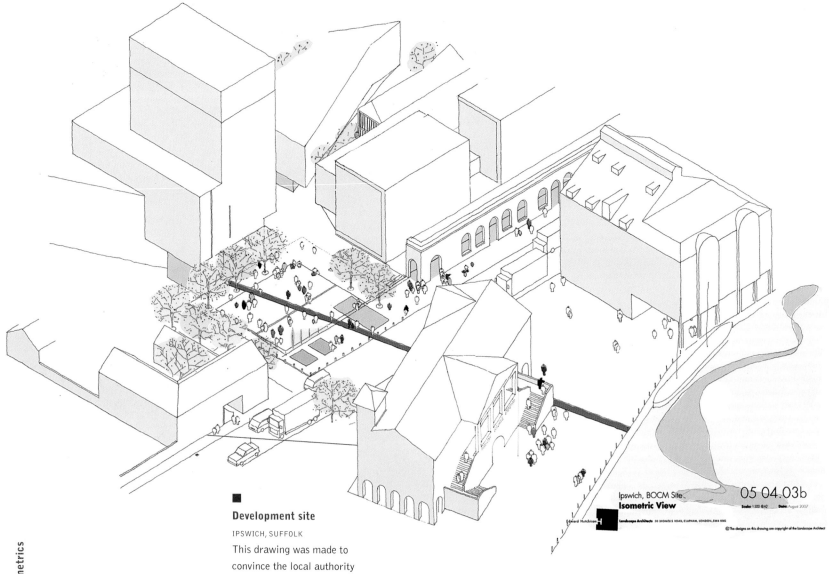

Ipswich, BOCM Site
Isometric View
Edward Hutchison
Landscape Architects 30 330MELS 30AS, CLAPHAM, LONDON, SW4 0BG
Scale: 1:300 @A2   Date: August 2007
© The designs on this drawing are copyright of the Landscape Architect

05 04.03b

■
Development site
IPSWICH, SUFFOLK
This drawing was made to
convince the local authority
that the landscape – the
'planning gain' associated with
the new development – would be
built to a very high standard.
The design was developed
in tandem with the massing
studies of the architecture
to ensure the success of the
resulting spaces.

Rotring 0.18 technical pen on
A2 tracing paper, scanned and coloured in
Photoshop; 2 days.

Isometrics may be scanned and
rendered with flat colours to
create more mechanical-looking
drawings. This adds 'punch', and
is an effective combination of
computer-generated design and
drawings created by hand.

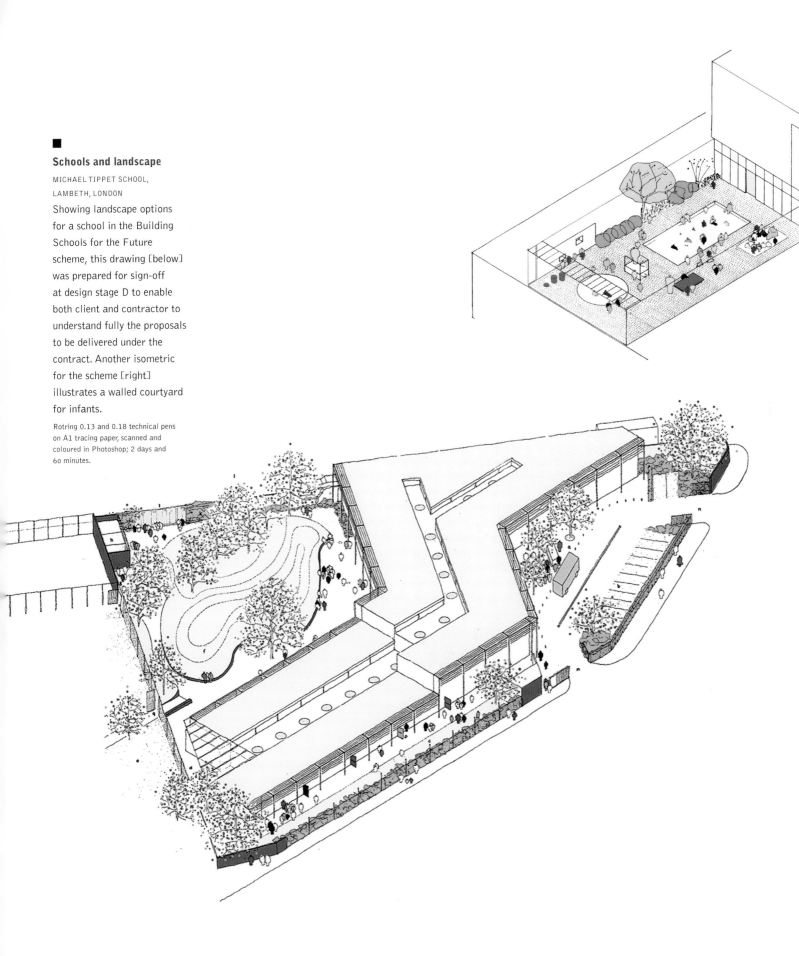

Schools and landscape

MICHAEL TIPPET SCHOOL,
LAMBETH, LONDON

Showing landscape options
for a school in the Building
Schools for the Future
scheme, this drawing [below]
was prepared for sign-off
at design stage D to enable
both client and contractor to
understand fully the proposals
to be delivered under the
contract. Another isometric
for the scheme [right]
illustrates a walled courtyard
for infants.

Rotring 0.13 and 0.18 technical pens
on A1 tracing paper, scanned and
coloured in Photoshop; 2 days and
60 minutes.

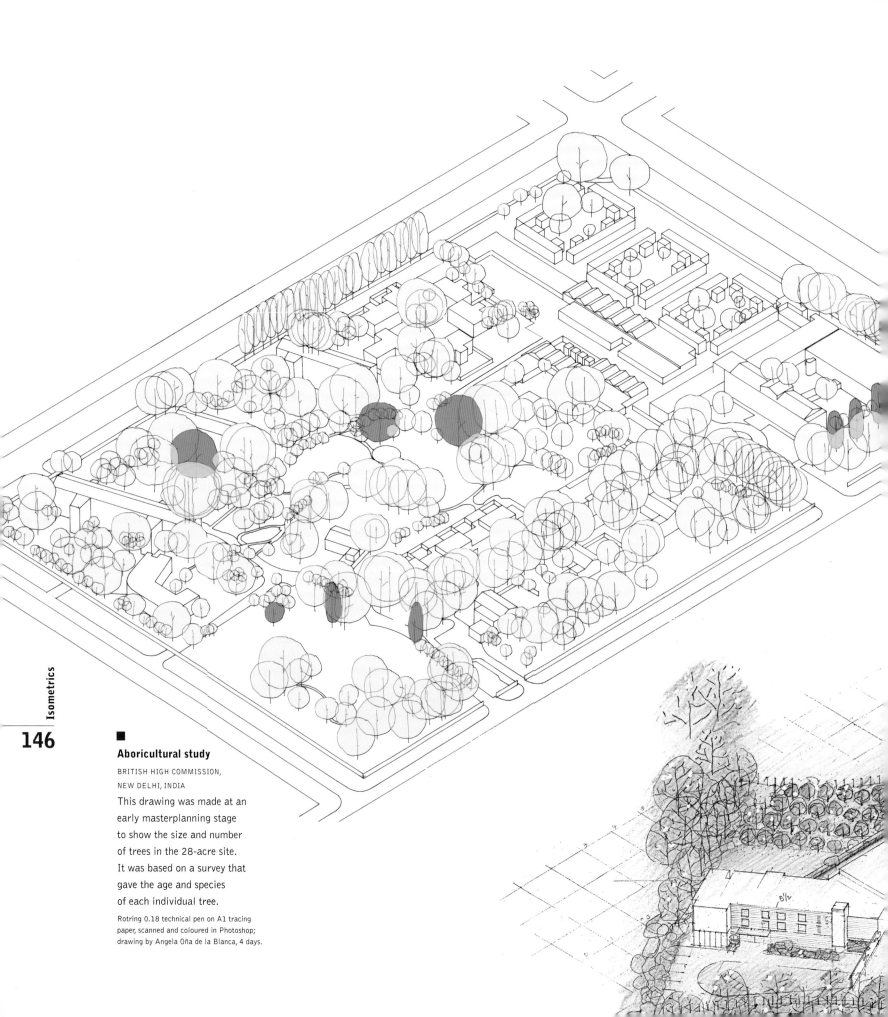

Aboricultural study

BRITISH HIGH COMMISSION,
NEW DELHI, INDIA

This drawing was made at an
early masterplanning stage
to show the size and number
of trees in the 28-acre site.
It was based on a survey that
gave the age and species
of each individual tree.

Rotring 0.18 technical pen on A1 tracing
paper, scanned and coloured in Photoshop;
drawing by Angela Oña de la Blanca, 4 days.

There are few designs that
do not benefit immeasurably from
being drawn in three dimensions.

■

Design and build

HASTINGS, EAST SUSSEX

One of the drawings that
formed part of a competition
bid to provide care homes for
the elderly within a 'design-
and-build' contract [below].
By stressing the importance
of the surrounding landscape,
the design aimed to lessen
the institutional look of the
homes. As the budget was
extremely tight, the proposals
had to be kept as simple
as possible.

3H 5mm pencil and Staedtler Ergosoft
coloured pencils on A1 tracing paper,
printed on smooth cartridge paper; 1 day.

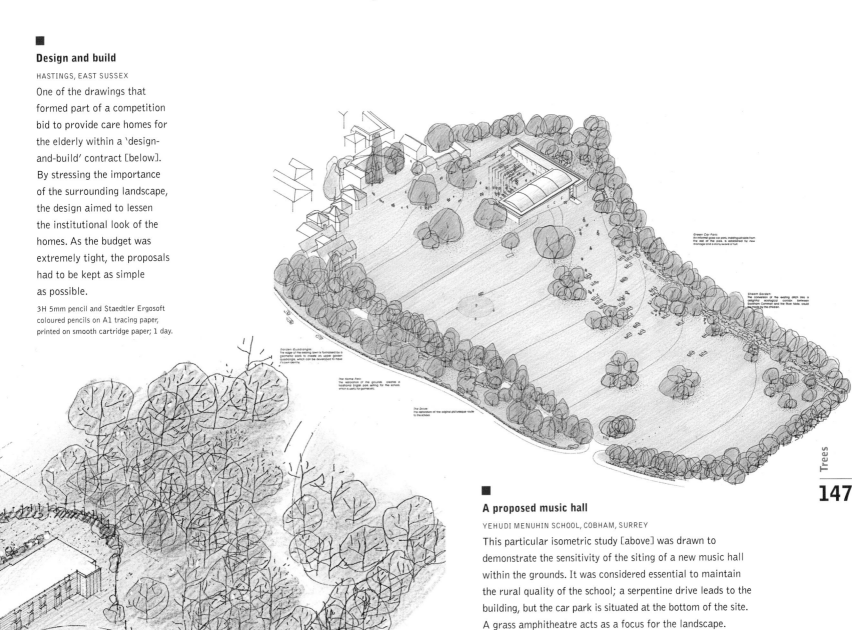

■

A proposed music hall

YEHUDI MENUHIN SCHOOL, COBHAM, SURREY

This particular isometric study [above] was drawn to
demonstrate the sensitivity of the siting of a new music hall
within the grounds. It was considered essential to maintain
the rural quality of the school; a serpentine drive leads to the
building, but the car park is situated at the bottom of the site.
A grass amphitheatre acts as a focus for the landscape.

Rotring 0.18 technical pen and Berol Karismacolor pencils on tracing paper,
printed on smooth cartridge paper; 3 days.

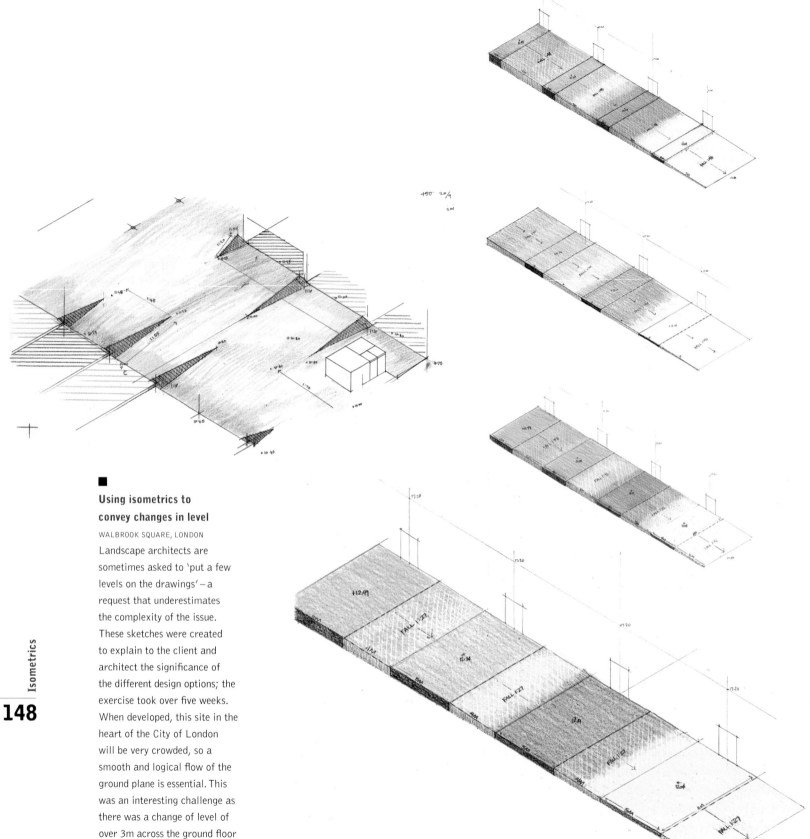

■

Using isometrics to convey changes in level

WALBROOK SQUARE, LONDON

Landscape architects are sometimes asked to 'put a few levels on the drawings' – a request that underestimates the complexity of the issue. These sketches were created to explain to the client and architect the significance of the different design options; the exercise took over five weeks. When developed, this site in the heart of the City of London will be very crowded, so a smooth and logical flow of the ground plane is essential. This was an interesting challenge as there was a change of level of over 3m across the ground floor of the building.

2H 5mm pencil and Staedtler Ergosoft coloured pencils on A3 tracing paper; 2 hours each.

Ramp-to-plane proportions

WALBROOK SQUARE, LONDON

Spot-heights on a plan cannot sufficiently indicate the significance of a change in level. These coloured drawings [right, above and below] were produced to explore the different proportions of ramp-to-flat-plane in a proposed street. The necessity of level paving outside each shopfront affected the steepness of the intermittent ramps along the street.

2H 5mm pencil and Staedtler Ergosoft coloured pencils on A3 tracing paper; 3 hours each.

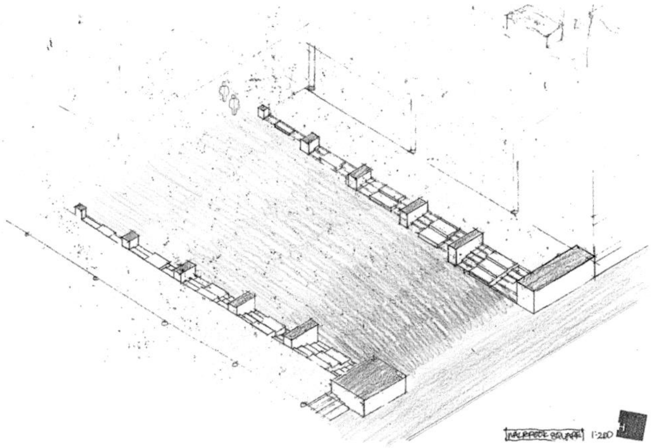

Circulation patterns

WALBROOK SQUARE, LONDON

This study [below] explores the relationship between the square and the surrounding levels of the shops, together with pedestrian circulation.

2H 5mm pencil and Staedtler Ergosoft coloured pencils on A3 tracing paper; 3 hours.

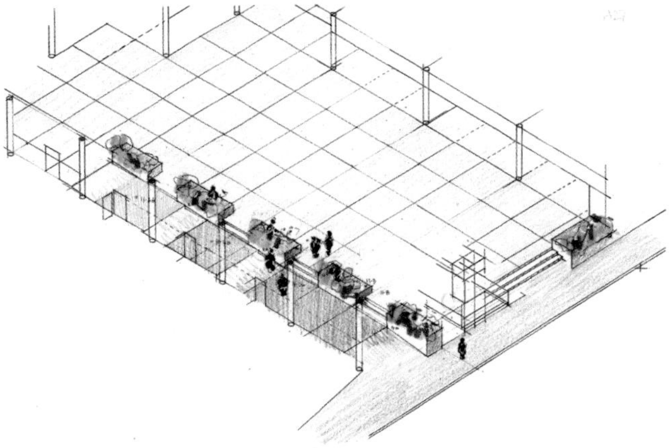

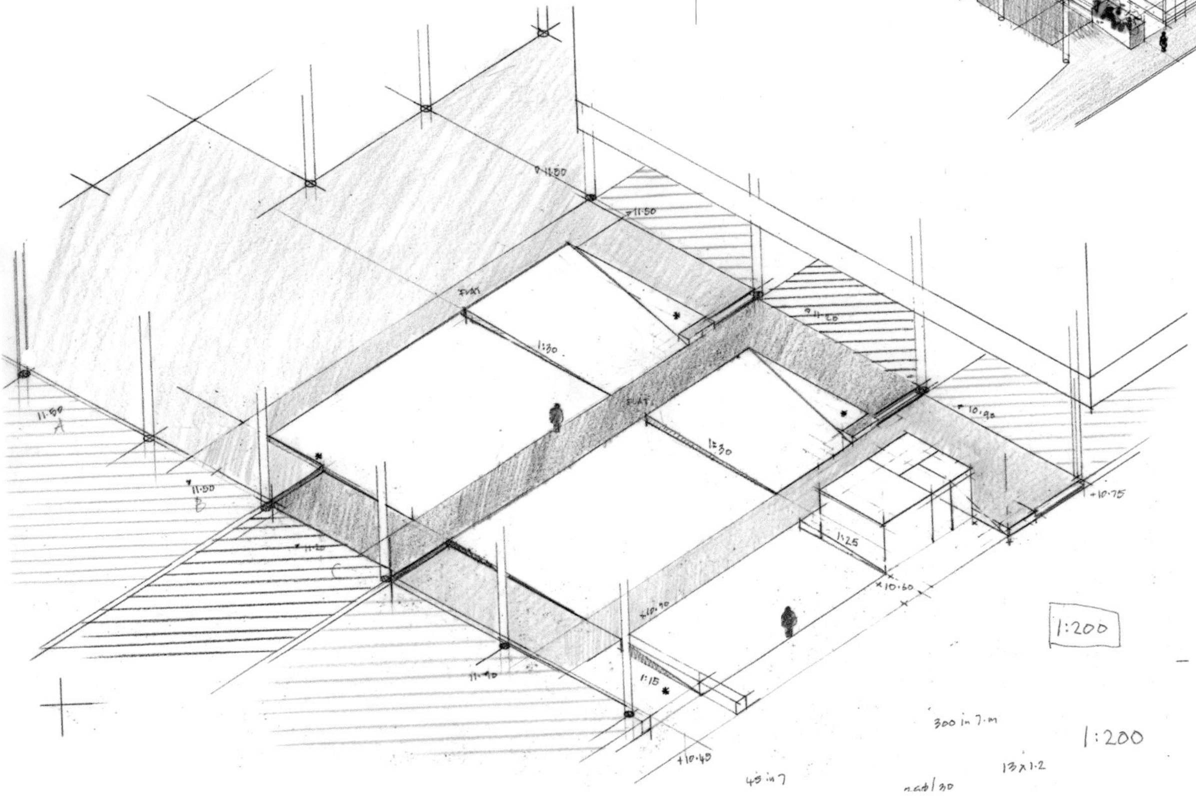

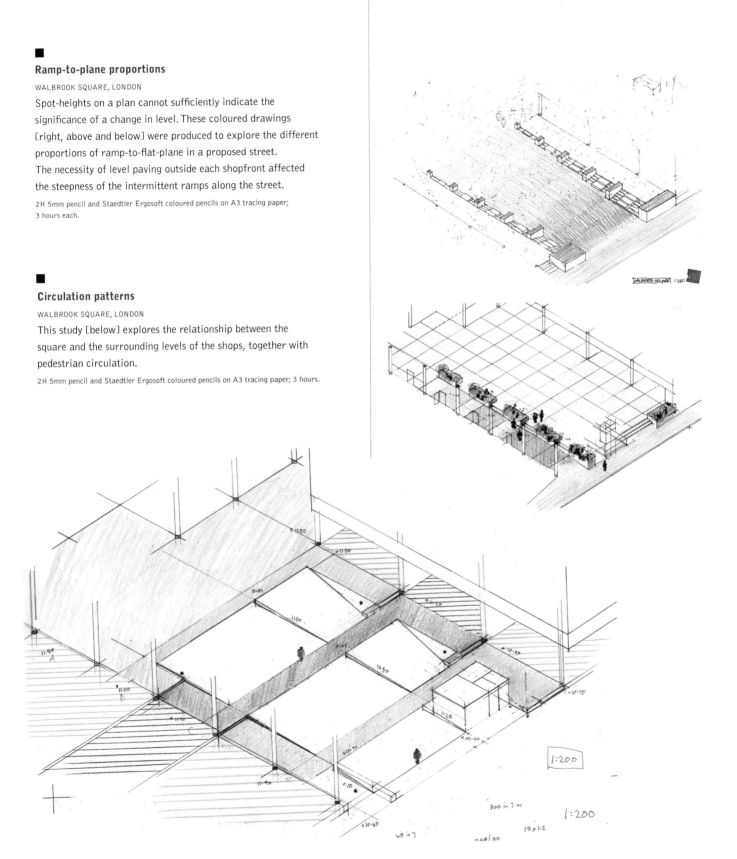

Isometrics for two colleges

IMPERIAL COLLEGE LONDON + SUSSEX DOWNS COLLEGE, EAST SUSSEX

Isometric drawings that describe the possible uses of a design proposal are key for testing ideas at an early stage. They are also an excellent way of presenting the three-dimensional reality of a scheme to the client in a relaxed, friendly manner. Drawings such as these of Imperial College London [below and opposite, bottom] and Sussex Downs College [right and opposite, top] may prove a more useful and appealing medium than the conventional perspective 'animated' by people.

Berol Karismacolor coloured pencils; 2–3 days each.

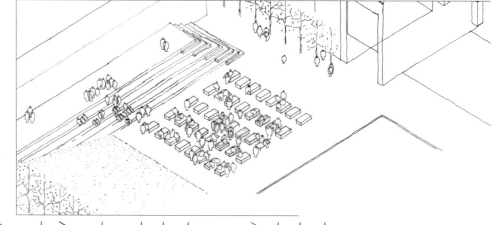

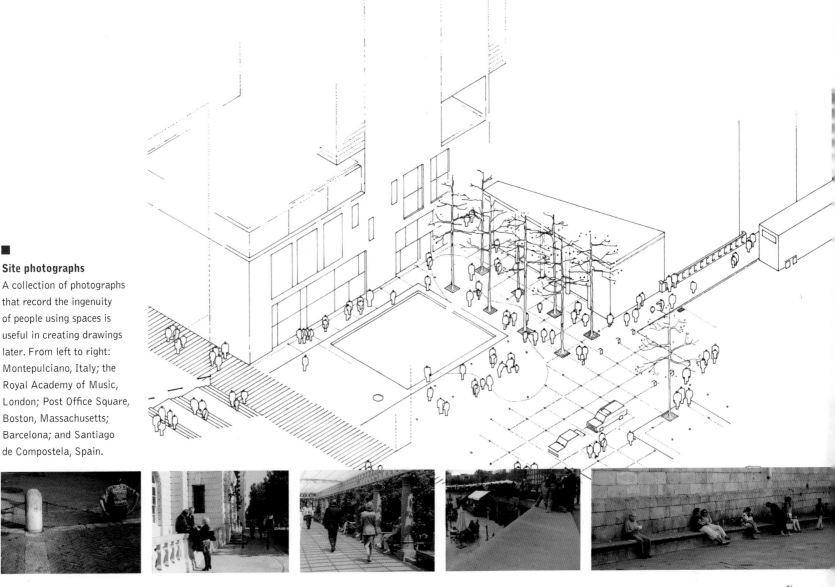

Site photographs
A collection of photographs that record the ingenuity of people using spaces is useful in creating drawings later. From left to right: Montepulciano, Italy; the Royal Academy of Music, London; Post Office Square, Boston, Massachusetts; Barcelona; and Santiago de Compostela, Spain.

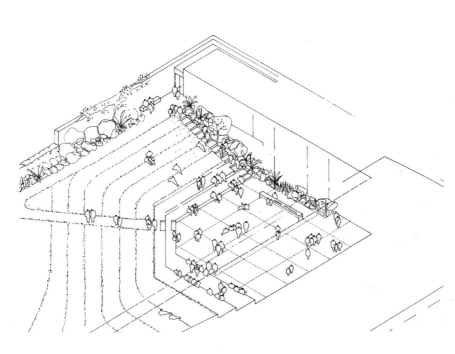

Much has been written on the many and varied ways that people use external space. An inner-city public park, for example, can offer a surprising degree of privacy. As a designer, it is important to understand the principles of creating a place that people will want to spend time in.

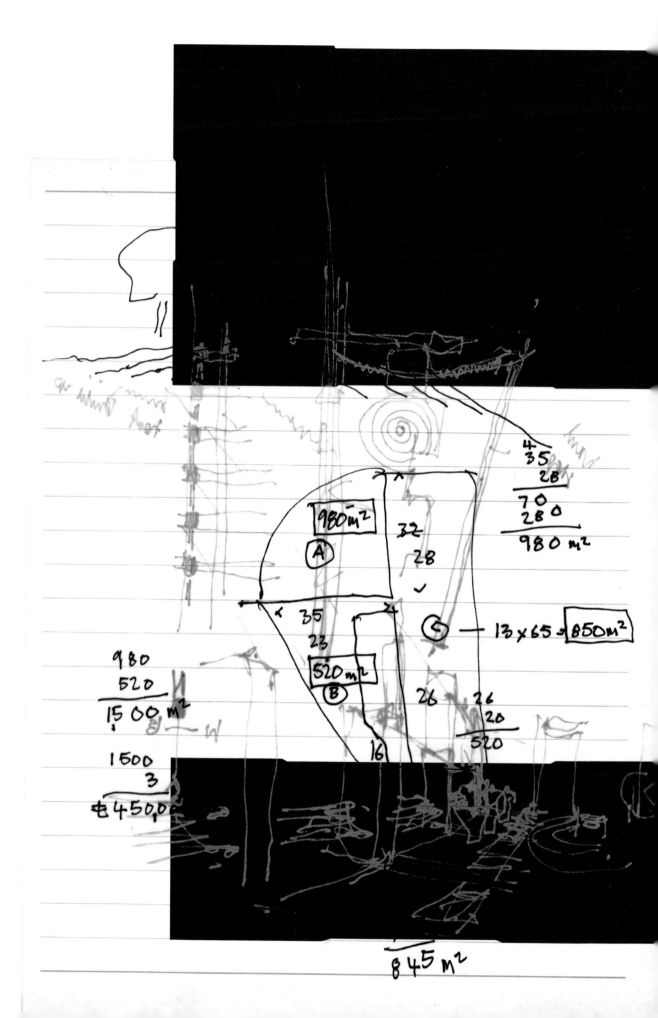

980 m²

A

32

28

4
35
2B
70
280
980 m²

35

23

520 m²

B

26   26
20
520

13 × 65 = 850 m²

980
520
1500 m²

1500
3
₺450,00

845 m²

7

Money drawings

■

Equating areas to a budget

COVENTRY PEACE GARDEN,
WARWICKSHIRE
On p. 152: These rough
sketches identified, at the start
of the project, the difficulty of
delivering an appropriate scheme
for the city centre within a
reduced budget.

Edding 55 fineliner pen, A4 notebook;
20 minutes.

■

It is often the case, particularly with larger architectural projects, that the initial budget earmarked for landscape design is inadequate, as it is not considered a high-priority part of the scheme. This makes it difficult from the start to achieve a good result. In the UK, unlike many other parts of the world, it is unusual to pay for high-quality landscape work. Project managers, quantity surveyors and clients can be resistant to the idea of setting aside enough money; many times they are just unused to experiencing the difference a well-designed landscape can make to the finished scheme, and it is not until the end of a project that its contribution is fully recognized.

There can frequently be an element of 'smoke and mirrors' when defining landscape costs within a larger project. In a highly competitive marketplace, the cost may render the project over budget. With this in mind, in 2004 we began to make 'money drawings' for each project, allowing us to have greater understanding and control of the landscape budget. These drawings, with their bold, simple graphics, illustrated the breakdown of costs to the design team. Their huge advantage is that any revision made to a drawing can be easily assessed for its financial implications, thus avoiding a negative reaction to the inevitable changes that take place during the development of the design. Quantity surveyors, even though they might be initially resistant, will generally find these drawings helpful. During their preparation, it is necessary to undertake a considerable amount of the measuring of the scheme, not usually part of the landscape architect's commission, in order to achieve an accurate idea of the budget. As a result, the quantity surveyor is more likely to be sympathetic and generous in the presentation of the landscape within the cost reports.

Bright colours are specifically chosen to define these diagrams, and the strong tones force a question over the landscape choices: how and why have these colours been selected? Grass is not represented by green, but – perhaps – by a bright red to highlight its importance and subsequent maintenance implications. Intense and lengthy discussions over schedules of prices become wearisome, and the significance and relevance of an item can become lost within the columns and columns of figures itemized on a spreadsheet. Colourful, diagrammatic drawings help to create a focus on a particular element. They bring a more relaxed approach to budget discussions and subliminally raise the spirits, even affecting the eventual decisions reached. While not pretending to be alternatives to conventional bills of quantities, prepared by the quantity surveyors from the architect's drawings, the simplicity of these naive images directly summarize the elements of a project. This allows cost decisions to be made by members of the design team, maintaining a balanced overview of the project far more easily than the more usual process of trying to cross-reference plans and section details against the relevant column in a price schedule.

Inevitably, there are critical moments in the development of a project when a landscape scheme has to be justified on cost grounds. It is at this stage that money drawings play an invaluable role in defending a design. During a lengthy cost meeting on a scheme in Coventry (the Coventry Peace Garden; see p. 214), five members of the team attempted to find savings without compromising the design ideas. At the end of the discussion, no cuts were made and the budget for the landscape was significantly increased. In this case, the money drawing's clarity of display and coherence of reason played a critical role in achieving the desired result.

■

The first money drawing

BEDALES SCHOOL, HAMPSHIRE

This electronic drawing conveys the full implications of the limited budget allocated to the landscape. The specified areas and shading give authenticity to the message.

Vectorworks software program; drawing by Claudia Corcilius.

Fixes	
Drop off	1,240m²
Excavation	3,880m²
Brick path	270m
Steps and retaining wall	1m
Edging	
Drainage	
Sub-total	
Prelims @ 12 per cent	
Sub-total	
Overheads and profit	
Sub-total	
Design contingency @ 3 per cent	
Sub-total	
Rate/m² ($167,000–$80,000)	
Budget	
Landscape costs	
Total	

There is little point in drawing up a design if it is unaffordable, though the process may be useful in its ability to tease out opportunities for discussion. This method for establishing a budget, however, is very time-consuming for a designer.

Development drawings

BEDALES SCHOOL, HAMPSHIRE

These drawings [right, above and below] were made to explain two variants on the overall design, using a limited palette of materials that had been approved by the school governors' building committee. The site photographs [bottom] illustrate, from left to right, Coleford handmade bricks; turf; semi-mature trees, 30–35cm girth; and stabilized gravel in Ritterings, a grass paving system.

Vectorworks software program; drawing by Claudia Corcilius.

Drainage	640m²
Nidoplast	245m²
Naturex	265m²
Brick path	265m²
Steps and retaining wall	33m²
Edging	1m
Scrapes	34m
Grass	2500m²
Planting native	185m²
Trees	13
Lights	60
Sub-total:	
Prelims @ 12 per cent	
Sub-total:	
Overheads and profit @ 7.5 per cent	
Sub-total:	
Design contingency @ 3 per cent	
Sub-total:	
Rate/m² ($294,000–$80,000)	
Budget:	
Landscape costs	
Total:	

Key
- Naturatex
- Brick
- Tactile paving
- Nidoplast
- Walls and steps
- Grass
- Planting
- Trees
- Scrapes

The choice of bright colours helps to
bring a lighthearted approach to the budget,
and to dispel the idea that the landscape is
a predictable part of the project.

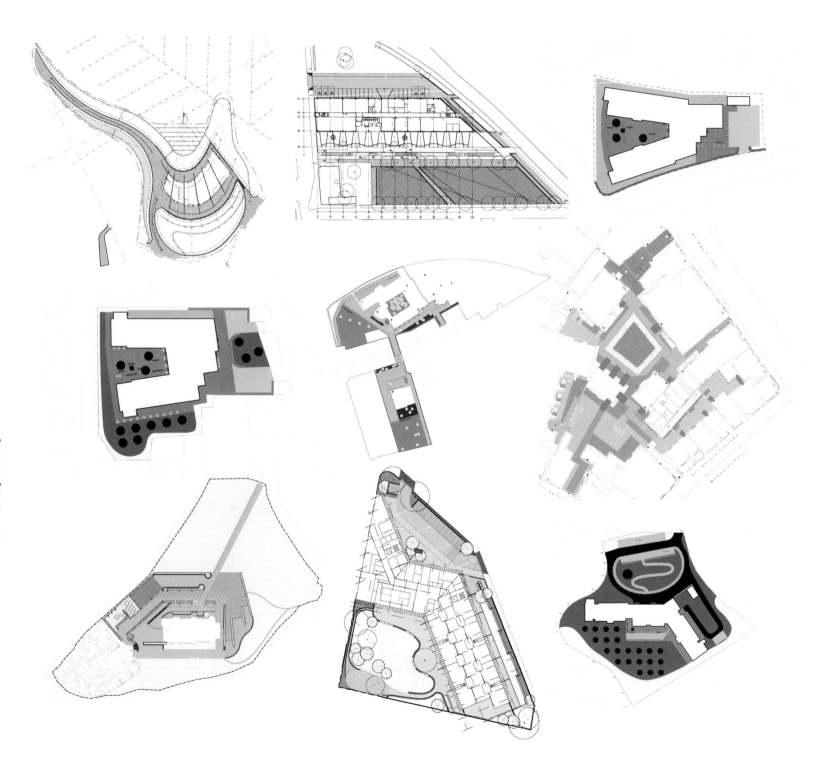

A group of isometrics

These isometrics [opposite] were created for a number of different projects. Top row, left to right: Avenham Park Pavilion, Preston, Lancashire; Pocket Park, Hull History Centre, East Yorkshire; Agewell, Ringmer, East Sussex. Middle row, left to right: Agewell, Wealden, East Sussex; Sussex Downs College, East Sussex; St John's College, Cambridge. Bottom row, left to right: Headland Hotel, Newquay, Cornwall; Michael Tippett School, London; Agewell, Hastings, East Sussex.

Vectorworks software program; drawings by Claudia Corcilius, Heidi Hundley, Matilda Jones and Julia Zimmermann.

Garden and grounds

BRITISH EMBASSY,
DAMASCUS, SYRIA

The British Foreign Office planned to convert two large, rather drab villas near Damascus into the new embassy and ambassador's residence. This drawing [right] shows the extent of the proposed landscape; the design intention was to enhance the experience of guests and dignitaries during their visit to the embassy. At the time, the supply of nursery-grown plants in Syria was limited, challenging the feasibility of a large-scale planting scheme. A solution was suggested by a nursery in Beirut, whose staff researched the practicality and costs of legitimately importing mature stock from Italy or Lebanon. Due to the demands of the tight programme, the project manager issued this drawing to a contractor to obtain a tender.

Vectorworks software program; drawing by Heidi Hundley.

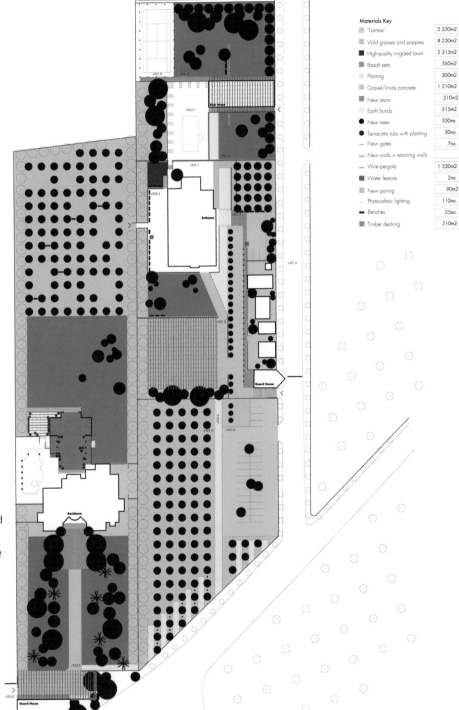

Materials Key	
'Tarmac'	2 230m2
Wild grasses and poppies	8 230m2
High-quality irrigated lawn	5 315m2
Basalt setts	560m2
Planting	300m2
Gravel/In-situ concrete	1 210m2
New stairs	210m2
Earth bunds	515m2
New trees	350no.
Terracotta tubs with planting	50no.
New gates	7no.
New walls + retaining walls	
Wire pergola	1 530m2
Water feature	2no.
New paving	90m2
Photovoltaic lighting	110no.
Benches	25no.
Timber decking	310m2

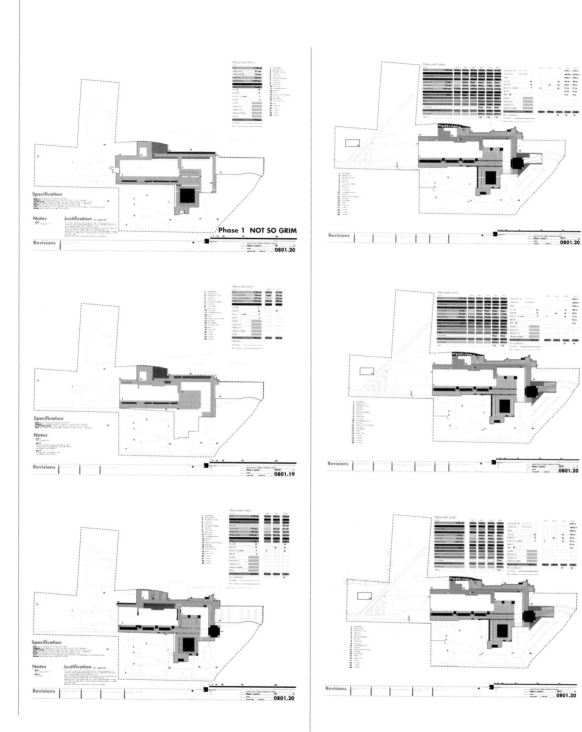

Phase 1 NOT SO GRIM

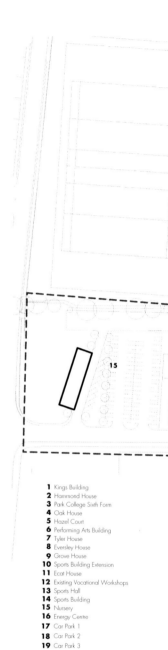

1 Kings Building
2 Hammond House
3 Park College Sixth Form
4 Oak House
5 Hazel Court
6 Performing Arts Building
7 Tyler House
8 Eversley House
9 Grove House
10 Sports Building Extension
11 Ecat House
12 Existing Vocational Workshops
13 Sports Hall
14 Sports Building
15 Nursery
16 Energy Centre
17 Car Park 1
18 Car Park 2
19 Car Park 3

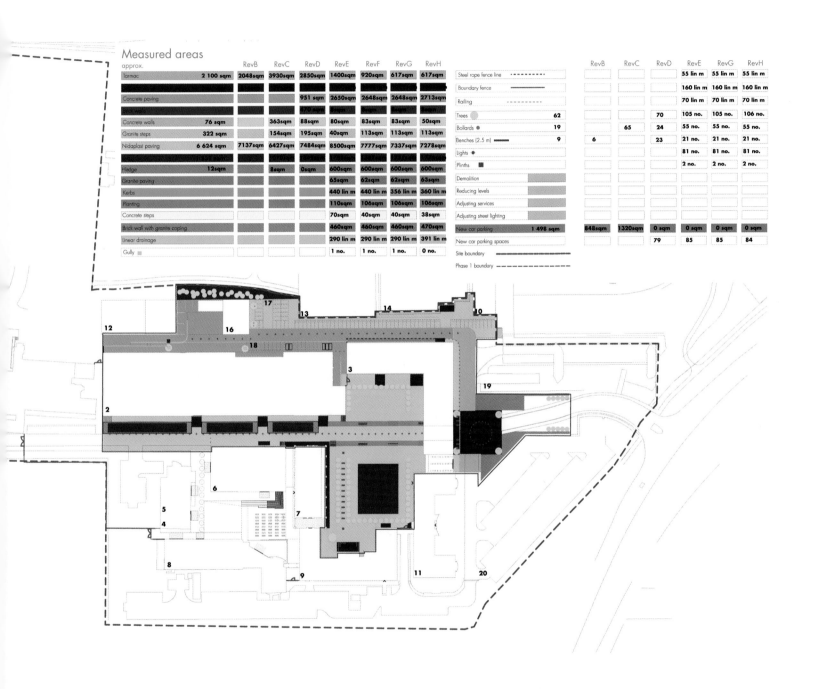

Measured areas

approx.	RevB	RevC	RevD	RevE	RevF	RevG	RevH
Tarmac	2 100 sqm	2048sqm	3930sqm	2850sqm	1400sqm	920sqm	617sqm	617sqm
Concrete paving				951 sqm	2650sqm	2648sqm	2648sqm	2713sqm
Brick walls				670 sqm				
Concrete walls	76 sqm		363sqm	88sqm	80sqm	83sqm	83sqm	50sqm
Granite steps	322 sqm		154sqm	195sqm	40sqm	113sqm	113sqm	113sqm
Nidaplast paving	6 624 sqm	7137sqm	6427sqm	7484sqm	8500sqm	7777sqm	7337sqm	7278sqm
Hedge	12sqm		8sqm	0sqm	600sqm	600sqm	600sqm	600sqm
Granite paving					65sqm	62sqm	62sqm	63sqm
Kerbs					440 lin m	440 lin m	356 lin m	360 lin m
Planting					110sqm	106sqm	106sqm	106sqm
Concrete steps					70sqm	40sqm	40sqm	38sqm
Brick wall with granite coping					460sqm	460sqm	460sqm	470sqm
Linear drainage					290 lin m	290 lin m	290 lin m	391 lin m
Gully					1 no.	1 no.	1 no.	0 no.

		RevB	RevC	RevD	RevE	RevG	RevH
Steel rope fence line					55 lin m	55 lin m	55 lin m
Boundary fence					160 lin m	160 lin m	160 lin m
Railing					70 lin m	70 lin m	70 lin m
Trees	62			70	105 no.	105 no.	106 no.
Bollards	19		65	24	55 no.	55 no.	55 no.
Benches (2.5 m)	9	6		23	21 no.	21 no.	21 no.
Lights					81 no.	81 no.	81 no.
Plinths					2 no.	2 no.	2 no.
Demolition							
Reducing levels							
Adjusting services							
Adjusting street lighting							
New car parking	1 498 sqm	848sqm	1320sqm	0 sqm	0 sqm	0 sqm	0 sqm
New car parking spaces				79	85	85	84

Site boundary
Phase 1 boundary

Landscaping phases

SUSSEX DOWNS COLLEGE, EAST SUSSEX

This drawing formed part of a sequence of illustrations that demonstrated
the phasing of the proposed landscape over a five-year period. The forceful colours
highlight areas of construction that required more detailed thought.

Vectorworks software program; drawing by Matilda Jones.

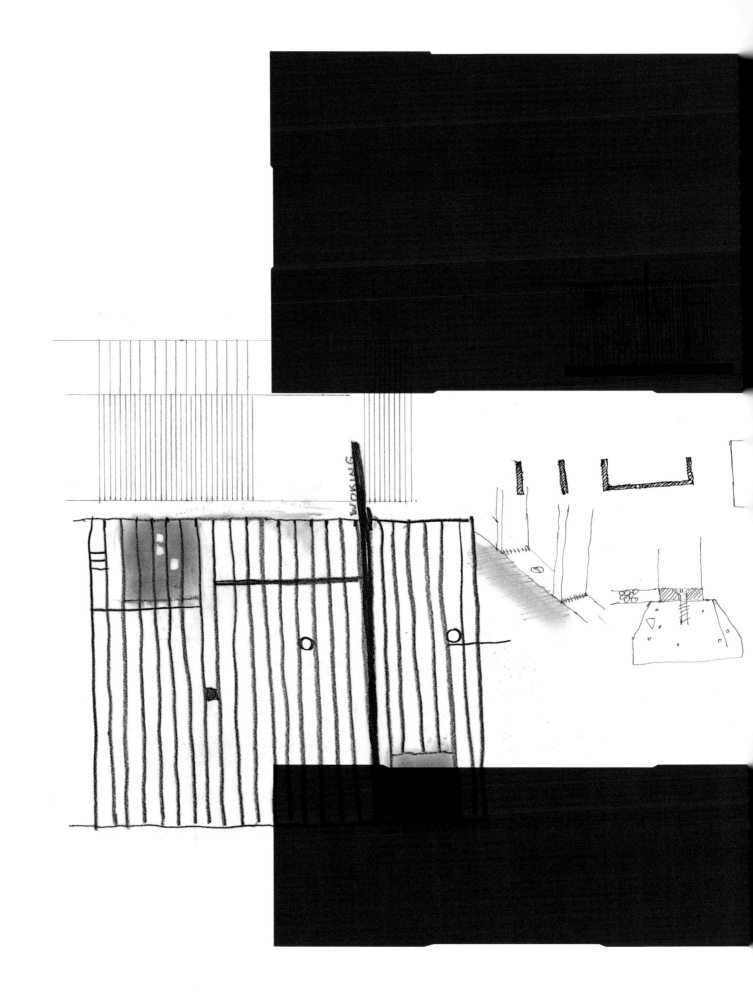

8

Construction details

■

Proposals for metalwork

THE LIGHTBOX, WOKING, SURREY
On p. 162: In the assessment
of a design, seemingly messy
sketches will reflect aspects
of a proposal more accurately
than very neat drawings.

Faber-Castell TG1.S technical pen and
2B 10mm and 2H 5mm pencils on
A3 tracing paper; 4 hours.

■

Construction detailing can be one of the most creative aspects in
landscape design. Careful consideration of how a particular detail is
to be put together requires equally careful commitment of thought
and time on the part of the designer, involving discussions with
suppliers, the further development and refinement of shop drawings,
and the production of mock-ups. All of this extra work may be hard
to justify on commercial grounds, but the process encourages the
creation of a collection of details, which can be used in a modified
form for another project. Craftsmen, too, take pleasure in completing
a job beautifully, although initially they may need convincing that
an unusual detail is strictly necessary. A unique design both helps
to define a 'house style' and brings individuality to a project, setting
it apart from other commissions and generating interest within
the profession. Post-construction photographs of the site will
frequently persuade new clients of the dedication you will give to
their own project.

Drawings that explain the ideas behind a new construction
detail are best done across a range of scales and media to test them
from different perspectives. Drawing a detail up at a very large
scale is an especially useful aid, as the exaggeration highlights any
incompatibility between the various elements, such as ingress
of water by capillary action, poor drainage, uncontrolled movement,
and so on. Isometric drawings of the corners and junctions are also
extremely important, as they explain the design intention clearly,
making it relatively easy for contractors to put the detail together.
The choice of graphics in construction drawings is always essential
in enabling a clear understanding of the materials used, and
more often than not it is quicker and easier to achieve this sensitivity
on paper. Craftsmen, who after all use their own hands in their
profession, feel a certain empathy with hand-drawings, perhaps
because these sketches reflect the reality of the workbench and
the site conditions.

In the majority of multidisciplinary contracts the landscape is the final element to be constructed, so it is essential that the drawings of the design concept are accurate and easily understood. Money and time are at a high premium towards the end of a project, and any substantial mistakes in the landscape package have to be paid for by cuts to the scope of works. It is advisable, therefore, to release a set of high-quality drawings, as complete as possible, at the tendering stage so that changes are not required later.

One frequently learns invaluable lessons when following the design and manufacturing process of an original concept detail from start to finish. Witnessing the ease and practicality, or sometimes difficulty, of construction and justifying the additional effort expended in changing the design from the accepted norm is a salutary experience. There is, however, an immense reward in creating an 'original' detail. By possessing an innate understanding of the requirements of a problem – whatever the scale of the design – one can make a personal contribution to the ongoing development of contemporary landscape design. More immediately, it is flattering to see one's own details copied by others. It is unfortunate that providing production information is all too often delegated to relatively inexperienced members of staff. In the past, experienced technicians formed part of the office team were delegated this work, thus ensuring the practicality of a detailed design, even if the result was at the cost of innovation.

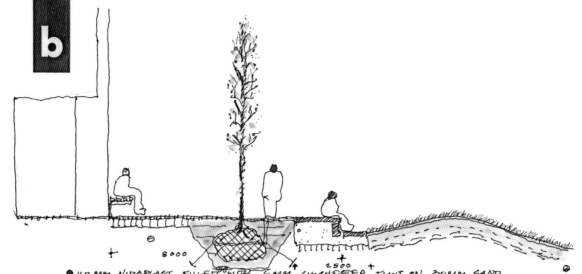

b

● 40 MM NIDAPLAST FILLED WITH 6 MM CHICHESTER FLINT ON 30 MM SAND
BEDDING ON 200 MM MOT TYPE 1 ● 100 MM CHINESE GRANITE · PINK GREY
TO BE BEDDED ON 1:2:4 LIGHTLY REINFORCED CONCRETE · ALLOW FOR
STAINLESS STEEL FIXING DOWELS ● STONE TO BE TREATED WITH 2
COATS METALIFFE SEALANT ● HARD WEARING TURF TO BE LAID ON GRADED
SOIL/TOPSOIL 250 MM DEEP ON 50 MM DRAINAGE GRAVEL. ● ALLOW
FOR 75 MM LAND DRAINS @ 6000 C/S FOR THE TURFED AREA
● 35/40 CMS ESPALIERED TREE IN 3 × 3 × 1·2 MM URBAN TREE SOIL
ALLOW FOR UNDERGROUND GUYING ● ALLOW £2,000 PER TREE FOR THE SUPPLY ONLY
ADD PLANTING ● ALLOW FOR PURPOSE MADE CORTEN STEEL BRACKETS TO SUPPORT
50 × 70 OAK SLATS FIXED WITH STAINLESS STEEL SCREWS.
● ALLOW FOR DEMOLITION + REMOVING ALL THE EXISTING SPOIL FROM THE SITE.
● ALLOW FOR PURPOSE MADE CORTEN STEEL SMOKERS BINS @ 10M CENTRES

Quick, freehand perspectives explore, and then establish, the overall character of a project, reinforced later by construction details. The tentative quality of these preliminary drawings reflects the early design stage, and are helpful in describing the mood of the landscape concept to the design team and client. More refined, hard-edged drawings require greater development and additional time at this stage to look convincing.

gravel.
ancillae

MAKE ROADS LESS ROADLIKE.

NO KERBS.
NO DRAINAGE

● NATRATEX ROAD SURFACE 30 MM DEEP ON 60MM DENSE BITUMEN MACADAM ON 80MM DBM ON 400MM MOT TYPE 1 ON 400 MM CAPPING LAYER. EDGING TO ROAD TO BE 100×100 ALUMINIUM EDGING - NO CONCRETE KERBS.
● 200 MM DIA ROLLED CORTEN POSTS 800 MM LONG TO BE HAUNCHED IN CONCRETE POSTS TO BE @ 2.500 MM CENTRES ● NIDAPLAST ● TOPSOIL AND WILD GRASS TURF ● INSTANT HEDGE 1.2 M HIGH HEDGE MATERIAL ALLOW THE COST OF £180 PER M FOR THE SUPPLY ADD COST OF PLANTING + 800 MM TOPSOIL
● FASTIGATE TREES @ 5M CENTRES. ALLOW £1,500 FOR THE SUPPLY . ADD PLANTING COST / UNDERGROUND GUYS TOPSOIL DRAINAGE GRAVEL
● ALLOW FOR LAND DRAINS TO CONNECT TO A RAINWATER HARVESTING SCHEME LIGHTING.

COUNTRY - GRASS & SCRUB

■ **Country-road details**

SUSSEX DOWNS COLLEGE, EAST SUSSEX

These typical sections, with people and vehicles included to give scale, accompanied by handwritten specification notes, are a fast and economical way of issuing information. From such apparently informal drawings, a quantity surveyor is able to build up a cost plan. When speed is of the essence and there are many other demands on the funds, these early drawings are important in establishing a reasonable budget for the landscape in a multidisciplinary project.

Zebra Drafix 01 pen and Pentel felt-tip pen, A4 Rowney sketchbook; 3 hours each.

■

Granite sett paving

IMPERIAL COLLEGE LONDON

In most urban projects, a large proportion of the landscape budget can be allocated to paving. When selling an idea to a client (in this case, the use of granite setts), it is important to convey the true quality of the material: its imperfections; the significance of the joints between the stone; the bond and integration of the service covers. The stack bond, much favoured by designers but not by pavers, is much less forgiving than a staggered bond. The durability of granite, which has a possible lifespan of over one hundred years, convinced the college that it was a more cost-effective solution than concrete.

2H 0.5mm pencil and Berol Karismacolor coloured pencils on A1 Mylar film; 4 hours.

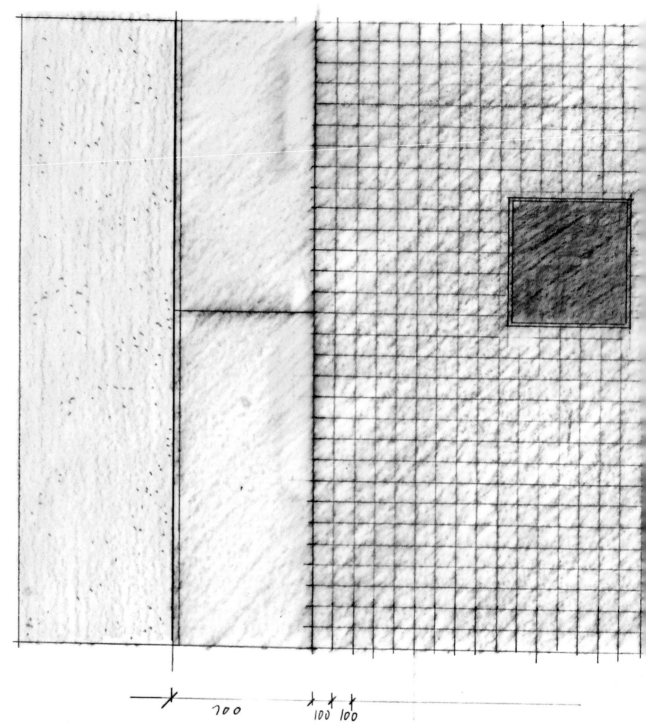

700   100 100

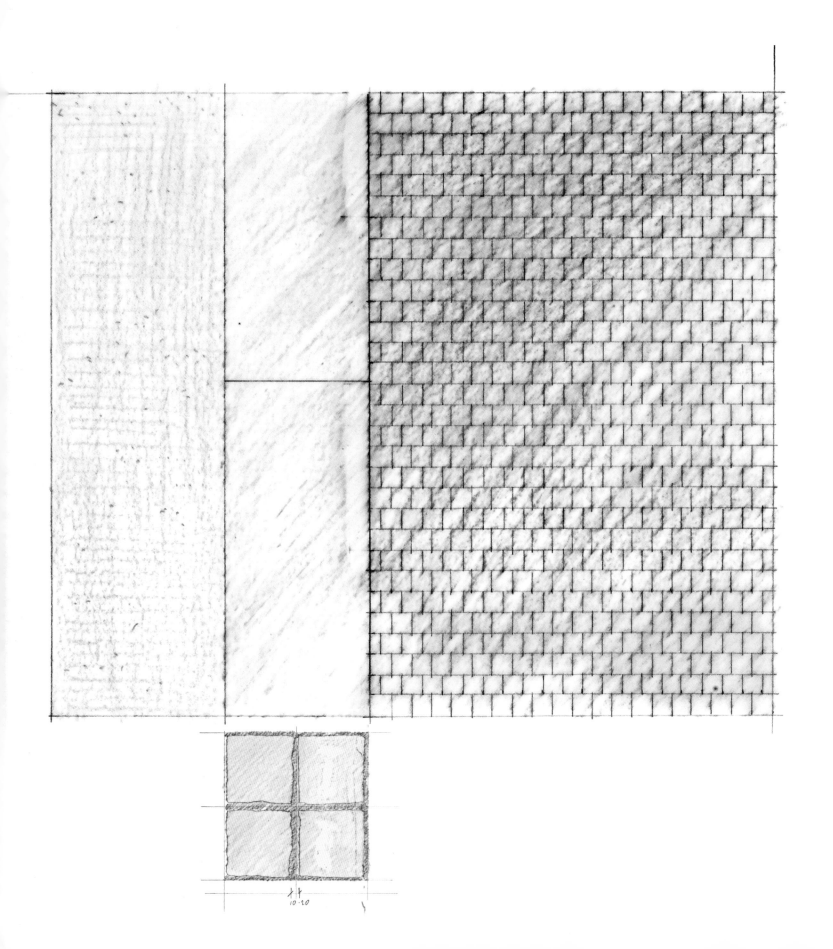

A curved bench

AVENHAM PARK, PRESTON, LANCASHIRE

The site for a new pavilion is located at the junction of
two parks designed by landscape architect Edward Milner in
the 1860s. Milner had worked previously for Sir Joseph
Paxton at Birkenhead Park in Liverpool, a scheme that
became the inspiration for Frederick Law Olmsted's designs
for Central Park in New York City. This robust new
bench, though modest in scale, respects the significance of
the historical context – in particular through its serpentine
curves, a hallmark of Victorian design – and forms an elegant
edge to the café terrace. The curved steel plates anchor
the hardwood slats to ensure they hold their shape and to
prevent vagrants from sleeping rough on the bench.
The photographs show the bench in situ [bottom] and the
completed pavilion [below, right].

Zebra Drafix 01 pen, Faber-Castell 0.18 and 0.35 technical pens, 0.5mm pencil
and Stabilo Layout 37 permanent marker on A3 tracing paper.

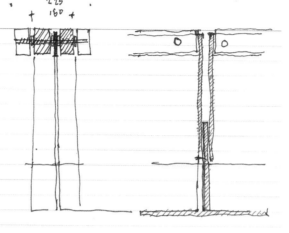

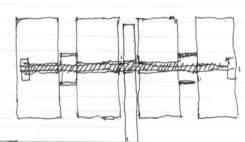

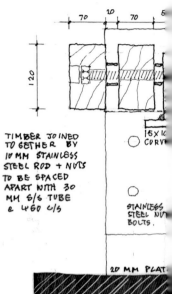

Section thro

TIMBER JOINED
TOGETHER BY
10 MM STAINLESS
STEEL ROD + NUTS
TO BE SPACED
APART WITH 30
MM S/S TUBE
@ 460 C/S

15×10
CURV

STAINLESS
STEEL NUT
BOLTS.

20 MM PLAT

SECTION OF MID PO

Plan of se

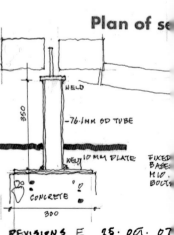

WELD

-76.1MM OD TUBE

WELD 10 MM PLATE   FIXED
BASE.
MID.
BOLTS

CONCRETE

300

REVISIONS E 25.0cn.07
METAL PLATES RAISED
PT INTRODUCED IN BENCH T

Section details

AVENHAM PARK, PRESTON,
LANCASHIRE

This construction drawing
[right] specifies in detail
the elevational sections of the
seat and bicycle stand.

Faber-Castell TG1.S 0.18 and 0.25
technical pens, Stabilo Layout 37
permanent marker, 0.5mm pencil and
Edding Brilliant paper marker on
A3 tracing paper.

170

Construction details

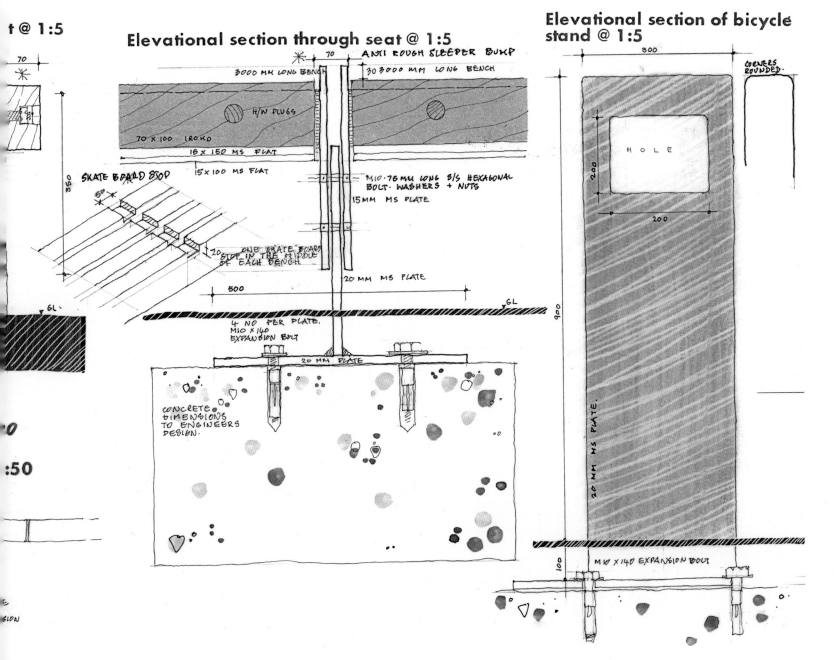

t @ 1:5

70

Elevational section through seat @ 1:5

ANTI ROUGH SLEEPER BUMP

70

3000 MM LONG BENCH

30 3000 MM LONG BENCH

H/W PLUGS

70 X 100 IROKO

16 X 150 MS FLAT

15 X 100 MS FLAT

M10·75 MM LONG S/S HEXAGONAL
BOLT· WASHERS + NUTS

15 MM MS PLATE

SKATE BOARD STOP

5°

20

ONE SKATE BOARD
STOP IN THE MIDDLE
OF EACH BENCH

20 MM MS PLATE

500

GL

4 NO PER PLATE.
M10 X 140
EXPANSION BOLT

20 MM PLATE

CONCRETE
DIMENSIONS
TO ENGINEERS
DESIGN.

350

GL

:50

Elevational section of bicycle stand @ 1:5

300

CORNERS
ROUNDED.

200

HOLE

200

900

20 MM MS PLATE.

100

M10 X 140 EXPANSION BOLT

Bench design

A comfortable bench

HULL HISTORY CENTRE, EAST YORKSHIRE

A 90m-long concrete plinth [below] forms the boundary between the Hull History Centre and a new 'pocket park' to the south. Set on the edge of the plinth, a low-level bench features a curved profile that gives a greater degree of lumbar support than a simple flat bench would. A mock-up of the bench in the workshop, and the finished article on site [bottom].

Zebra Drafix 01 pen and Faber-Castell TG1.S 0.18 and 0.25 technical pens on A3 tracing paper; 2 hours.

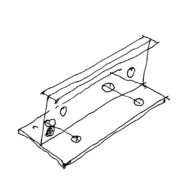

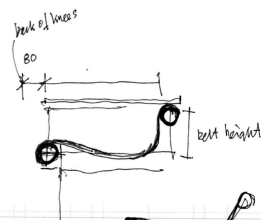

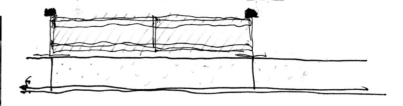

Construction details

172

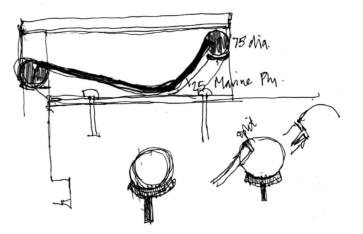

Concept to realization

HULL HISTORY CENTRE, EAST YORKSHIRE

These initial sketches [above and opposite, top] demonstrate the curved profile of the timber benches.

Pilot G-Tec-C4 pen on A3 tracing paper; 15 minutes each.

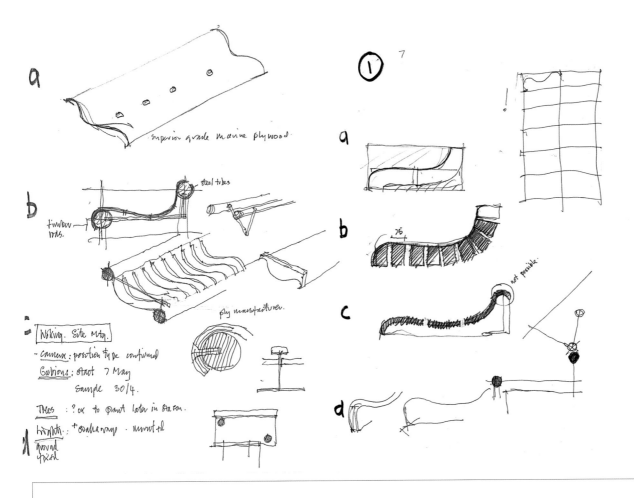

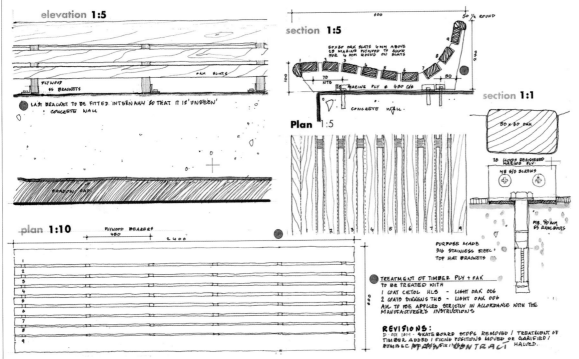

Working out the details

HULL HISTORY CENTRE,
EAST YORKSHIRE

Part of a detailed drawing for
the construction of the bench.

Pilot G-Tec-C4 pen, Faber-Castell TG1.S
0.18 and 0.25 technical pens, Edding
Brilliant paper marker and 0.3mm pencil,
with Swann-Morton scalpel on
A3 tracing paper.

Drawing details freehand and in colour is a useful way to articulate the different elements in the construction, and to identify the various trades involved. A drawing that uses fewer colours, for example, indicates a cheaper, more simplified option, involving less coordination in the production.

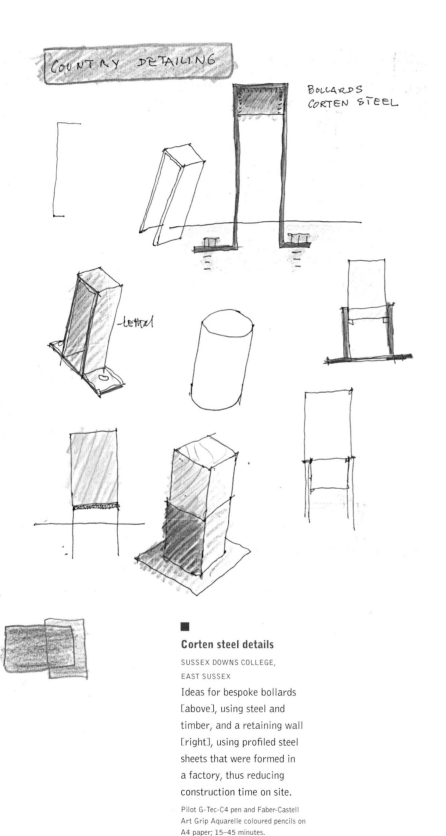

Corten steel details

SUSSEX DOWNS COLLEGE,
EAST SUSSEX

Ideas for bespoke bollards [above], using steel and timber, and a retaining wall [right], using profiled steel sheets that were formed in a factory, thus reducing construction time on site.

Pilot G-Tec-C4 pen and Faber-Castell Art Grip Aquarelle coloured pencils on A4 paper; 15–45 minutes.

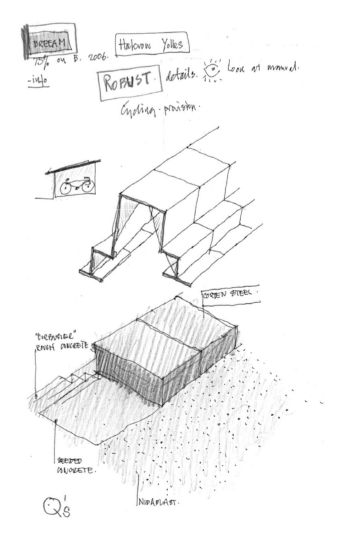

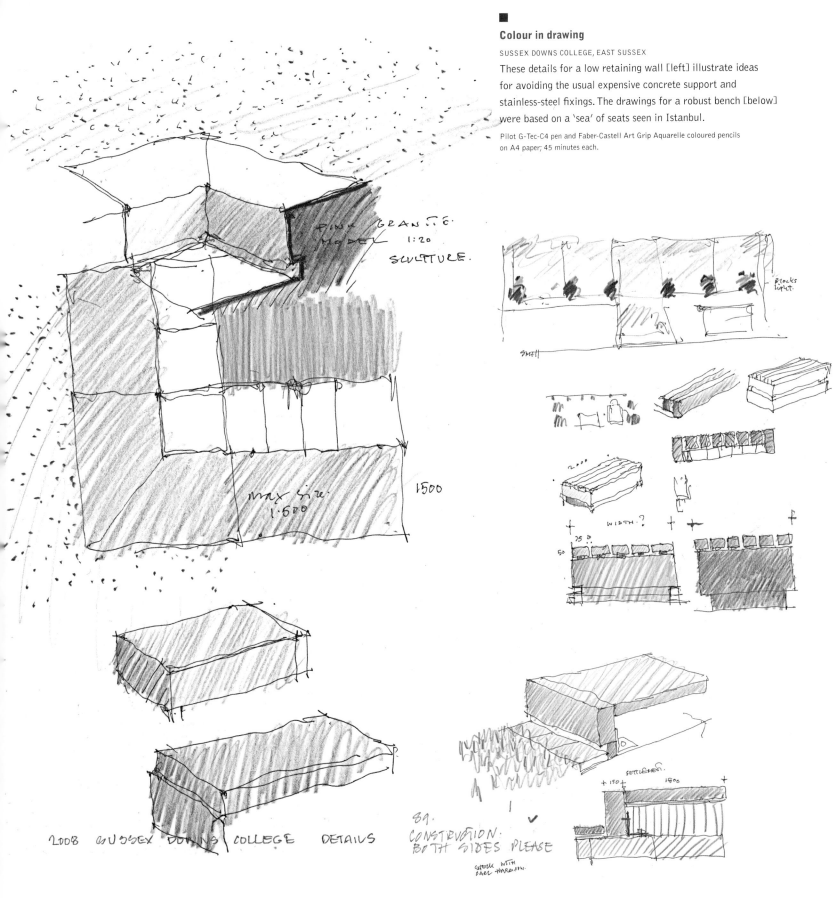

■

Colour in drawing

SUSSEX DOWNS COLLEGE, EAST SUSSEX

These details for a low retaining wall [left] illustrate ideas
for avoiding the usual expensive concrete support and
stainless-steel fixings. The drawings for a robust bench [below]
were based on a 'sea' of seats seen in Istanbul.

Pilot G-Tec-C4 pen and Faber-Castell Art Grip Aquarelle coloured pencils
on A4 paper; 45 minutes each.

PINK GRANITE.
MODEL 1:20
SCULPTURE.

max size
1:500

1500

Blocks
light.

SMELL

2,000

WIDTH ?

25 D

50

2008 SUSSEX DOWNS COLLEGE DETAILS

89.
CONSTRUCTION.
BOTH SIDES PLEASE

CHECK WITH
EARL HARADON.

SETTLEMENT.

+150+   1500

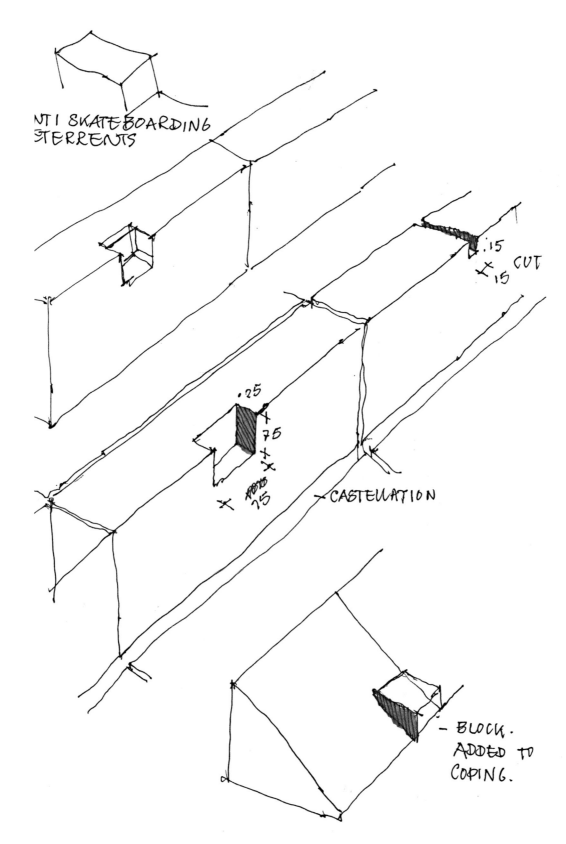

NT I SKATEBOARDING
STERRENTS

.15
+
15 CUT

.25
+
75
+ +
+ X
ADDED
75
+

CASTELLATION

BLOCK.
ADDED TO
COPING.

A site for skateboarders
COVENTRY PEACE GARDEN,
WARWICKSHIRE
These drawings [left]
explore ideas for
skateboarding deterrents.
The photograph [below] is a
close-up of the stone textures
in the finished design.
Pilot G-Tec-C4 pen and Tombow ABT
felt-tip pen on A4 paper; 30 minutes.

The benefits of stone
COVENTRY PEACE GARDEN,
WARWICKSHIRE
Designing with custom-
made stone elements allows
a great deal of freedom
regarding sizes and shapes
[opposite]. But the wide range
of materials and finishes
achievable make it important
to establish basic rules of
design at an early stage to
avoid becoming overwhelmed
by choice.
Pilot G-Tec-C4 pen and Tombow ABT
felt-tip pen on A4 paper; 30 minutes.

6dine.

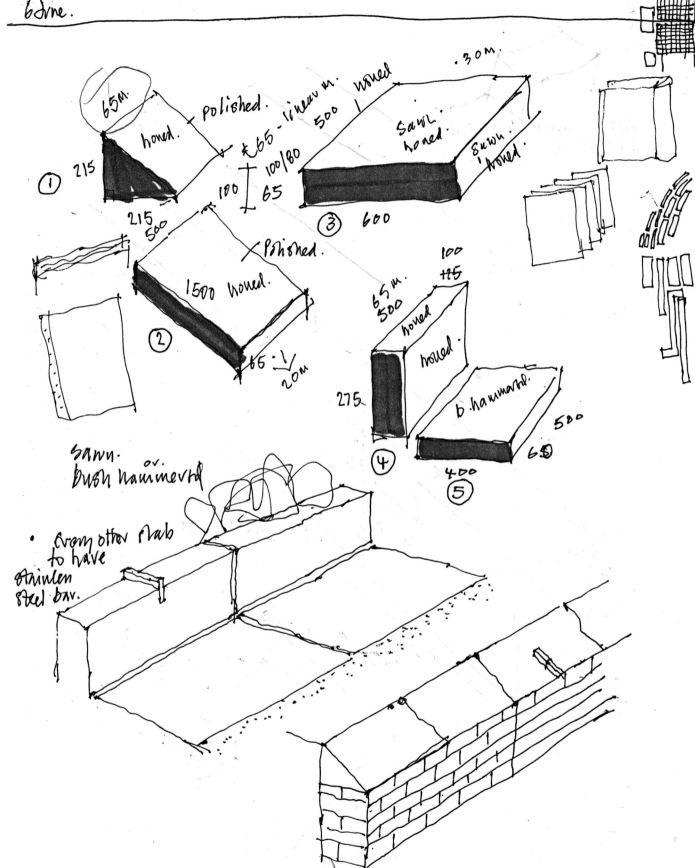

65m.

① 215   honed.   Polished.

x 65 - linear m.   .30m.

500   honed

Saur. honed.

Saw. honed.

100/80

180   65

③   600

215
500

Polished.

1500   honed.

②

65 .1
2.0m

65 m.
500

honed

honed

100
+75

275

b. hammered.

④

500

65

⑤   400

Saw. or. Bush hammered

• every other slab to have stainless steel bar.

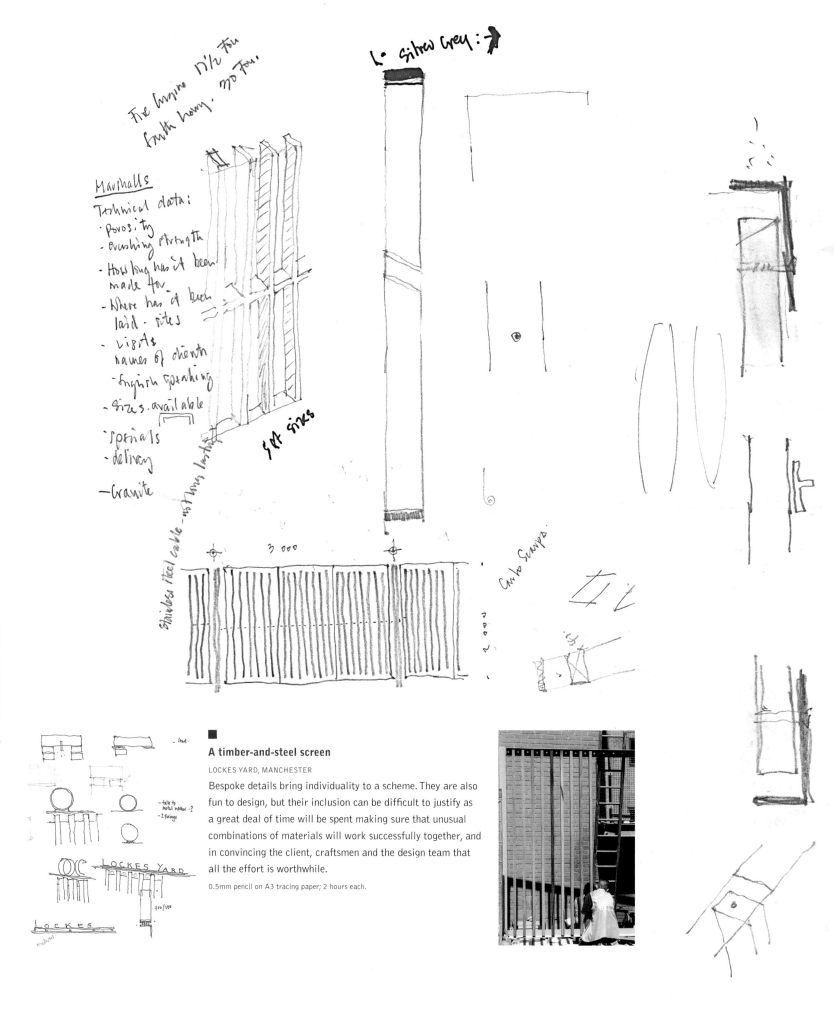

Fire Engine 17½ Ton
forth hony. 330 Ton.

Marshalls
Technical data:
- Porosity
- Crushing strength
- How long has it been made for.
- Where has it been laid - sites
- Lists names of clients
- English speaking
- Sizes available
- specials
- delivery
- Granite

Stainless steel cable - nothing instant

get sizes

3 000

L• Silver Grey :→

Carlo Scarpa

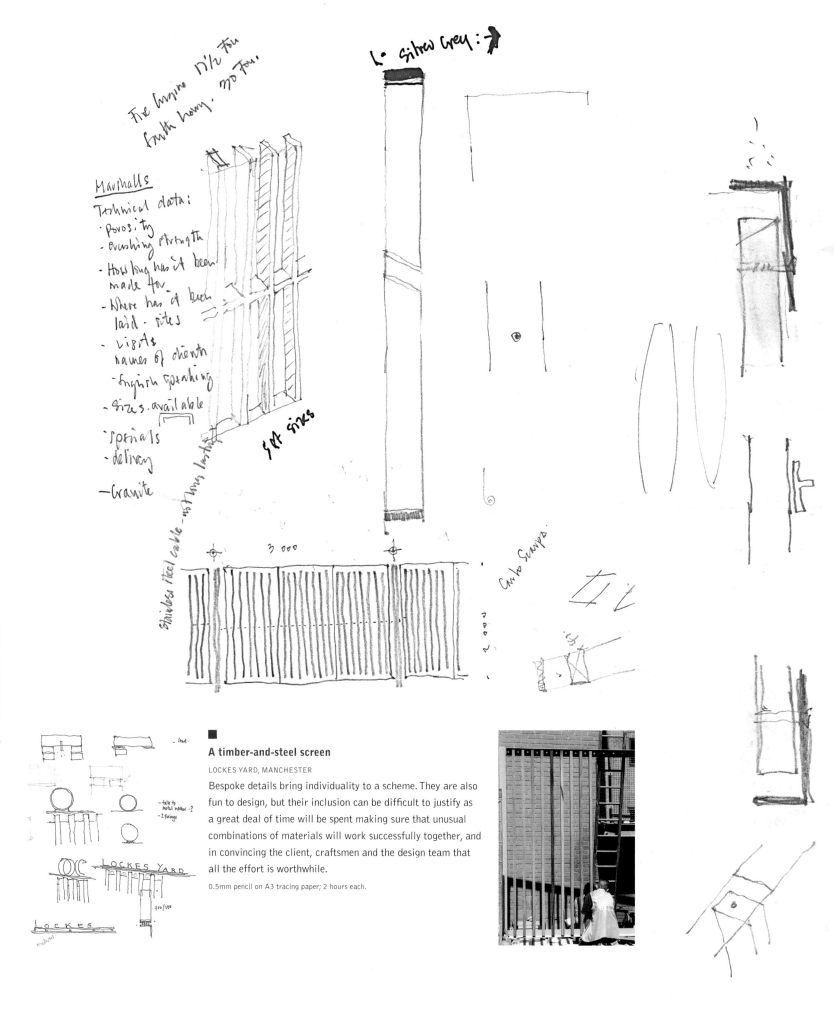

LOCKES YARD

LOCKES

178

■
A timber-and-steel screen

LOCKES YARD, MANCHESTER

Bespoke details bring individuality to a scheme. They are also
fun to design, but their inclusion can be difficult to justify as
a great deal of time will be spent making sure that unusual
combinations of materials will work successfully together, and
in convincing the client, craftsmen and the design team that
all the effort is worthwhile.

0.5mm pencil on A3 tracing paper; 2 hours each.

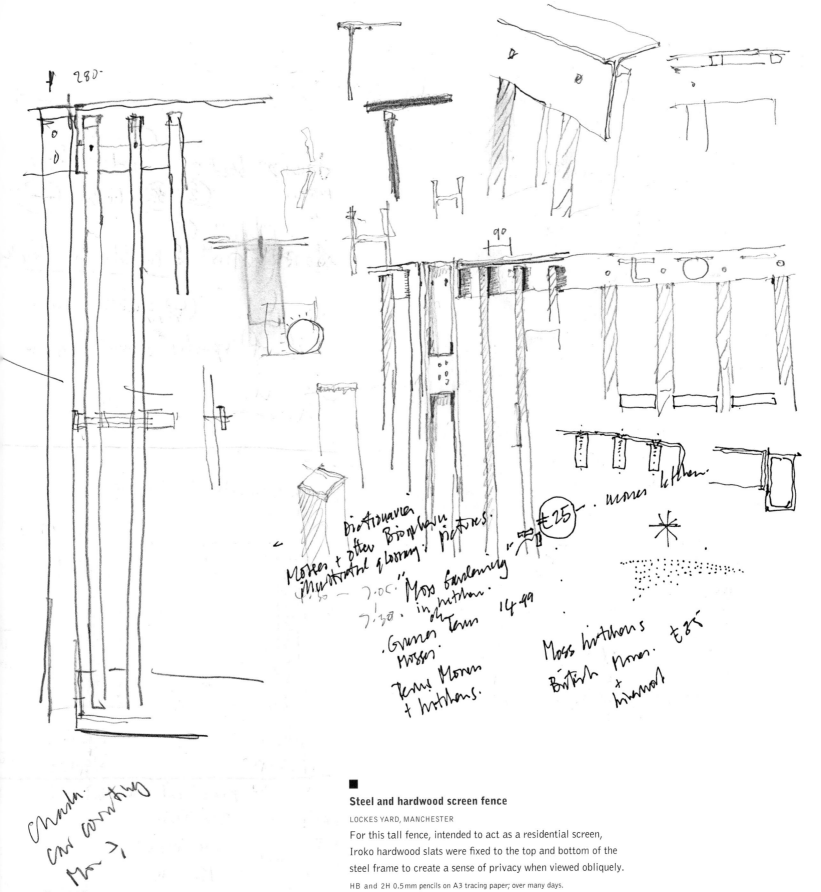

■

Steel and hardwood screen fence

LOCKES YARD, MANCHESTER

For this tall fence, intended to act as a residential screen,
Iroko hardwood slats were fixed to the top and bottom of the
steel frame to create a sense of privacy when viewed obliquely.

HB and 2H 0.5mm pencils on A3 tracing paper; over many days.

section through the dwarf wall to the sunken lawn

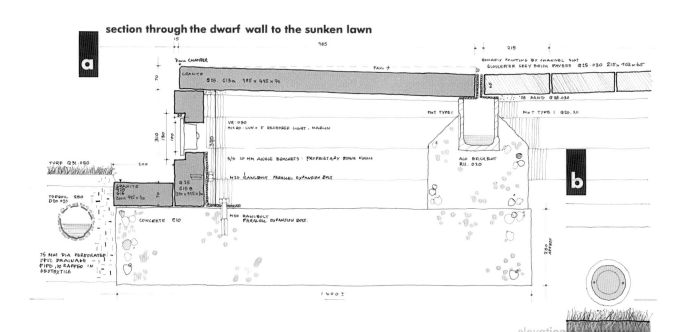

Low retaining walls

ST JOHN'S COLLEGE, CAMBRIDGE

Retaining walls can be
extremely expensive
to construct if the stone is
merely treated as cladding.
The necessary detailing
and coordination of the
stainless-steel fixings
and concrete wall are all
hidden costs.

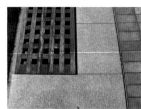

Granite blocks

ST JOHN'S COLLEGE, CAMBRIDGE

Detail of the oak seat, set
flush with the surface of the
retaining wall.

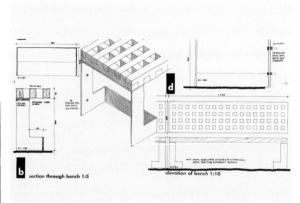

b   section through bench 1:5

elevation of bench 1:10

Bench details

ST JOHN'S COLLEGE, CAMBRIDGE

The care put into the
construction drawings, both
hand-drawn [top] and created
on screen [above], made a
favourable impression on
the contractor. As a result,
the craftsmen rose to the
challenge and did a beautiful
job under difficult conditions.

Faber-Castell TG1.S technical pen,
HB pencil and Copic wide felt-tip pen
on A3 tracing paper.

Sometimes imagining oneself at
the scale of an ant is an effective
way of testing a particular detail
for practicality. This engagement is
especially helpful when talking
to craftsmen about making things
in an unorthodox way.

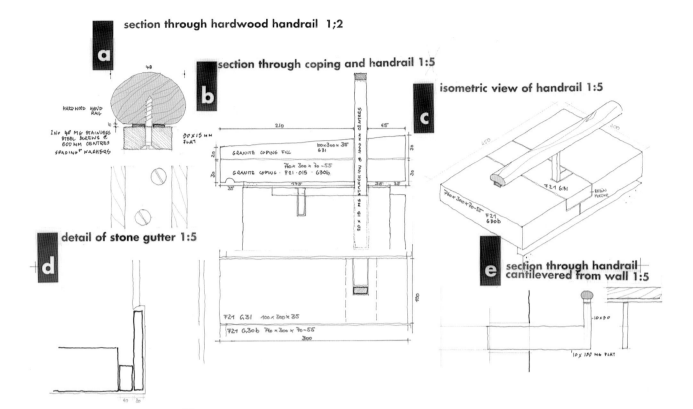

section through hardwood handrail 1;2

a

HARDWOOD HAND RAIL

2No 40 M6 STAINLESS STEEL SCREWS @ 600 MM CENTRES

SPADING? WASHERS

30×15 MM FLAT

48

section through coping and handrail 1:5

b

GRANITE COPING FILL   100×300×35 631

210   65

760×300×70~55

GRANITE COPING · F21·015 · 630b

35   175

20 18 MS STANCHION @ 1000 MM CENTRES

20 × 20

F21 631   100×300×35

F21 G30b   760×300×70~55

300

isometric view of handrail 1:5

c

650   500

F21 631

760×300×70~55   F21 630b

RESIN POCKET

F21 630b

detail of stone gutter 1:5

d

40   30

section through handrail cantilevered from wall 1:5

e

10×90

10 × 100 M6 FLAT

■

Handrails and drainage

ST JOHN'S COLLEGE, CAMBRIDGE

This drawing [above] addresses the problem of water-staining under a coping junction. The top face of the granite coping is cut at an angle, so that the water drains back to the planter, away from the face of the wall. A stone wedge sits in the rebated stone at the junction of the two copings. This is further refined where the steel support for the handrail occurs. The oak handrail is lifted off the steel flat, so that water does not collect at this point, and also to bring a quality of lightness. It is often ill-advised to involve structural engineers in small landscape structures, as their criteria for calculations are on a different scale and the solutions tend to be expensive. The completed design [left].

Faber-Castell TG1.S technical pen, HB pencil and Copic wide felt-tip pen on A3 tracing paper.

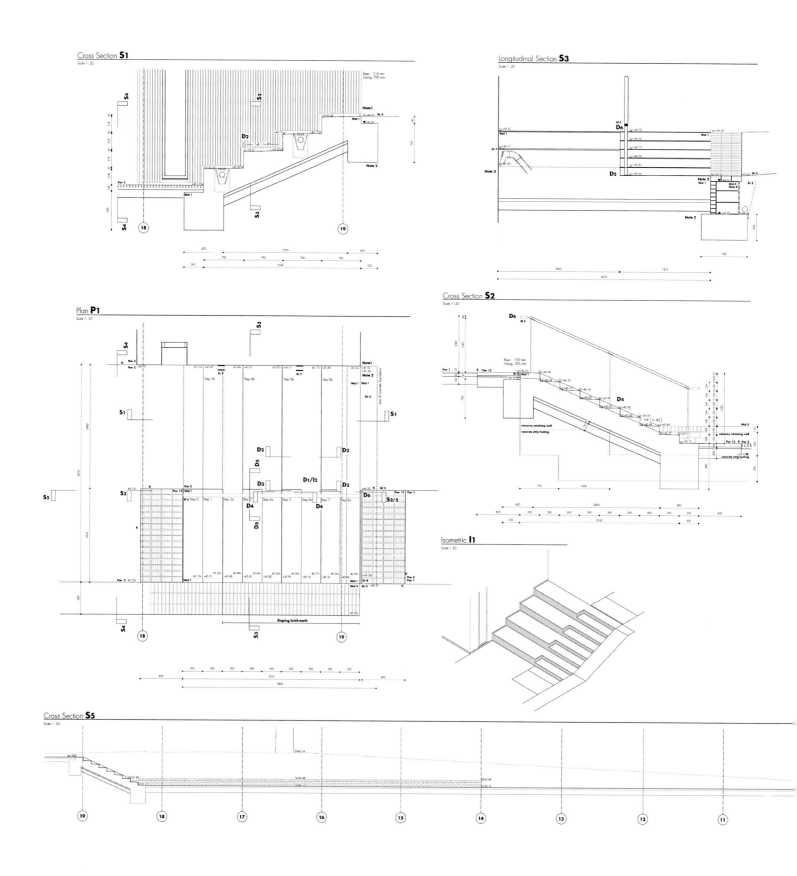

Brick steps

BEDALES SCHOOL, HAMPSHIRE

Painstakingly worked-out
drawings for steps [opposite],
to be made from handmade
bricks. The steps were dropped
as the cost proved beyond the
budget. This type of detail,
which otherwise brings a real
sense of quality to a landscape
scheme, needs to be authorized
an at early stage as it can
easily become sacrificed as an
unnecessary expense.

Vectorworks software program;
drawing by Claudia Corcilius.

Stone steps

COVENTRY PEACE GARDEN,
WARWICKSHIRE

Isometric details of stone
steps at Coventry [left],
which address the visibility
of the nosings. It was decided
to omit the projecting
stone block before the steps
were completed, but it was
reintroduced at a later stage
when skateboarding became
an issue. The small nosing
setts proved expensive to fix
individually in epoxy resin,
and were substituted for larger
granite blocks. The steps under
construction [above].

Faber-Castell TG1.S 0.18 and 0.25
technical pens, Edding Brilliant paper
marker and Stabilo Layout 37 permanent
marker on A3 tracing paper.

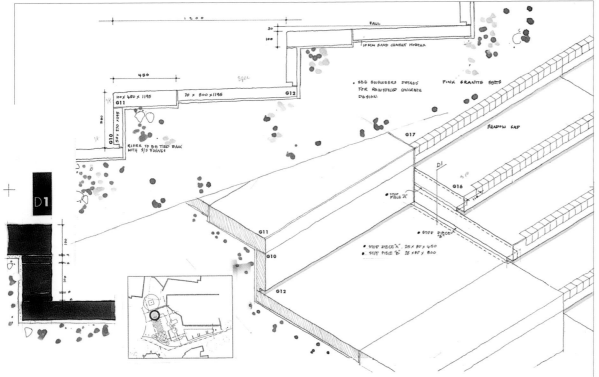

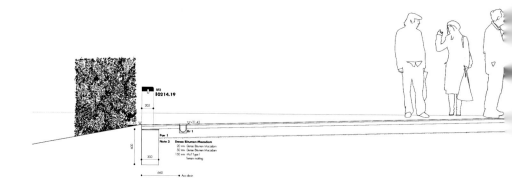

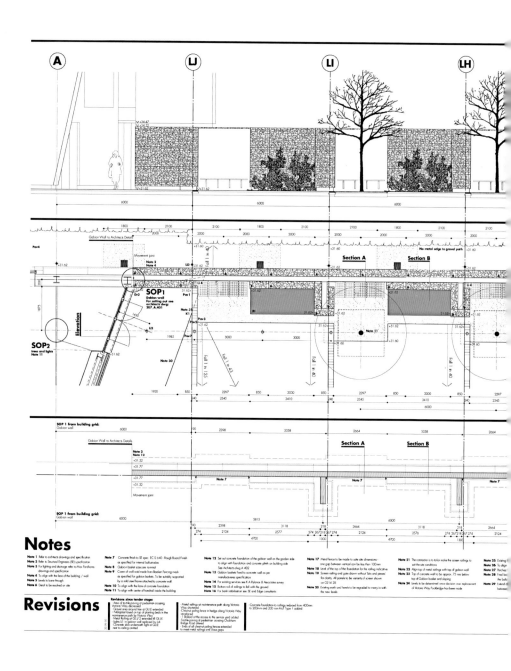

Gabion wall

THE LIGHTBOX, WOKING, SURREY

This garden wall for a new art gallery provides protection from the noise and pollution of nearby traffic. The design focuses on the articulation of the acoustic wall, creating a series of micro-spaces that isolate the garden from the road. The dimensions of the standard wire gabion baskets dictate the setting out of the bays and height of the wall, while the inner concrete core is expressed behind the seats. As this was an expensive detail in a limited budget, it was important that the design and dimensions were thoroughly considered, transforming the engineering elements into component parts of the garden architecture.

Vectorworks software program; A0 drawing by Claudia Corcilius.

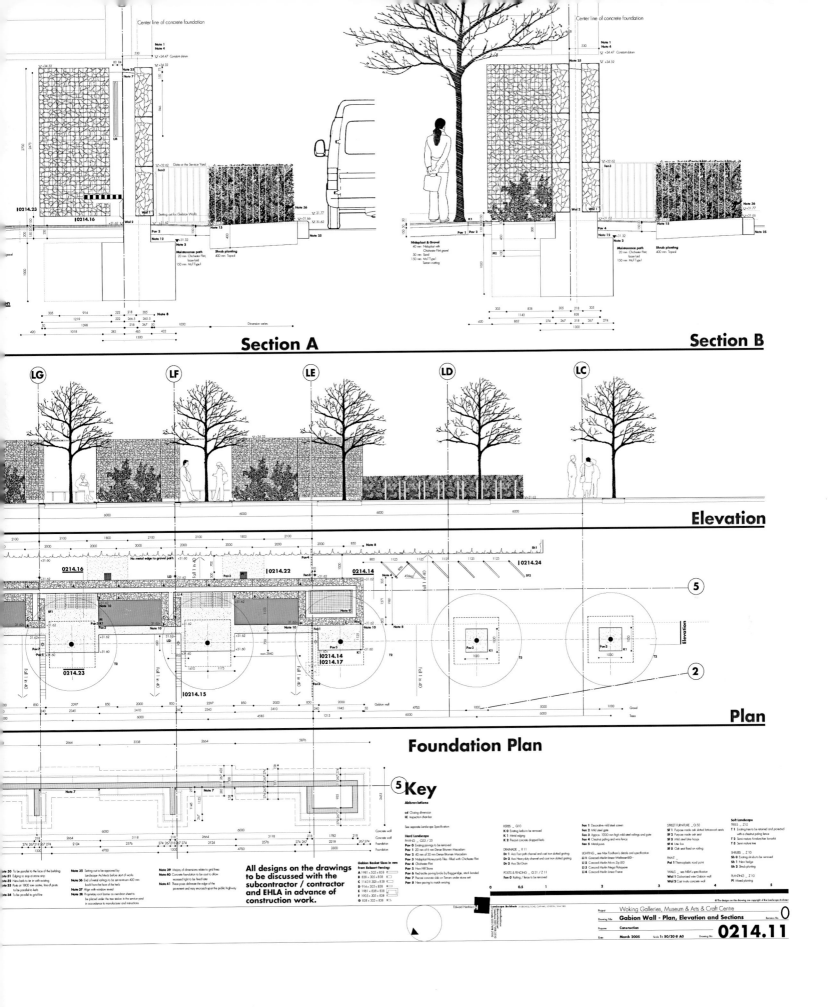

Section A

Section B

Elevation

Plan

Foundation Plan

Key

All designs on the drawings to be discussed with the subcontractor / contractor and EHLA in advance of construction work.

Project **Woking Galleries, Museum & Arts & Craft Centre**
Drawing Title **Gabion Wall - Plan, Elevation and Sections**
Purpose **Construction**
Date **March 2005**   Scale **1: 50/20 @ A0**   Drawing No

0214.11

Computer drawings

9

Completed work
St John's College, Cambridge
Coventry Peace Garden

■

The brief for a site owned by **St John's College, Cambridge** involved the creation of residences for forty graduates and fellows, the formation of three new courtyards for the private use of this community, and the restoration of the old shops that surrounded the triangular-shaped site. The neighbouring properties had become run down, and the enclosed courtyards had turned into overgrown urban jungles. But the city's planning department considered this quiet backwater to represent a valuable archetype in the history and development of Cambridge; the college, therefore, required the buildings to be sympathetically restored, and to include at the centre of the project a suitable landscape.

Landscape briefs are often vague. The full potential of the site was explored through a series of presentations to the building committee over a period of eighteen months. Over the past five hundred years, the university has commissioned some of the most beautiful urban landscapes in England, and the thrill of adding to this legacy was balanced by the practicalities of modern student living; an overly intellectual design approach to the site was considered irrelevant. The new landscape scheme had to be designed and finalized before the site was disturbed in any way. With trees and undergrowth concealing much of the space, it was necessary to make detailed microclimatic studies that illustrated how sunlight would penetrate the site in the morning, at midday and in the afternoon at three key times of the year. It was remarkable to appreciate the importance of this work when, in reality, demolition was ongoing and sunlight would continually light up previously dark corners.

In order to minimize disruption, the building operation had to be discreet: no overhead cranes were allowed and all materials were brought to site by hand. This placed an onerous responsibility on the construction team to make drawings and schedules that worked in the circumstances given. The landscape contractor, in particular, rose to the challenge and demonstrated craftsmanship at the highest level.

In Coventry, the competition for an extension to the city's existing Herbert Art Gallery and Museum offered the opportunity to upgrade the urban landscape and setting of the building. It was decided to simultaneously redesign the square between the new cathedral and university, which would be fronted on one side by the new extension. Several remnants of the old city had survived the Blitz in 1940, and the new design traced their location: a medieval cellar, which can be visited, was represented on the surface paving by huge sandstone blocks; a 50mm-wide bronze strip delineated the fronts of ancient buildings; brick pavers defined their internal areas; and granite setts marked the external walls. Ten Corten steel plates, which followed the party walls of historic houses along Bayley Lane, were inscribed with the names and occupations of inhabitants dating back to 1540 and created the greatest visual impact. The view of the old cathedral up Bayley Lane is framed by the alignment of the steel edges, echoing the sense of enclosure that prevailed before 1940. The inner edges were corroded to reflect the destruction caused by the bombs.

The re-establishment of the **Coventry Peace Garden** included two stone sculptures, resited in the new landscape setting, together with the addition of an old, gnarled olive tree as a symbol of peace. A small lawn was set at a raised level to give the grass protection and to provide an informal seating area for visitors and students on the wide, brick edging. Further seating was provided by broad steps leading from Priory Square to the entrance of the museum. A clump of multi-stemmed Amelanchier trees defined the edge of the garden, creating a sense of intimacy and adding a froth of white blossom in springtime, while a tall sandstone retaining wall formed a dramatic edge to the scheme. Hard landscape exploited the considerable change of level across the site. The garden has become a popular and well-established open space in the city, despite the limited size of the overall scheme, and decisions taken during the course of the project to resolve the many issues at stake can be seen to have worked.

St John's College, Cambridge

Brief: To provide accommodation for graduates and fellows, form three new courtyards and restore the old shops surrounding the site.

■

The site

With the decision made to develop the underused Triangle Site for residential use, some of the buildings were found to be in an advanced stage of decay and the grounds were very overgrown. It was recognized that the new design would be most evident in the landscape of the three new courtyards, as the historic buildings would be carefully restored.

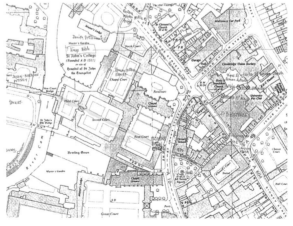

■

Topography

Observations of the landscape were recorded on a photocopy of a historic map [left], a useful practice for becoming acquainted with a site's history. Aerial photography is also an instant means of accessing the site from above.

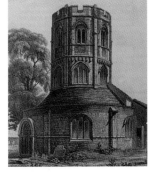

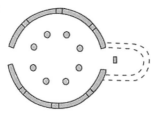

■

Archaeology

The history of Cambridge has touched the site in a variety
of ways. Bridge Street to the north was originally a straight
Roman road, becoming less direct during the MiddleAges.
Vikings arrived in the Fenlands in AD 850, ameliorating the
low-lying town by cutting a network of drainage ditches
in the marshy ground. One of these ditches lies immediately
beneath the central axis of the three main courts of the College.
In the 12th century, crusaders returning from the Holy Land
built a number of round churches, including an example on
Bridge Street [above], to echo the Holy Sepulchre in Jerusalem.
Bridge Street's Round Church is one of only five such
structures in Britain.

191

It is important to assess the nature of a site
from all aspects: archaeology, history, heritage,
demographics. Photography, in addition to site
drawings, is an instant visual record. The thorough
understanding of a site from as many aspects as
possible encourages a surprising freedom to think
and design in an unrestrained manner.

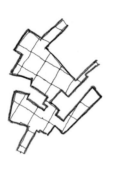
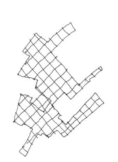
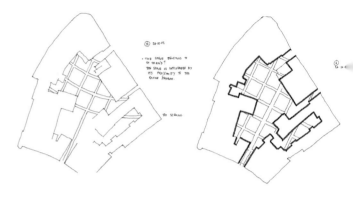

800 M² :GARDEN
125 M² FIRST

Appreciating accurately the scale of external spaces can be difficult. Comparisons made to tennis courts, which cover 625m², are useful.

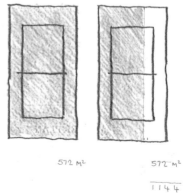

572 M²   572 M²
              ‾‾‾‾‾
               1144

Isometric sketches
These drawings [below] show
an idea for a conservatory,
which was abandoned in the
fear that the space would
become impractical.

Zebra Grafix 01 pen on A3 tracing paper.

⑧ 26·10·02

③

25 Oct. 02

? DPO. SIZE

**Creating order from
the medieval muddle**
Early design studies [above
and right] aimed to link the
Triangle Site to the College's
three courtyards by extending
the geometry of the path on
the central axis. In contrast to
the formality of the existing
large courts, our initial scheme
proposed a more user-friendly
site, with areas of grass and
water and a conservatory.
Several different landscape
options were presented, but the
planning authority questioned
the overall formality of what
was previously an informal
space, and we were forced to
reconsider our approach.

Zebra Grafix 01 pen on A3 tracing paper;
60 minutes each.

+ VIEW points.
bicycles.
North end treatment.

- CREATE ORDER
FROM MEDIEVAL
'MUDDLE'

inspiration.

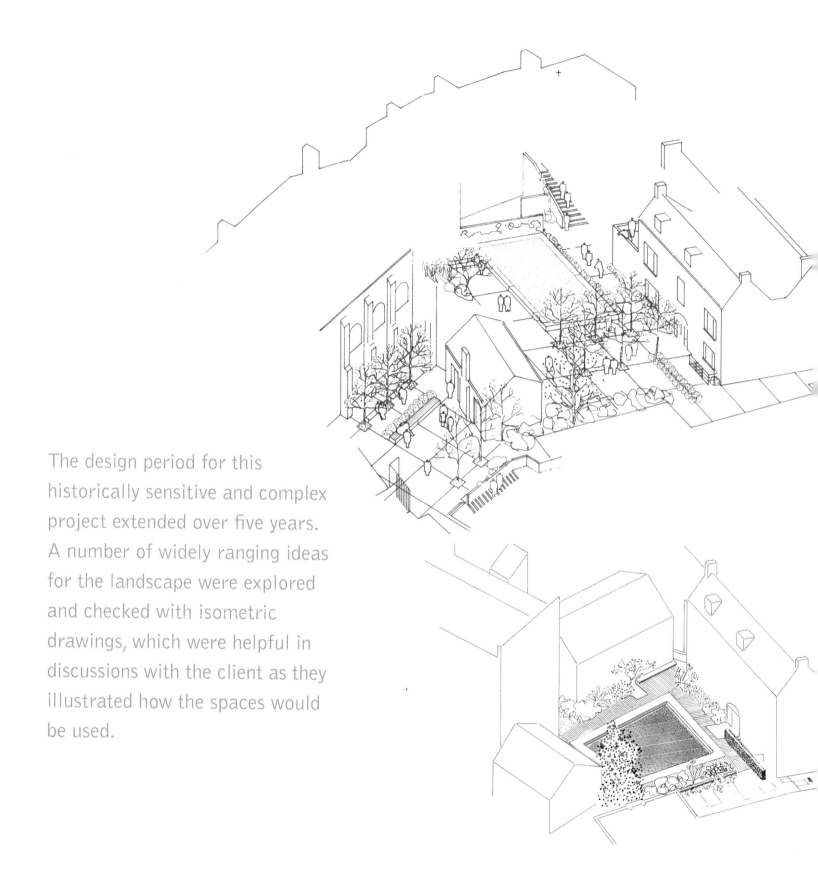

The design period for this historically sensitive and complex project extended over five years. A number of widely ranging ideas for the landscape were explored and checked with isometric drawings, which were helpful in discussions with the client as they illustrated how the spaces would be used.

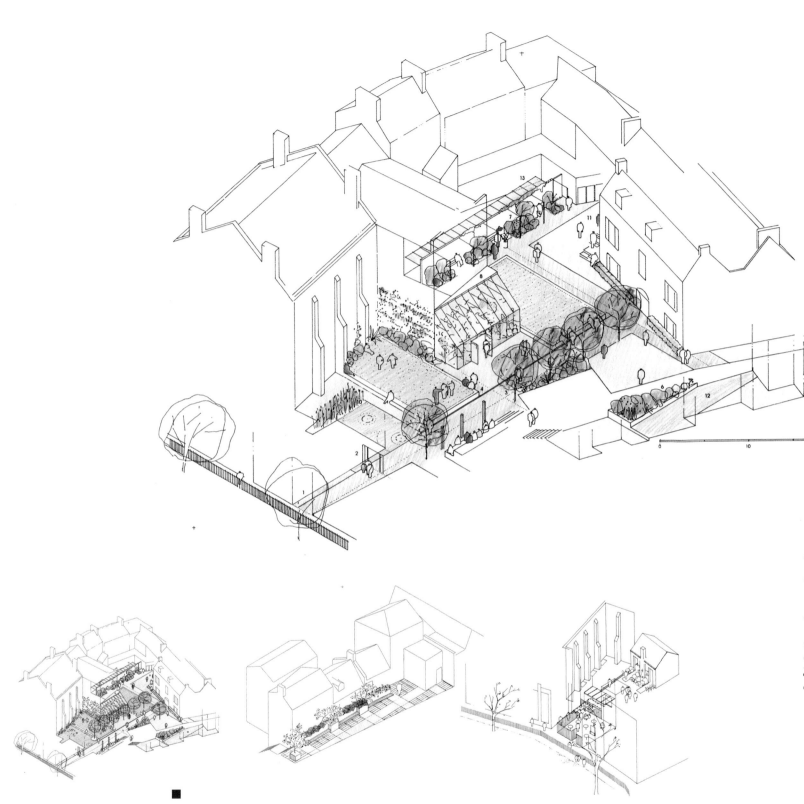

Isometric drawings

These drawings, produced over the length of the project, explore the use of different elements in the courtyards: water, a conservatory, trees, raised lawns, planting and paving patterns.

Rotring 0.18 technical pen, Pilot G-Tec-C4 pen, HB pencil and Berol Karismacolor pencils on tracing paper (30cm × 42cm); 1 day each.

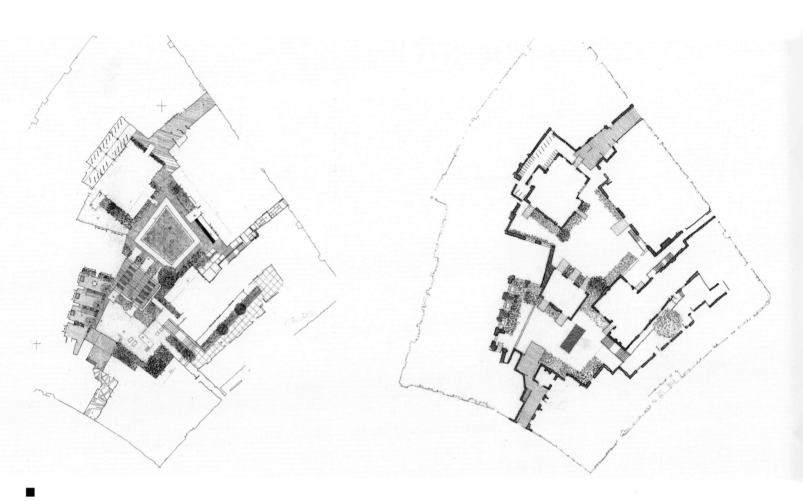

Planting and paving studies

These two drawings show the development of the built scheme. The first [above, left] was made as a design check to show the relationship between the planting texture and the paving design. The second [above, right] shows the spaces created at the edges of the buildings, softened and reinforced by planting. A wide variety of media was used on both sides of the paper in an attempt to capture the light and complexity of the planting. To make the image more complex, the initial pencil and ink marks were modified by Tipp-Ex, an eraser and a razor blade.

Zebra Grafix 01 pen and HB and 2H pencils on A1 tracing paper; 1 day and 4 hours.

These two stitched-together computer plans are full of construction information. Most of the awkward junctions, created by the random layout of the existing buildings, were worked out in sketch form before being transferred to computer. The advantage of using the computer at this stage is that practical design details can be resolved with total precision. Importantly, the sparkle of the earlier hand-drawings has not been entirely lost in the process, which is lengthy but absorbing.

Vectorworks software program; A0 drawing by Claudia Corcilius, Julia Zimmermann and Heidi Hundley; 40 hours.

Proposals

197

Coordinating levels, materials and dimensions

This, the first electronic drawing for the project, describes in two dimensions the concept for the landscape regarding levels, materials and planting. It established the design principles that ensured the built landscape would fit like a glove within the existing buildings. Although the drawing was issued to the contractor, the information was not detailed enough for construction. It did, however, help to give a good idea of the design intent. Some contractors are grateful for this type of drawing as a supplement to strictly functional information.

Vectorworks software program;
A0 drawing by Claudia Corcilius.

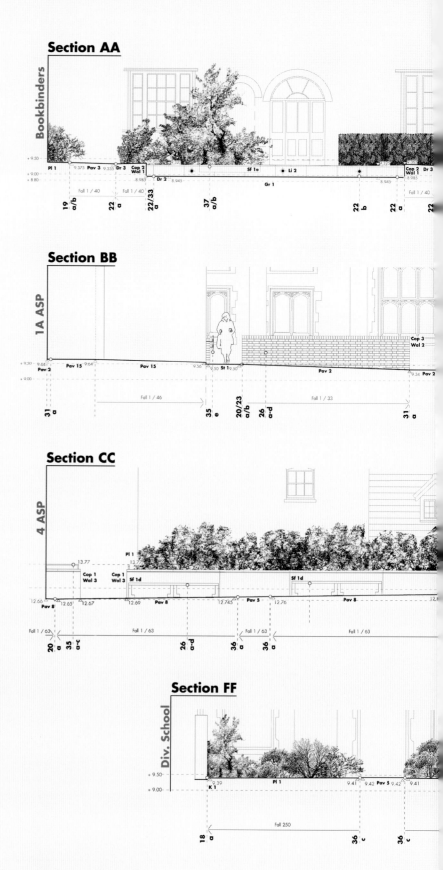

Key

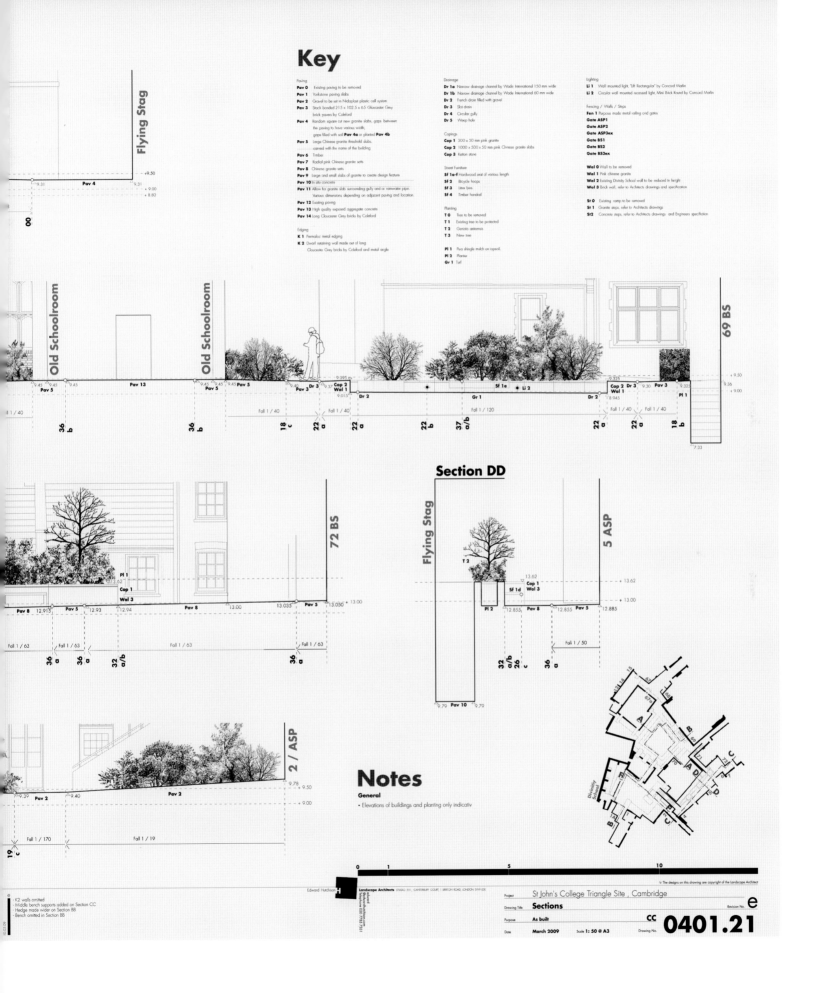

Section DD

Notes

General

• Elevations of buildings and planting only indicativ

Edward Hutchison

Landscape Architects STUDIO 551, CANTERBURY COURT, 1 BRIXTON ROAD, LONDON SW9 6DE

Project **St John's College Triangle Site , Cambridge**

Drawing Title **Sections**

Purpose **As built**

Date **March 2009**   Scale **1: 50 @ A3**

Drawing No. **0401.21**   CC   e

Revision No.   e

© The designs on this drawing are copyright of the Landscape Architect

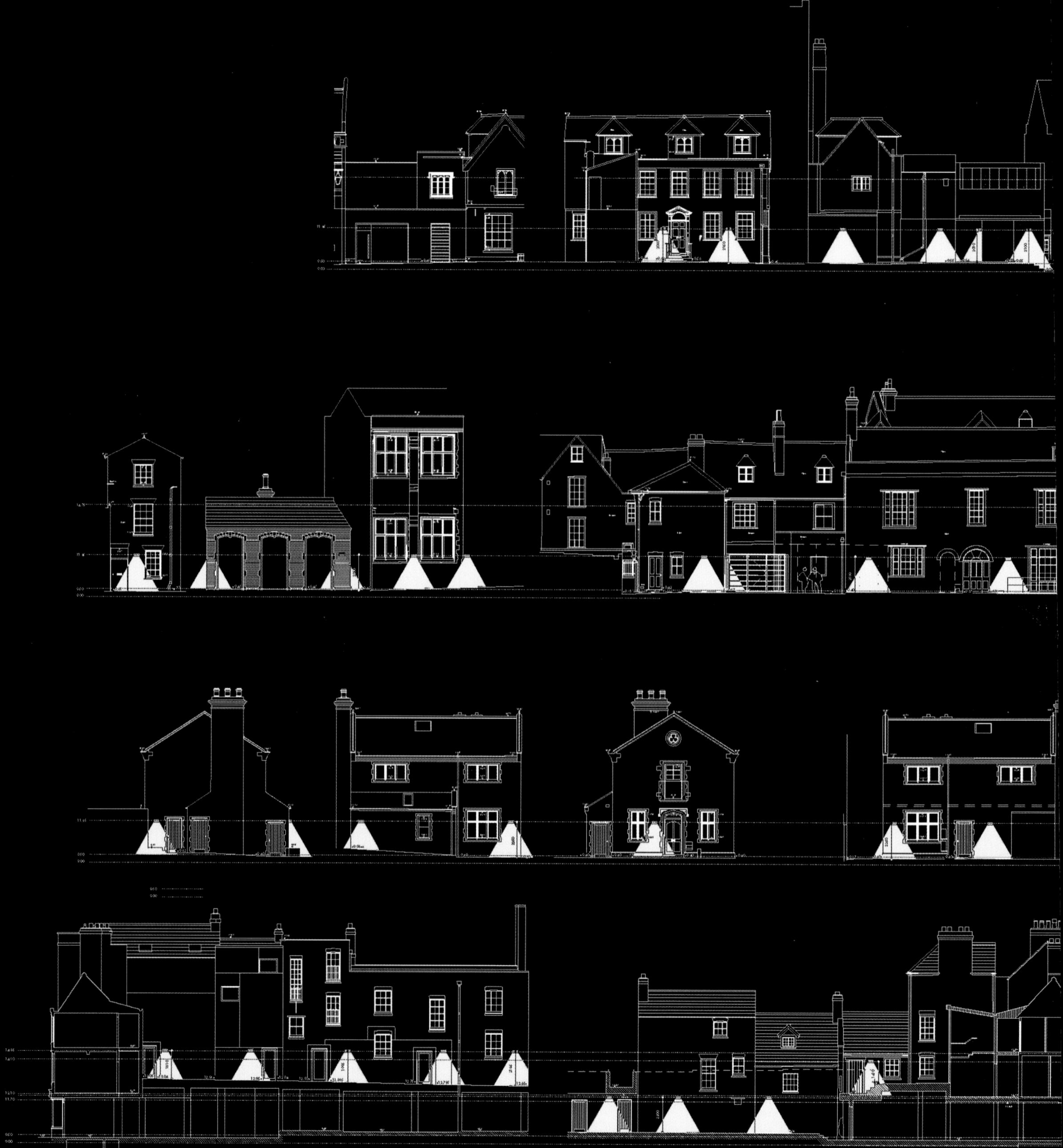

Balancing light design

Lighting design is a delicate art. Just the right amount of light is a difficult balance to achieve: too much, and the area becomes brashly overlit, too little and the scheme becomes potentially unsafe. Due to the nature of the layout, the spaces were very random, and it was decided to make a virtue of this informality. Discreet, purpose-made light fittings were designed to be mounted at a constant height and spacing, drawing attention to the walls of the different courtyards and delineating the edges of the site.

Vectorworks software program; drawing (84cm × 120cm) by Claudia Corcilius + Van Heyningen & Haward.

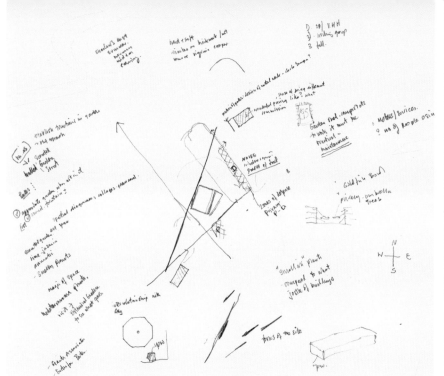

Developing ideas

The concepts in this sketch are too preliminary and fragile to be presented to a client, but the drawing does serve as a way to put down basic ideas about a site to help in formulating a planting strategy.

HB 5mm pencil on A3 tracing paper.

 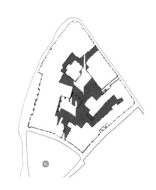  

Anticipating microclimates

The ability to understand the eventual character of a space several years before it is constructed is learned through experience. A good tool in this process is the construction of a series of accurate diagrams that illustrate the projected microclimates on site. These help the designer to interpret future growing conditions across a range of areas.

Planting design is highly personal. There are so many possibilities, and an endless choice of plants and plant combinations available. The skill lies in creating a scheme that has integrity as an overall design.

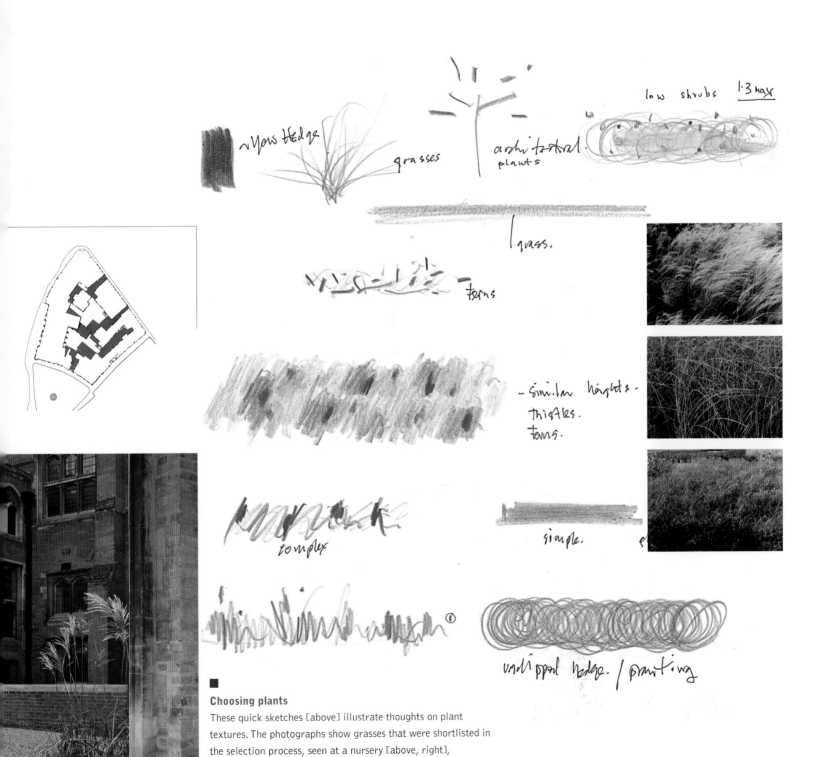

low shrubs 1·3 max

~~yew~~ hedge

grasses

architectural
plants

grass.

ferns

- similar heights.
  thistles.
  ferns.

complex

simple.

unclipped hedge. / planting

Choosing plants

These quick sketches [above] illustrate thoughts on plant
textures. The photographs show grasses that were shortlisted in
the selection process, seen at a nursery [above, right],
and those used in the completed work [left].

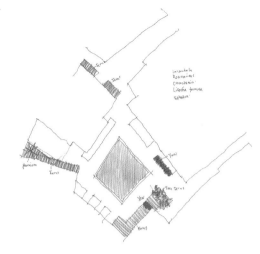

When testing out ideas for a new planting scheme, it is important to work in as carefree a manner as possible. There are relatively few constraints on the design at this stage, and it is vital to keep an open mind.

Planting textures

This drawing [left], created while experimenting with a range of media, was enjoyable to make. Rubbing the back of the tracing paper with graphite gives depth to the planting textures, while erased areas and white Tipp-Ex imply sunlight and shadow. This method of drawing can be developed to make relatively realistic planting plans. The photographs show the completed scheme, with juvenile planting around the courtyard.

Faber-Castell TG1-S technical pen, HB and 2H 5mm pencils, Stabilo Layout 37 permanent marker and Pilot Sign pen on A1 tracing paper.

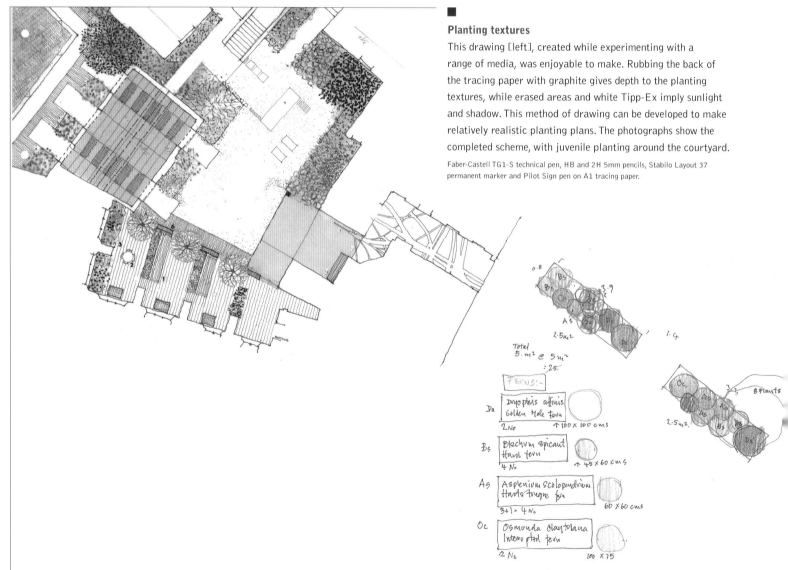

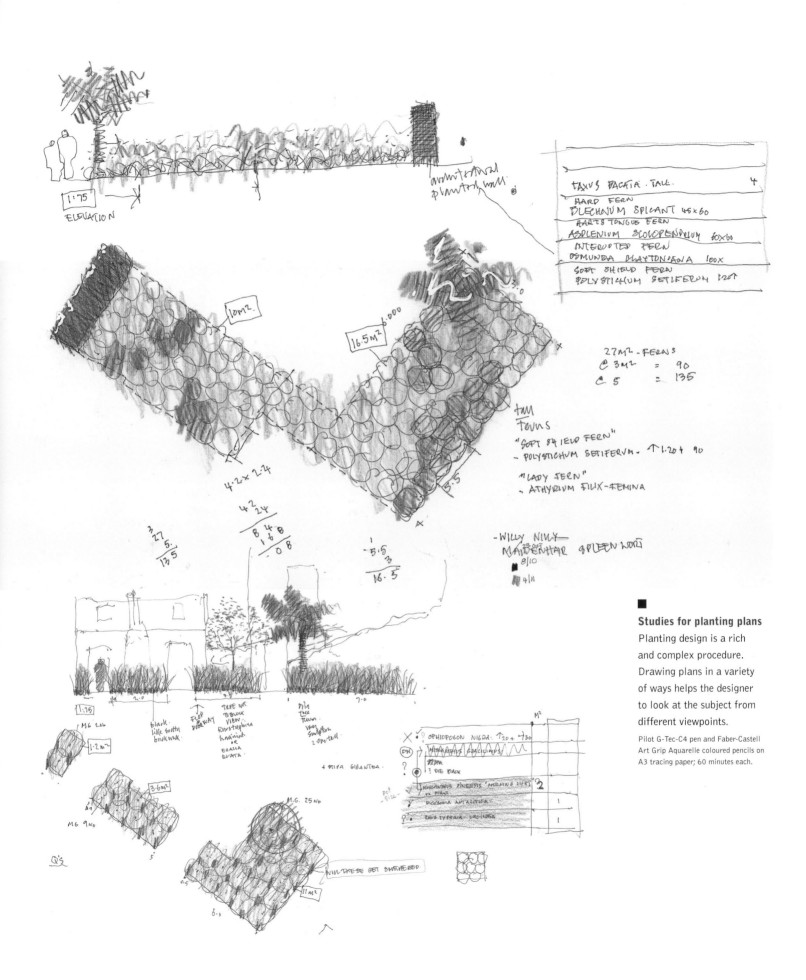

Studies for planting plans

Planting design is a rich and complex procedure. Drawing plans in a variety of ways helps the designer to look at the subject from different viewpoints.

Pilot G-Tec-C4 pen and Faber-Castell Art Grip Aquarelle coloured pencils on A3 tracing paper; 60 minutes each.

Planting design

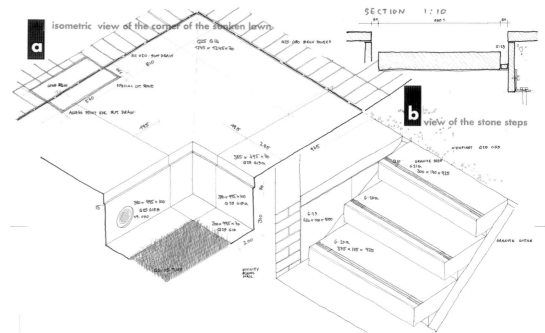

SECTION 1:10

a isometric view of the corner of the sunken lawn

b view of the stone steps

■

Refining plans

A construction drawing of the corner of the sunken lawn [top, right]. In the design for the first planning application, the Old Schoolroom was to be demolished in order to maximize the amount of open space. The planners objected to this proposal, and the building was retained as an open loggia [above]. The complex geometry of the site was echoed in the paving patterns of handmade bricks and granite [right]. The coordination of the underground services with the surface landscape was relatively complicated.

Faber-Castell TG1.S 0.18 and 0.25 technical pens and 0.5mm and 0.3mm pencils on A3 tracing paper.

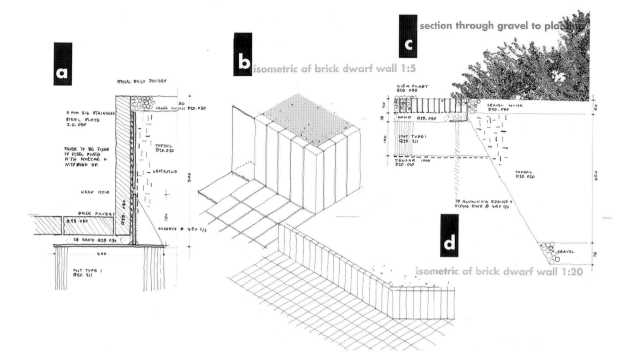

SPECIAL BRICK PAVERS

5 MM 316 STAINLESS
STEEL PLATE
2.11.050

PAVER TO BE FIXED
TO STEEL PLATE
WITH MORTAR &
NITOBOND EP.

WEEP HOLE

BRICK PAVERS
Q25.030

25 SAND Q25.030

400

MOT TYPE I
Q20.211

GRAVEL MULCH D20.030

TOPSOIL
D20.020

GEOTEXTILE

50

GUSSETS @ 450 C/s

500

150

NIDA PLAST
Q18.050

SAND Q18.050

MOT TYPE I
Q20.211

TENSAR 1000
D20.010

GRAVEL MULCH
D20.030

40

25

150

78 ALUMINIUM EDGING &
FIXING PINS @ 450 C/s

TOPSOIL
D20.010

GRAVEL

60

450

75

Brick edging

As the bricks were handmade,
it was possible to develop a small kerb
wall that was faced in long bricks,
as demonstrated in this construction
drawing [above].

Faber-Castell TG1.S 0.18 and 0.25 technical
pens and 0.5mm and 0.3mm pencils on A3
tracing paper.

Radial setts

The granite setts were originally
set out with the centre of
the circle in the Round Church.
The curves, however, proved to
be too shallow to be significant.

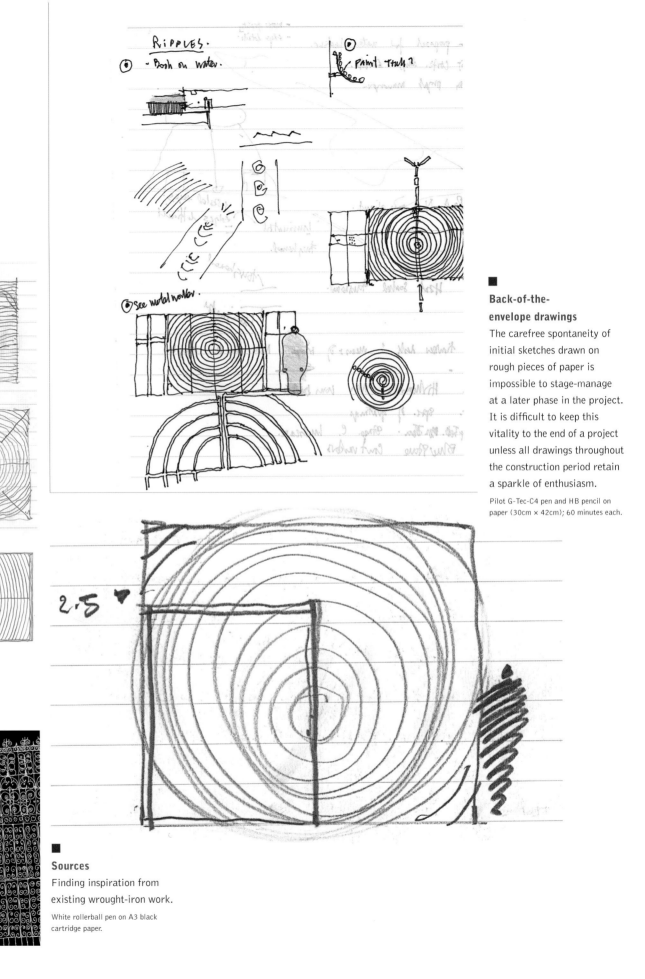

Back-of-the-envelope drawings

The carefree spontaneity of initial sketches drawn on rough pieces of paper is impossible to stage-manage at a later phase in the project. It is difficult to keep this vitality to the end of a project unless all drawings throughout the construction period retain a sparkle of enthusiasm.

Pilot G-Tec-C4 pen and HB pencil on paper (30cm × 42cm); 60 minutes each.

Sources

Finding inspiration from existing wrought-iron work.

White rollerball pen on A3 black cartridge paper.

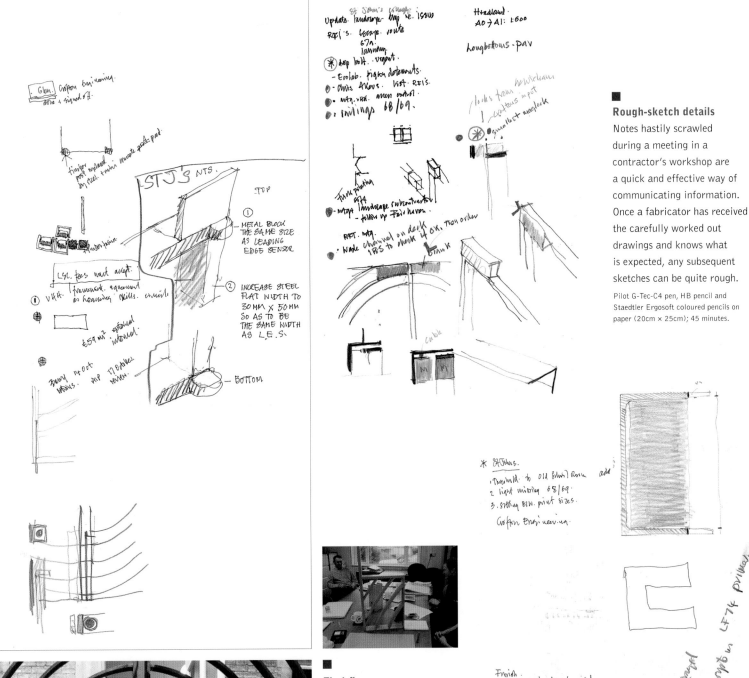

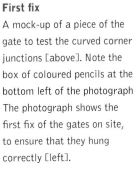

Rough-sketch details

Notes hastily scrawled during a meeting in a contractor's workshop are a quick and effective way of communicating information. Once a fabricator has received the carefully worked out drawings and knows what is expected, any subsequent sketches can be quite rough.

Pilot G-Tec-C4 pen, HB pencil and Staedtler Ergosoft coloured pencils on paper (20cm × 25cm); 45 minutes.

First fix

A mock-up of a piece of the gate to test the curved corner junctions [above]. Note the box of coloured pencils at the bottom left of the photograph! The photograph shows the first fix of the gates on site, to ensure that they hung correctly [left].

Elevation gate - BS 1

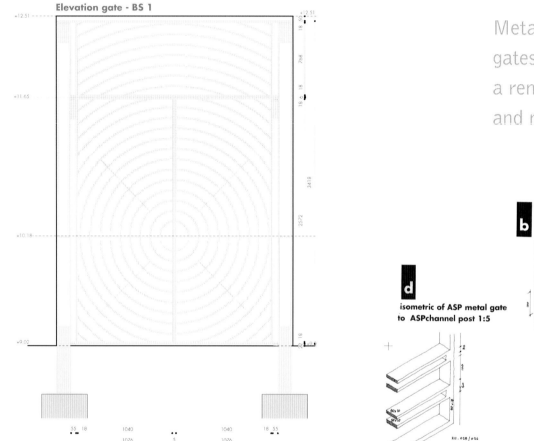

Metalwork in general, and gates in particular, can consume a remarkable amount of time and money to get right.

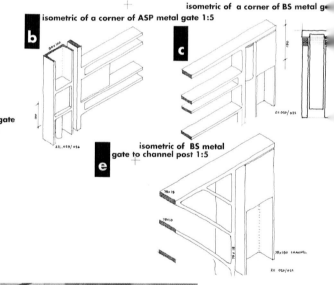

isometric of a corner of BS metal ga

isometric of a corner of ASP metal gate 1:5

b

c

d

isometric of ASP metal gate to ASPchannel post 1:5

e

isometric of BS metal gate to channel post 1:5

Metalwork drawings
Elevation of the gates [above],
and a sketch of the completed
work [right]. Isometric
drawings of typical details,
including corners and channel
post [top, right].

Rotring 0.18 technical pen, Pilot G-Tec-C4
pen, HB pencil and Berol Prismacolor
pencils on A3 tracing paper.

Translating the design
Section from the metal-fabricator's shop drawing.

It is essential that any drawings made in the workshop truly reflect the designer's intentions. It is at this stage that the original spirit of the design can get lost through a lack of understanding by all parties of the significance of details.

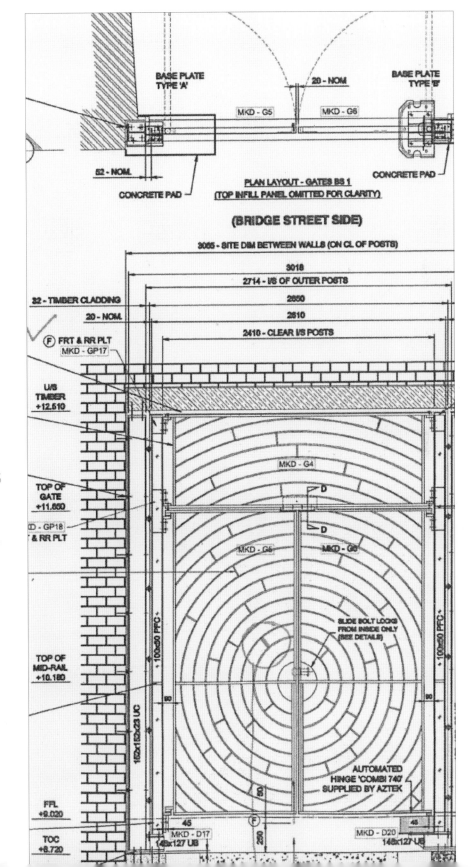

BASE PLATE TYPE 'A'

20 - NOM

BASE PLATE TYPE 'B'

MKD - G5

MKD - G6

52 - NOM.

CONCRETE PAD

CONCRETE PAD

PLAN LAYOUT - GATES BS 1
(TOP INFILL PANEL OMITTED FOR CLARITY)

(BRIDGE STREET SIDE)

3055 - SITE DIM BETWEEN WALLS (ON CL OF POSTS)

3018

2714 - I/S OF OUTER POSTS

2650

32 - TIMBER CLADDING

2610

20 - NOM.

2410 - CLEAR I/S POSTS

(F) FRT & RR PLT
MKD - GP17

U/S
TIMBER
+12.510

MKD - G4

D

TOP OF
GATE
+11.650

D - GP18
& RR PLT

D

MKD - G5

MKD - G6

TOP OF
MID-RAIL
+10.180

SLIDE BOLT LOCKS
FROM INSIDE ONLY
(SEE DETAILS)

80

80

AUTOMATED
HINGE 'COMBI 740'
SUPPLIED BY AZTEK

FFL
+9.020

45

45

MKD - D17
146x127 UB

F

MKD - D20
146x127 UB

TOC
+8.720

The value of endless analysis and sketches of different options becomes evident in the final built scheme. Over many changes during the course of the project, the design concept had to be very clear to avoid being watered down.

Skyline
The idea of celebrating the rich skyline found in the middle of Cambridge – by having no trees in the design to block the view – only became obvious towards the end of the contract period, when the scaffolding was struck. Similarly, the little sunken lawn was seen to full powerful effect, well beyond its size, and therefore 'punches above its weight'.

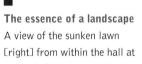

The essence of a landscape
A view of the sunken lawn
[right] from within the hall at
68/69 Bridge Street. This
drawing [left] was made at
the completion of the project,
and aimed to distil many of
the elements considered
during a lengthy and complex
design process.

Faber-Castell coloured pencils on
A3 Bristol board; 45 minutes.

Coventry Peace Garden
Brief: To provide a landscape for
the extension to the Herbert Art
Gallery and Museum.

■

Coventry at war

Coventry was never the same after the night of 14 November
1940. Approximately 515 Luftwaffe bombers, unchallenged,
methodically criss-crossed the city and dropped 500 tons
of high-explosive bombs in retaliation for the earlier bombing
of Munich. The destruction included the 14th-century
St Michael's Cathedral in the medieval part of the city, and
after the end of the war, the process of healing was
concentrated in this quarter with the construction of a new
cathedral by Sir Basil Spence. In the 1960s, Coventry was
recognized as the world centre of 'Peace and Reconciliation',
and further attempts at coming to terms with the trauma
of the war were consolidated two decades later with the
creation of the Peace Garden, opened by the Queen Mother.
An opportunity arose to reconsider the design of this garden
with the redevelopment of the Herbert Art Gallery and
Museum. The city centre in 1851 [left], from a map produced
by the Board of Trade. An Ordnance Survey map from 1905,
second edition [left, below].

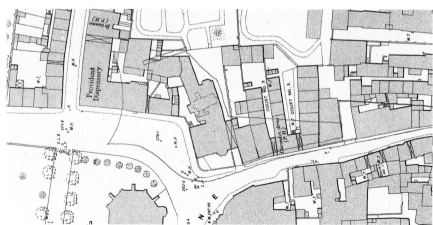

■
The cathedral in ruins
The cathedral on the day after the Blitz [top]; the masonry was still hot from the fire. Coventry's football team is called the Sky Blues in recognition of the roofless structure. A view up Bayley Lane towards the cathedral [top, right], and the Peace Garden at the start of the competition [above].

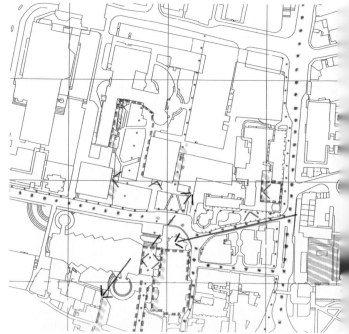

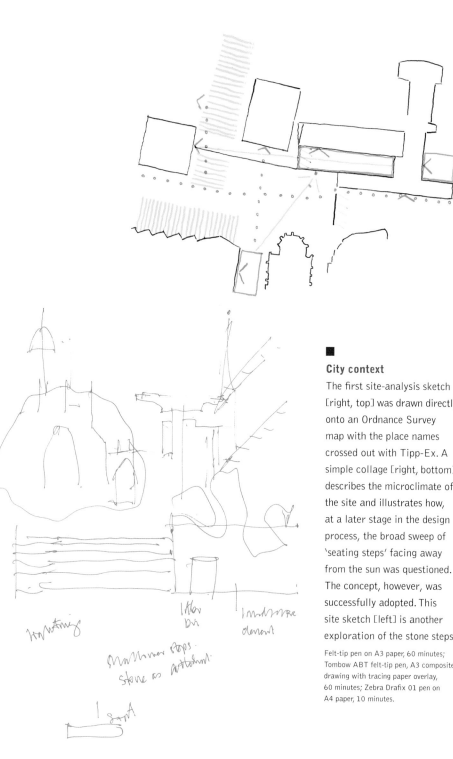

Basic analysis

This crude, initial diagram [left] concentrates on the essential elements – views, entrances, pedestrian routes and green space – which remained the key concerns throughout the seven-year project. The resolution of pedestrian circulation became a critical issue, with the 2m change of level adding to the complexity and interest of the site.

Felt-tip pen on A3 paper; 60 minutes.

City context

The first site-analysis sketch [right, top] was drawn directly onto an Ordnance Survey map with the place names crossed out with Tipp-Ex. A simple collage [right, bottom] describes the microclimate of the site and illustrates how, at a later stage in the design process, the broad sweep of 'seating steps' facing away from the sun was questioned. The concept, however, was successfully adopted. This site sketch [left] is another exploration of the stone steps.

Felt-tip pen on A3 paper, 60 minutes; Tombow ABT felt-tip pen, A3 composite drawing with tracing paper overlay, 60 minutes; Zebra Drafix 01 pen on A4 paper, 10 minutes.

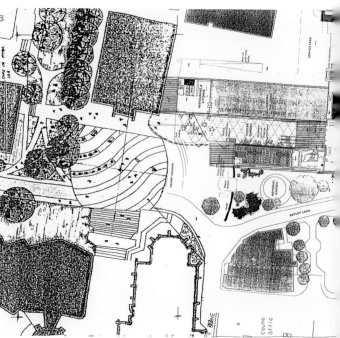

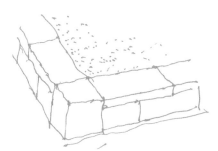

- anval / join photos
- views in / out
- unluckbnuts.
- nukenne.
- pedestrian routes.
- sketches.

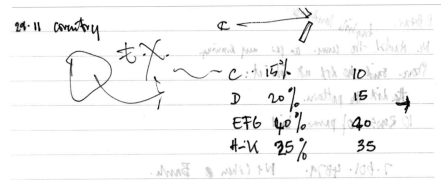

29.11 coventry

C ⟶

~ C : 15%   10
  D   20%   15
  EFG 40%   40
  H-K 25%   35

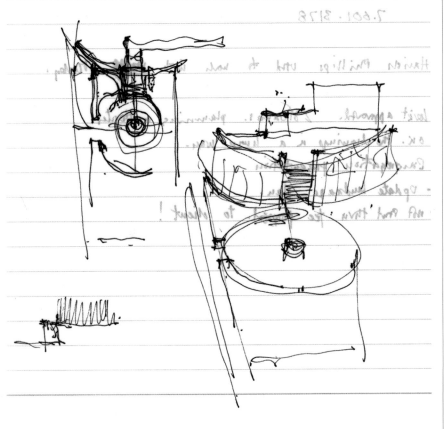

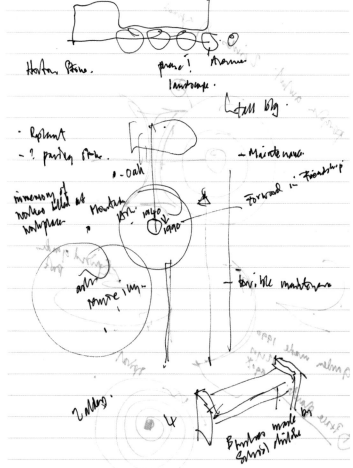

Horton Stone.   phase !   Morris
                 landscape.

- Replant
- ?. parking stue.   — Maintenance.
        - Oak
in memory of   — Forward in Friendship
nurses killed at   Morton
                   1940
workplace.   1990
                   — too. the maintenance

Zollers.   Buildras made
                                by artist / Mitchie

■

Initial sketches

These tentative drawings
explored the potential
significance of a memorial
sculpture within the Peace
Garden, together with
thoughts on fees.

Zebra Drafix 01 pen on A4 paper;
30 minutes.

217

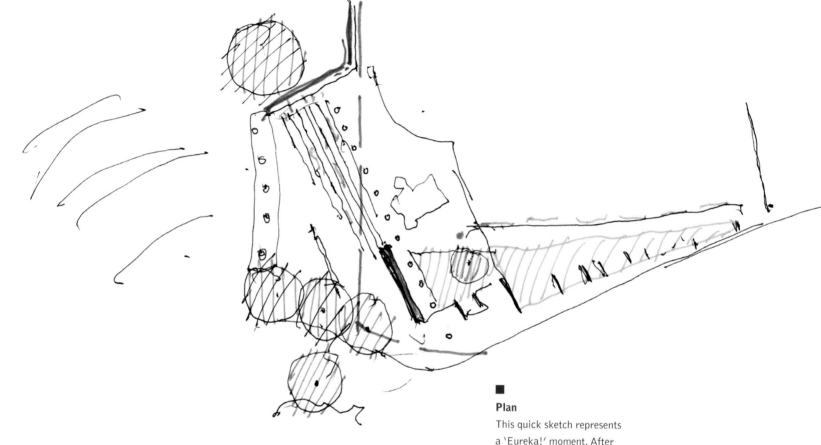

■
Plan
This quick sketch represents
a 'Eureka!' moment. After
working for two years on the
project, suddenly the design
solution became evident.
Although presented crudely,
all of the elements are
represented: steps, trees, grass
and steel fins.

Staedtler Triplus Fineliner and Pilot
G-Tec-C4 pen on A3 paper; 20 minutes.

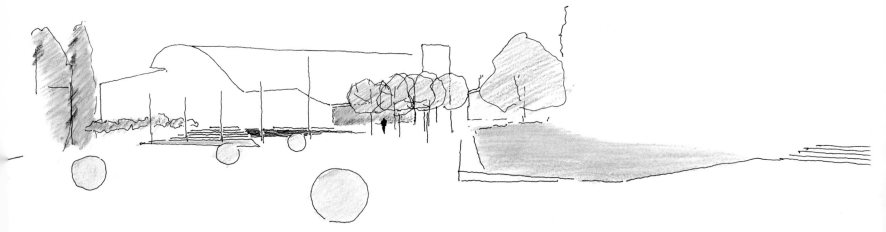

This type of drawing is relatively easy to make, and is useful for testing the proposed design in a 'postcard' fashion. Time needs to be taken to coordinate the set-up of the perspectives of the photograph and digital drawing, in terms of vanishing points, scale and so on, for the image to be completely convincing. It is easy to be misled by the apparent authority of the wire-frame drawing; in this case, the angle of the roofline was incorrect.

■

Perspective

A simplified perspective of one design option, showing the view from the bottom of the cathedral steps. The image was drawn onto tracing paper over site photographs and a wire-frame computer drawing.

Zebra Drafix 01 pen and Berol Karismacolor felt-tip pen on A3 tracing paper; 2 hours, excluding CAD set-up.

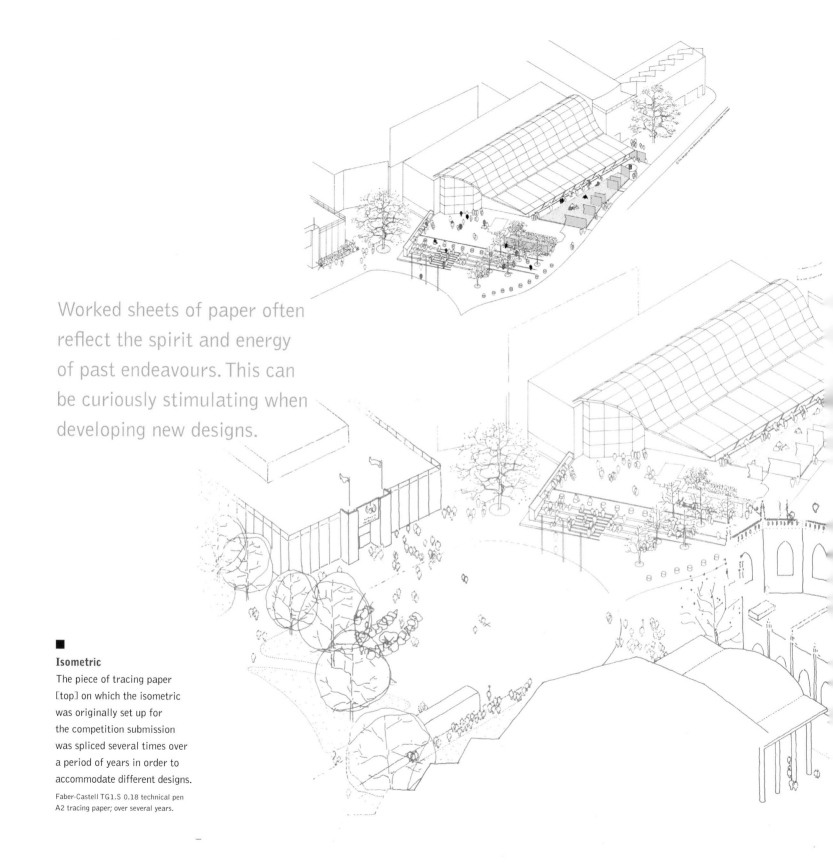

Worked sheets of paper often
reflect the spirit and energy
of past endeavours. This can
be curiously stimulating when
developing new designs.

■
Isometric
The piece of tracing paper
[top] on which the isometric
was originally set up for
the competition submission
was spliced several times over
a period of years in order to
accommodate different designs.

Faber-Castell TG1.S 0.18 technical pen
A2 tracing paper; over several years.

Incomplete perspective

This drawing was created by
placing tracing paper over
a CAD wire-frame drawing and
site photograph.

Faber-Castell TG1.S 0.18 technical pen
and 2H 0.3mm pencil on A3 tracing
paper; 4 hours.

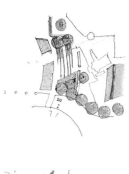

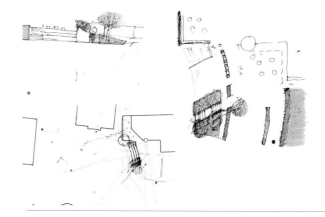

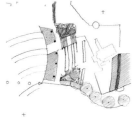

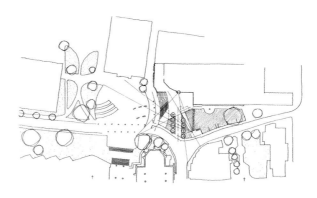

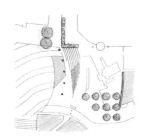

Pedestrian desire lines

The new public space opposite the cathedral was designed before the completion of the plans for the museum extension. These drawings formed part of the extensive investigations into the predicted pedestrian desire lines leading to the museum entrance, and ultimately led to the modification of the design of Priory Square. The concept of a 'green border' proved impractical through this work, which was undertaken over a twelve-month period.

Felt-tip pen on A3 paper; 30 minutes each.

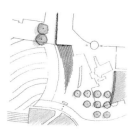

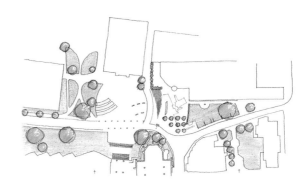

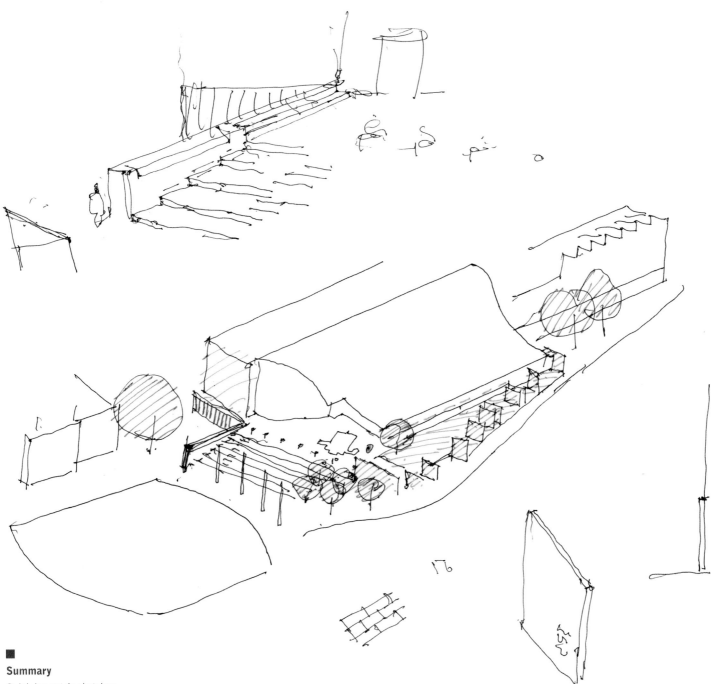

■
Summary
Quick isometric sketches
often come quite easily at the
end of a long and difficult
design period. The brain, having
assimilated a wide range of
information, can direct the hand
with confidence.

Pilot G-Tec-C4 pen and Berol Karismacolor
pencils on A3 tracing paper.

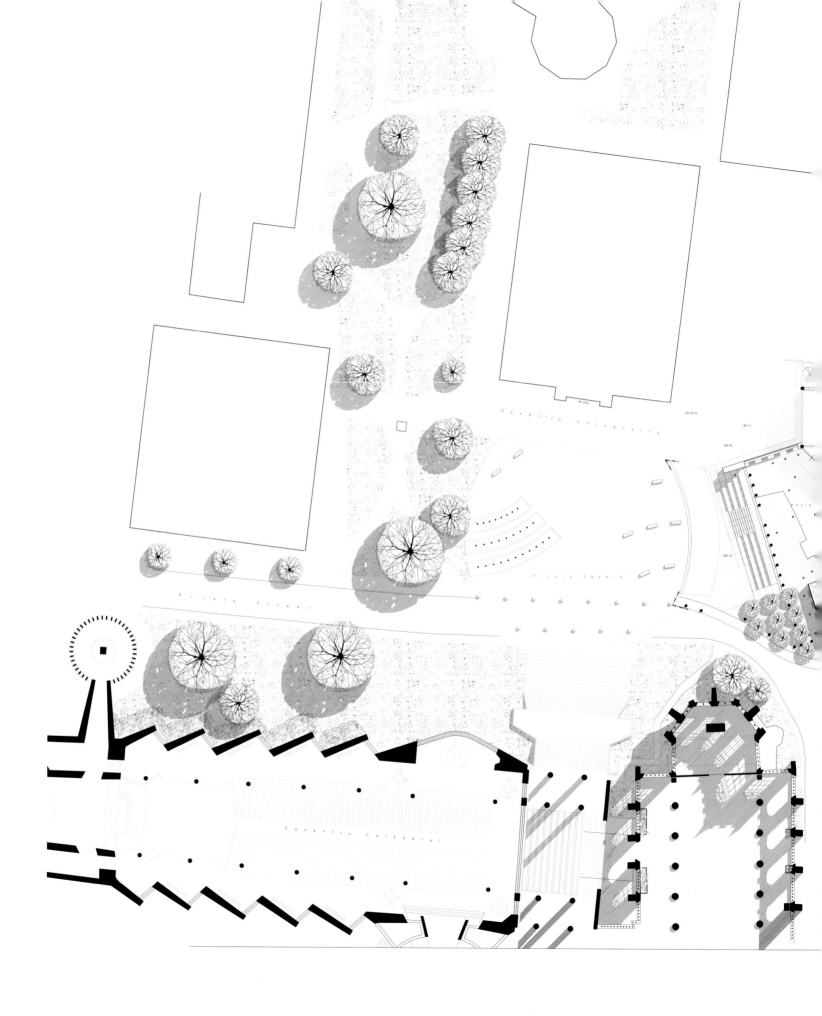

Coventry Peace Garden

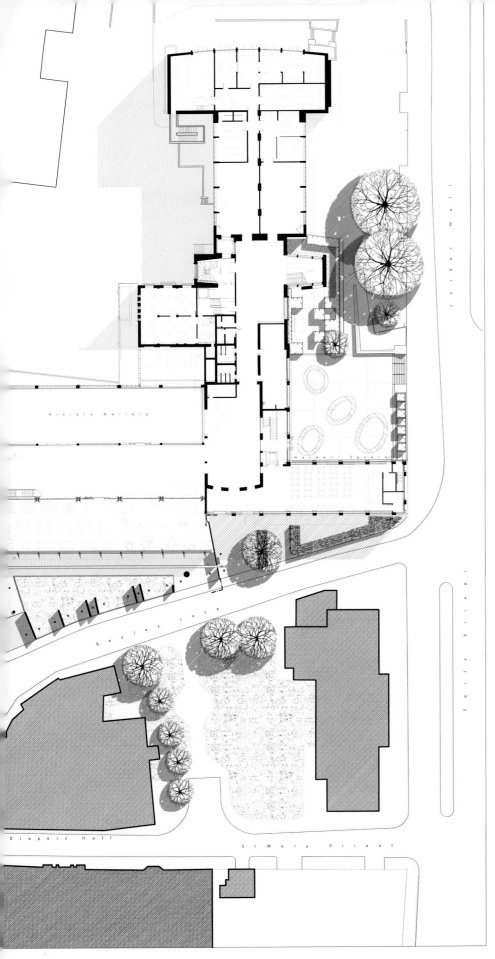

■

Design in context

This drawing shows the landscape proposals in context, and describes the relationship of the public spaces, both internal to external, and the new Peace Garden to the old cathedral.

Vectorworks software program; A0 drawing by Sarah Mackay, Claudia Corcilius and Heidi Hundley; over 4 years.

It is always a privilege to be given the responsibility of designing public space. A careful drawing that recognizes the importance of the commission is a useful resource during discussions about the design.

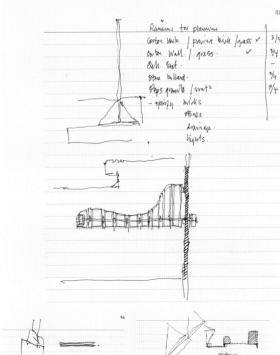

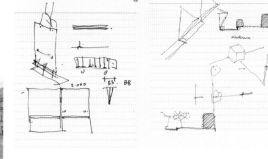

A link to the past

The process of water-jet cutting allows steel to be cut with great accuracy. Here, sheets of Corten steel, 15–20mm thick, have been incised with letters in the Futura Light typeface. The steel, whose earthy red colour reflects the local sandstone, delineates the alignments of party walls that belonged to the medieval houses that originally stood on the site. The incised lettering spells out the names of the previous inhabitants and their occupations back to the mid-16th century.

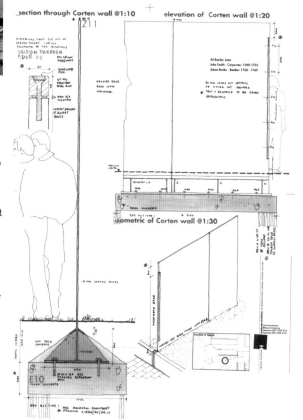

section through Corten wall @1:10

elevation of Corten wall @1:20

isometric of Corten wall @1:30

Minimizing deflection

The client was persuaded against adding a safety strip to the edge of the steel sheets. The steel absorbs heat from the sun, which tends to dry out the adjoining grass. Since the individual sheets flex in the wind, despite their thickness, small blocks of steel were welded in the 20mm gap to the tops of the sheets to minimize this deflection[right]. Another sketch [top, right] illustrates how to handle the steel sheets.

Pilot G-Tec-C4 pen and Staedtler Triplus Fineliner pen on A4 paper; 60 minutes.

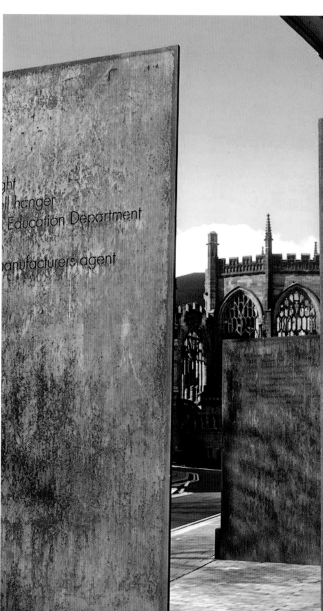

Corten steel's initial high cost is offset by the lack
of any need for maintenance and the material's
ability to weather in a sympathetic and natural way.

Construction details

The combination of the thickness
of the Corten steel and the
different backdrops created a
ghostly quality, unplanned but
appropriate [above]. The metal
bridges were designed to be
vertical, thus avoiding a strong
horizontal line running through
the wording [left, middle]. A
detail elevation for construction
[left, top].

Vectorworks software program;
A1 drawing by Claudia Corcilius.

Selecting the right trees for a site can be an exciting process. Often the choice is limited, but there are occasions when an opportunity arises to plant a striking alternative to the obvious. An example of this is in Manhattan, where small trees, relating to the scale of humans, resonate a connection with the natural world against an environment of skyscrapers.

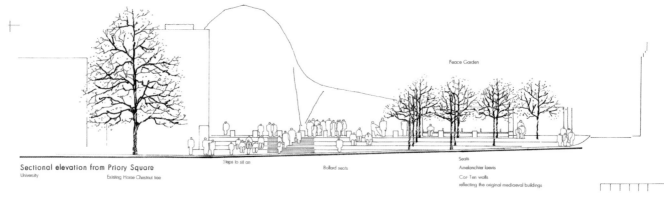

Sectional elevation from Priory Square
University
Existing Horse Chestnut tree
Steps to sit on
Bollard seats
Peace Garden
Seats
Amelanchier laevis
Cor-Ten walls
reflecting the original mediaeval buildings

Trees for peace

The Snowy Mespilus was chosen to create an intimate space at the edge of the Peace Garden, overlooking the two cathedrals. The trees form a grove beside the seating benches, adding a sense of protection and equanimity. These unusually large specimens of multi-stemmed Amelanchier lamarckii [right] were kept for the project for over three years without any payment by a German tree nursery sympathetic to the significance of the project. Elevations of the trees and steps [above and top, left].

Vectorworks software program; A0 drawing by Claudia Corcilius.

Paving and trees

A construction drawing [below], and details of the paving
and trees [bottom]. Most design issues for planting new trees in
an urban landscape are below ground and invisible.

Faber-Castell TG1.S technical pen, Stabilo Layout 37 permanent marker and Edding
Brilliant paper marker, with a razor blade, on A3 tracing paper.

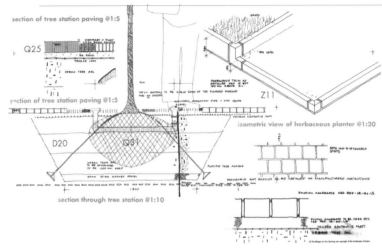

section of tree station paving @1:5

section of tree station paving @1:5

isometric view of herbaceous planter @1:20

section through tree station @1:10

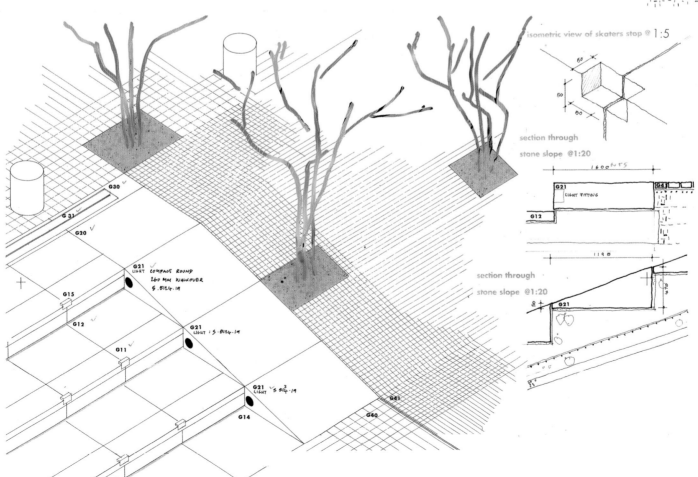

isometric view of skaters stop @ 1:5

section through
stone slope @1:20

section through
stone slope @1:20

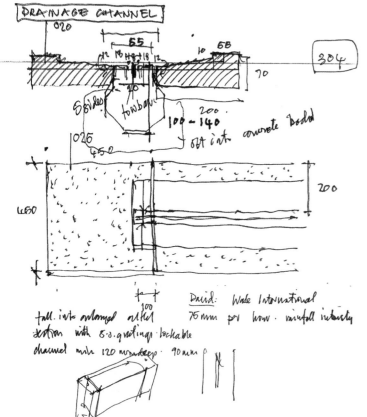

Paving and drainage have been core requirements of good landscape design ever since the Romans introduced the concept of the cambered road to Britain in the first century AD. Traditionally paving was bold laid, falling steeply to well-defined drainage channels. The scale and durability of stone elements have ensured that numerous examples of this style have survived. Contemporary drainage is different: steep falls are seldom acceptable, and proprietary channels and gullies are manufactured economically.

■

Drainage-channel details
These studies [far left] demonstrate the combination of modern and traditional drainage systems. The central 'ACO' system is invaluable: the channel can be laid flat as the falls are incorporated into the varying depth of the sub-surface chamber. A quantity of rainwater can be collected in the stone half-channels, before entering the relatively sophisticated metal system. The staff of the manufacturer's technical department were both helpful and intrigued by this design. The general layout drawing [left] shows the drainage channel in situ. The channel under construction [above].

Vectorworks software program; drawing by Claudia Corcilius.

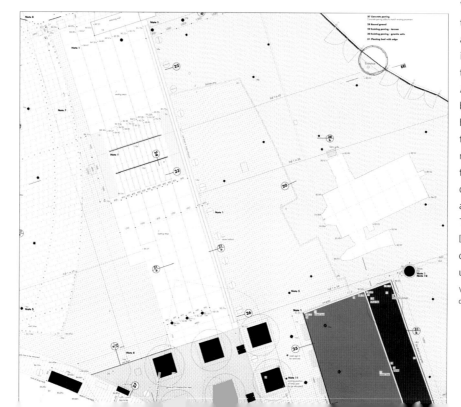

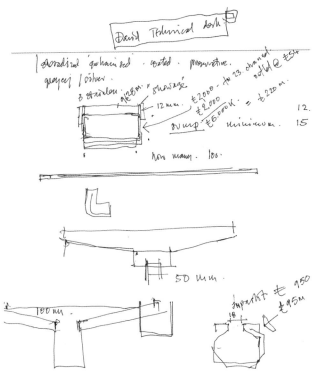

Function and form

These sketches were drawn as a way of understanding the drainage sump [left]. The channel helps to define the space, and introduces a strong perspective [below]. Construction detail drawings [bottom].

Pilot G-Tec-C4 pen on A4 paper; Faber-Castell TG1.S 0.18, 0.25 and 0.5 technical pens, and Edding Brilliant paper marker on A3 tracing paper.

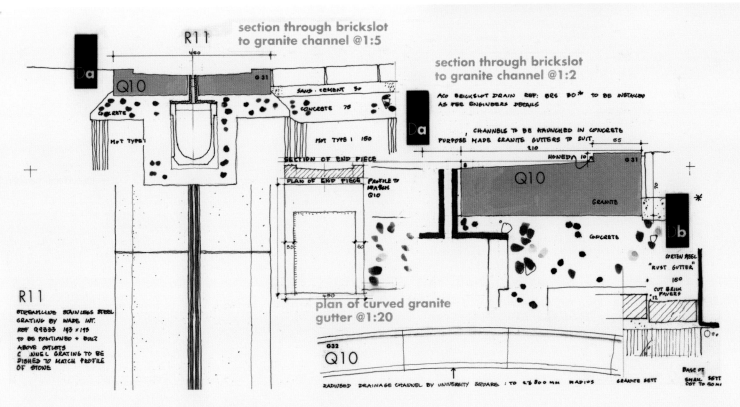

section through brickslot to granite channel @1:5

section through brickslot to granite channel @1:2

plan of curved granite gutter @1:20

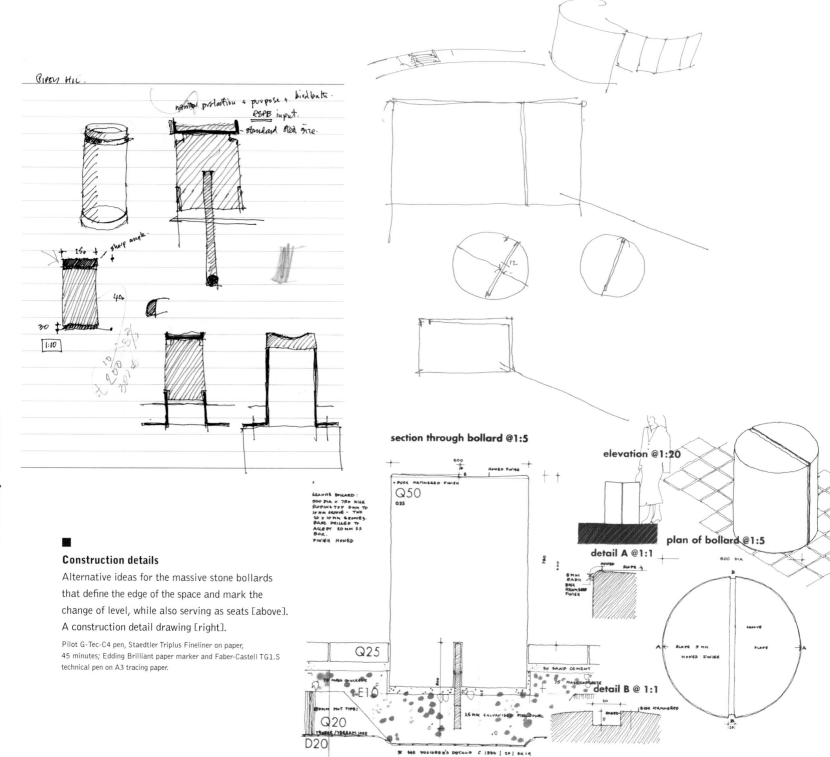

section through bollard @1:5

elevation @1:20

plan of bollard @1:5

detail A @1:1

detail B @1:1

Q50

Q25

Q20

D20

Construction details

Alternative ideas for the massive stone bollards
that define the edge of the space and mark the
change of level, while also serving as seats [above].
A construction detail drawing [right].

Pilot G-Tec-C4 pen, Staedtler Triplus Fineliner on paper,
45 minutes; Edding Brilliant paper marker and Faber-Castell TG1.S
technical pen on A3 tracing paper.

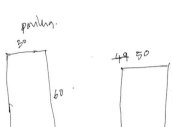

pavilio.

30
60

49 50
75

50
50

Ø5

A10. D 400/E 600
grating

Drainage solutions

To avoid rainfall forming puddles on top of the pure cylinders of the bollards, the plane was modified so that water drains to a central gutter and is shed down a vertical channel [right]. The 'butterfly tops' dry quickly, and the two angled planes are marginally more comfortable to sit on than a flat surface. An early sketch [opposite, top right], exploring an asymmetrical top and drainage from the bollard.

Faber-Castell TG1.S 0.18 technical pen on A3 tracing paper; Zebra Drafix 01 pen on A4 paper, 10 minutes.

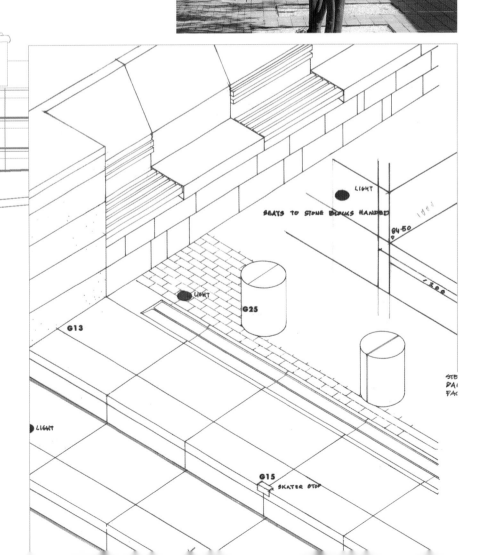

LIGHT

SEATS TO STONE BLOCKS HANDED

Ø450

G25

LIGHT

G13

LIGHT

STE
PA
FA

G15
SKATER STOP

The concept of genius loci, although often translated as 'the distinctive atmosphere or spirit of a place', is a difficult one to define. This site in Coventry, as with much of the city in 1940, experienced great destruction, and the city's trauma is still tangible. The area has become a rendezvous for young people in the city, perhaps because they have picked up in the design a certain atmosphere and link with the past.

The finished scheme

A watercolour of the project,
one year after completion.

Winsor & Newton Artists' watercolours
on A3 hot-pressed paper.

Project credits

Agewell Homes for the Elderly
pp. 88, 90, 106–7, 124, 125,
146–47, 158, 159
Hastings, Lewes, Ringmer,
Rother and Wealden, East Sussex
Client: Kier Group
Architect: Greenhill Jenner
Architects

Avenham Park Pavilion
pp. 158, 159, 170–71
Preston, Lancashire
Client: Preston City Council
Architect: McChesney Architects
Contractor: John Turner & Sons

Axton Chase School
pp. 104–5
Longfield, Kent
Client: Kent County Council
Architect: Trevor Horne Architects

Bedales School
pp. 108, 110–11, 143, 156, 157,
182, 183
Petersfield, Hampshire
Client: Bedales Schools
Architect: Walters & Cohen
Contractor: R. Durtnell & Sons

British Embassy
pp. 52, 53, 78, 79, 122,
140–41, 159
Damascus, Syria
Client: The Foreign and
Commonwealth Office

British High Commission
pp. 57, 58, 59, 122, 146
New Delhi, India
Client: The Foreign and
Commonwealth Office
Architect: Marks Barfield
Architects
Architect: John McAslan &
Partners

Coventry Peace Garden
pp. 12, 152, 154, 155, 176, 177,
183, 214–35
Coventry, Warwickshire
Client: Coventry City Council
Architect: Pringle Richards
Sharratt Architects
Engineer: Alan Baxter & Associates
Quantity surveyor: Turner &
Townsend
Project manager: Gardiner &
Theobald
Access consultant: Earnscliffe
Davies Associates
Contractor: Galliford Try
Landscape contractor: Interlock
Paving
Supplier: ACO Building Drainage
Supplier: CED
Supplier: Treadstone
Supplier: Lorberg Nurseries

Duisburg Masterplan
pp. 54, 55
Duisburg, Germany
Client: Duisburg City Council
Architect: Foster & Partners

Glasgow Observation Tower
p. 130
Glasgow, Scotland
Client: Glasgow City Council
Architect: David Morley Architects
Engineer: Jane Wernick Associates

Headland Hotel
pp. 132–33, 158, 159
Newquay, Cornwall
Client: The Headland Hotel
Architect: Chapman Workhouse

Hull History Centre
pp. 74, 75, 128, 158, 159, 172,
173, 175
Hull, East Yorkshire
Client: Hull City Council
Architect: Pringle Richards
Sharratt Architects
Contractor: Interior Services Group
Landscape contractor: Blakedown
Landscapes
Supplier: R. Durtnell & Sons

Imperial College London
pp. 86, 87, 143, 150, 151, 168–69
South Kensington, London
Client: Imperial College London
Architect: Foster & Partners

The Lightbox
pp. 70, 72, 102–3, 138, 139, 162,
164, 184–85
Woking, Surrey
Client: Woking Galleries
Architect: Marks Barfield
Architects

Lloyd's Register of Shipping
p. 84
Fenchurch Street, London
Client: Lloyd's Register of Shipping
Architect: Richard Rogers
Partnership

The London Eye
p. 83
South Bank, London
Client: British Airways London Eye
Architect: Marks Barfield
Architects
Project manager: Mace
Landscape contractor: Waterers
Landscapes
Supplier: Lorberg Nurseries

Lord's Cricket Ground
pp. 85, 86
St John's Wood, London
Client: Marylebone Cricket Club
Architect: David Morley Architects

Macintosh Village
pp. 178, 179
Lockes Yard, Manchester
Client: Taylor Woodrow
Architect: Hurley Robertson &
Associates
Architect: Terry Farrell & Partners

Michael Tippett School
pp. 109, 145, 158, 159
Lambeth, London
Client: Lambeth Council
Architect: Marks Barfield
Architects

Pitzhanger Manor (competition)
pp. 60–63
Ealing, London
Client: London Borough of Ealing
Architect: Wright & Wright
Architects

Place de Carrée d'Art
pp. 48–50, 80
Nîmes, France
Client: Ville de Nîmes
Architect: Foster & Partners

St John's College
pp. 12, 87, 112–13, 158, 159,
180, 181, 186–213
University of Cambridge
Client: St John's College,
University of Cambridge
Architect: Van Heyningen &
Haward Architects
Project manager: Davis Langdon
Quantity surveyor: Davis Langdon
Contractor: Bluestone
Landscape contractor: Elmswell
Contractors
Landscape contractor: Land
Structure
Supplier: Crofton Engineering
Supplier: CED

Sevenoaks School
p. 82
Sevenoaks, Kent
Client: Sevenoaks School
Architect: Tim Ronalds Architects

Sussex Downs College
pp. 98–99, 150, 151, 158, 159,
160–61, 166, 167, 174, 175
East Sussex
Client: Sussex Downs College
Architect: Van Heyningen &
Haward Architects

Walbrook Square
pp. 76, 77, 100–1, 130, 131,
148, 149
Queen Victoria Street, London
Client: Stanhope
Architect: Foster & Partners

Walsall Manor Hospital
(competition)
pp. 126, 127
Walsall, West Midlands
Client: Walsall Hospitals
Architect: David Morley Architects

Worcester Library (competition)
pp. 13, 114–15, 129
Worcester, Worcestershire
Client: Worcester City Council
Client: Pringle Richards Sharratt
Architects

Worthing Swimming Pool
(competition)
pp. 64, 65
Worthing, West Sussex
Client: Worthing Borough Council
Architect: Pringle Richards
Sharratt Architects

Yehudi Menuhin School
p. 147
Cobham, Surrey
Client: Yehudi Menhuin School
Architect: Walters & Cohen

Further reading

Adams, Eileen, *Drawing: A Tool for Design,* Power Drawing series (Enfield, England: Campaign for Drawing, 2009).

———, *Power Drawing: Active Learning,* Power Drawing series (Enfield, England: Campaign for Drawing, 2009).

Berger, John, *Berger on Drawing* (Aghabullogue, Ireland: Occasional Press, 2005).

Ching, Francis D. K., *Architecture: Form, Space and Order* (New York: Van Nostrand Reinhold, 1979).

'Construction Drawing Practice: Guide for the Structuring and Exchange of CAD Data', document BSI BS 1192-5 (Denver, Colorado: IHS, 1998).

Craig-Martin, Michael, *Drawing the Line: Reappraising Drawing Past and Present,* cat., exh., Southampton City Art Gallery, 13 January–5 March 1995.

Doyle, Michael E., *Color Drawing Skills and Techniques for Architects, Landscape Architects and Interior Designers,* 2nd ed. (Hoboken, New Jersey: John Wiley & Sons, 1999).

Edwards, Betty, *Drawing on the Artist Within: How to Release Your Hidden Creativity* (London: HarperCollins, 1988).

Frankbonner, Edgar Loy, *Art of Drawing the Human Body* (New York: Sterling Publishing, 2003).

Gregory, Richard L., *Eye and Brain: The Psychology of Seeing* (Benson, Arizona: World University Library, 1966).

Hogarth, Paul, *Drawing Architecture: A Creative Approach* (London: Pitman Publishing, 1973).

Klee, Paul, *The Thinking Eye* (London: Lund Humphries, 1961).

Kovats, Tania, ed., *The Drawing Book: A Survey of the Primary Means of Expression* (London: Black Dog Publishing, 2007).

Lin, Mike W., *Drawing and Designing with Confidence: A Step-by-Step Guide* (New York: Van Nostrand Reinhold, 1993).

Olin, Laurie, *Transforming the Common/Place: Selections from Laurie Olin's Sketchbooks* (New York: Princeton Architectural Press, 1997).

Petherbridge, Deanna, *The Primacy of Drawing: Histories and Theories of Practice* (London: Yale University Press, 2010).

Reekie, Ronald Fraser, *Draughtsmanship: Drawing Techniques for Graphic Communication in Architecture and Building,* 3rd ed. (London: Hodder Arnold, 1976).

Ruskin, John, *The Elements of Drawing* (1857; London, A & C Black, 1991).

Sullivan, Chip, *Drawing the Landscape* (New York: Van Nostrand Reinhold, 1994).

Thompson, Ian, Torben Dam and Jens Balsby Nielsen, *European Landscape Architecture: Best Practice in Detailing* (Oxford: Routledge, 2007).

Treib, Marc, *Drawing/Thinking: Confronting an Electronic Age* (Oxford: Routledge, 2008).

———, *Thomas Church, Landscape Architect: Designing a Modern California Landscape* (San Francisco: William Stout, 2003).

Wester, Lari M., *Design Communication for Landscape Architects* (New York: Van Nostrand Reinhold, 1990).

Edward Hutchison

Following his studies at Kingston Art School (BA Interior Design), the Royal College of Art (MA Environmental Design), Thames Polytechnic (Dip LA Landscape Architecture) and the Architectural Association in London (AA Dip Architecture), Edward Hutchison worked from 1973 to 1984 in the Architectural Department at the London Borough of Hammersmith & Fulham (LBH&F), where he was responsible for the conceptual detailed design and running on site of a wide range of architectural and landscape projects, the majority of which received awards. From 1985 to 1991, he worked for Foster & Partners, where he was made an Associate in 1988 and was jointly responsible for the conceptual and detailed design of several prestigious projects that received international acclaim.

In 1991, Hutchison established Edward Hutchison Landscape Architects as a consultancy. Collaborations with leading architectural practices include: Allies & Morrison (A&M), Bennetts Associates (BA), Chapman Workhouse (CW), David Morley Architects (DMA), Foster & Partners (F&P), Future Systems, Hurley Robertson Architects (HRA), John McAslan & Partners (JM&P), Marks Barfield Architects (MBA), Pascall & Watson (P&W), Pringle Richards Sharratt (PRS), Richard Faulkner Architects (RFA), Richard Rogers Partnership (RRP), Sheppard Robson (SR), Sprunt Architects (S), Van Heyningen & Haward (VHH), Walters & Cohen (W&C), and Wright & Wright (W&W).

238

■
Landscape architecture
[Top to bottom] Lockes Yard, Macintosh Village, Manchester; The London Eye; Hull History Centre, East Yorkshire; Place de Carrée d'Art, Nîmes, France.

Urban spaces
Canal basins, Nancy, France, while at F&P
De La Warr Pavilion, Bexhill-on-Sea, East Sussex, JM&P
Devonshire Square, London, BA
Judiciary Courts, Bordeaux, France, RRP
Mitre Square, London, SR
Pierhead, Liverpool, A&M
Street repaving, Nîmes, France, while at F&P
Riverside offices, Battersea, London, while at F&P
South Bank redevelopment, RRP
South Quay Station, London, P&W
Main Square, Nîmes, France, while at F&P
Walbrook Square, London, F&P

Landscapes and museums
Herbert Art Gallery and Museum, Coventry, PRS
The Lightbox, Woking, Surrey, MBA
Pitzhanger Manor, Ealing, London, W&W

Public parks
Bayonne Park, Fulham, London, while at LBH&F
Blakes Park, Fulham, London, while at LBH&F
King's Cross Park, London, while at F&P
The London Eye, South Bank, London, MBA
Pocket Park, Hull History Centre, East Yorkshire, PRS

Masterplanning
Berlin Olympics 2000, MBA
Nîmes, France, while at F&P
Pennrhydeudraeth Business Park, Wales, DMA
Statue Square, Hong Kong, while at F&P
Terminal Zone, Stansted Airport, Essex, while at F&P

Sport
Ascot Racecourse, Berkshire, shortlisted with P&W
Lord's Cricket Ground, St John's Wood, London, DMA
Oasis Cycle Track, Stockwell, London, MBA

Street furniture
Range of street furniture, Stansted Airport, Essex,
    while at F&P
Blue engineering brick paver, while at F&P
Bus shelter, while at F&P

Corporate landscapes
Lloyd's Register of Shipping, London, RRP
Yapi Kredi Bank, Istanbul, JM&P

Schools and universities
Bedales Schools, Hampshire, W&C
Imperial College London, F&P
Sports and Events Centre, Liverpool University, DMA
Building Schools for the Future proposal, W&C
St John's College, Cambridge, VHH
Sussex Downs College, East Sussex, VHH
Thames Valley University, Slough, Berkshire, RRP
Michael Tippett School, Lambeth, London, MBA
Yehudi Menuhin School, Cobham, Surrey, W&C

Landscapes and housing
Banim Street Sheltered Housing, Hammersmith, London,
    while at LBH&F
Dorcas Estate Sheltered Housing, Fulham, London,
    while at LBH&F
Fairmead Sheltered Housing, Essex, S
Headland Holiday Village, Newquay, Cornwall, CW
Macintosh Village, Manchester, HRA
Marinefield Road Sheltered Housing, Fulham, London,
    while at LBH&F
Montevetro Battersea, London, RRP

Health
Walsall Hospital, West Midlands, DMA
The Kaleidoscope, Lewisham, London, VHH

Car parks
Canal basins, Nancy, France, while at F&P
Centre for Two St James, Gerrards Cross,
    Buckinghamshire, DMA
Imperial College London
Lord's Cricket Ground, St John's Wood, London, DMA
Terminal Zone, Stansted Airport, Essex, while at F&P

Gardens
Birkholme Manor, Lincolnshire
Glasgow Observation Tower, DMA
Kawana House, Japan, while at F&P
Spencer Road, Wimbledon

Embassies
British High Commission, New Delhi, India, JM&P
British Embassy and Residence, Damascus, Syria, RFA

Acknowledgments

This book stemmed from an exhibition entitled *Drawing Space*, held in 2009 at the Garden Museum, in Lambeth, London, which showed the working process of Edward Hutchison Landscape Architects.

My assistant Heidi Hundley, graphic designer Susan Scott and I selected content from plan chests and sketchbooks bursting with a lifetime's work. Ian Lambot, photographer, book designer and publisher (Watermark) of, among others, volumes on Norman Foster, guided us on the overall feel and structure of the book. Annabel Downs, former archivist of the Landscape Institute, asked penetrating and provocative questions; she also helped with the enormous task of labelling the illustrations. Sheila Harvey, former librarian of the Landscape Institute, was invaluable in raising issues covered, or not covered, in landscape design publications and drawing attention to the importance of pithy text. Eileen Adams, who has herself published several books on drawing, brought both insight and dynamism to our meetings.

I was advised by Jane Brown and Alan Gordon Walker, and was then very fortunate to have the professional support of everyone at Thames & Hudson. My artist son Jeremy gave input from a student's point of view, and my daughter Daisy, a professional photographer, captured the completed work in her photographs. I am grateful most of all to Polly, my wife, who acted as wordsmith and helpmeet.

I am deeply indebted to all of the above for their skills and their time. I would also like to thank my many tutors for their guidance and encouragement at the start of my career and my employers, fellow architects and clients, who have given a purpose to my life as a designer.

Picture credits

All drawings are by the author, except where noted in the text.

All photographs by the author. Additional photography by Rachel Elliott 201; Heidi Hundley 132–33, 204; Daisy Hutchison (www.daisyhutchison.com) 190, 191, 202, 203, 206, 207, 210, 212, 213, 214, 226, 227, 228, 229, 234; Marcus Robinson (www.marcusrobinsonphotography.com) 83.

The PCC of Holy Sepulchre Parish (St Andrew the Great Church) 191; Coventry City Archives 214; Times Newspapers Limited 215.

Photomontages by Susan Scott 234–5, 236.